# Building Our Own

This book is number six in the Litwin Books/Library Juice Press Series on Critical Race Studies and Multiculturalism in LIS, Rose L. Chou and Annie Pho, series editors.

# Building Our Own
Critiques, Narratives, and Practices by Community College Library Workers of Color

*Edited by*
Amanda M. Leftwich and Eva M.L. Rios-Alvarado

Library Juice Press
Sacramento, CA

Copyright 2024

Published in 2024 by Library Juice Press.

Litwin Books
PO Box 188784
Sacramento, CA 95818

http://litwinbooks.com/

This book is printed on acid-free paper.

Publisher's Cataloging in Publication

Names: Leftwich, Amanda M., editor. | Rios-Alvarado, Eva M.L., editor.
Title: Building our own : critiques, narratives, and practices by community college library workers of color / Amanda M. Leftwich and Eva M.L. Rios-Alvarado, editors.
Description: Sacramento, CA : Library Juice Press, 2024. | Series: Critical race studies and multiculturalism in LIS ; 6. | Includes bibliographical references and index.
Identifiers: LCCN 2024939114 | ISBN 9781634001366 (acid-free paper)
Subjects: LCSH: Academic librarians. | Minority librarians. | Minority library employees. | Community college libraries. | Academic libraries – Services to minorities.
Classification: LCC Z682.4.M56 B85 2024 | DDC 027.7--dc23
LC record available at https://lccn.loc.gov/2024939114

# Contents

VII   Acknowledgments
     *Amanda M. Leftwich and Eva M.L. Rios-Alvarado*

IX   Foreword
     *Dr. Kel Hughes Jones*

XV   Foreword
     *Lizeth Zepeda*

1   Introduction
     *Amanda M. Leftwich and Eva M.L. Rios-Alvarado*

## Honoring Our Communities    Building Our Own Practices

19   **Breaking the Bamboo Library Ceiling**   Asian American Women's Path to Community & Technical College Library Administration
     *Alyssa Jocson Porter, Jess Koshi-Lum, and Gerie Ventura*

38   **Communities of Practice**   Responsibility and Opportunities for Shared Praxis in Community College Libraries
     *Evangela Q. Oates*

53   **Unique Communities of Practice through Library Work**
     **A Dialogue on Building Connections at a Community College**
     *Amanda M. Leftwich, Fran L. Lassiter, Stephanie Nnadi, and Adriene Hobdy*

**Honoring Our Stories**   Frameworks, Identities, and Narratives

75   **Accepting My Own Worth**   Reflecting and Healing from "Imposter Experience" as a Latina Librarian in Academia
*Sally Najera Romero*

97   **Creating a Sense of Belonging for BIPOC Students in a Community College Library**
*Andrew Kuo*

114   **Student Success and Equity in the Library**   Looking at our Community Campus Library Collections
*Edeama Onwuchekwa Jonah*

131   **Testament of Perseverance**   A Journey Through Tenure
*Shamika Jamalia Morris Simpson*

**Honoring Our Labor**   Reflections on Our Work

147   **Learning from the Brown Body**   Xicana Feminism in the Community College Library
*Eva M.L. Rios-Alvarado*

169   **And Now We Are Strangers to Each Other**   Reflections on My Onboarding Process
*Dele Chinwe Ladejobi*

184   **Racelighting**   Understanding BIPOC community college library workers' experience with questioning their own realities
*Terezita Reyes Overduin*

201   About the Contributors

207   Index

# Acknowledgments

*Amanda M. Leftwich and Eva M.L. Rios-Alvarado*

This book wouldn't have been possible without our communities' constant support, empathy, and care. We thank the many people, systems, and organizations that helped us publish this book. This project exists because of you and is for you.

To our LIS communities, cohorts, and supporters, we humbly thank you for the time and energy you contributed to our careers. Your guidance and friendships have been fundamental to the work we do. To the planning crew Aisha Conner-Gaten, Jennifer Masunaga, Jessea Young, and Nataly Blas and fellow presenters at the People of Color in Library & Information Science (POCinLIS) Summit at Loyola Marymount in Los Angeles, California, in 2018, we thank you for uplifting the work of BIPOC library workers, especially community college library employees. This summit gave us the space, time, and opportunity to develop the ideas that gave this book life. Allowing us to center our experiences as people of color within the field created invaluable access to the community. We cannot thank you enough for sharing your lived ideas and experiences for our collective profession's betterment.

Special thank you to Rose L. Chou and Annie Pho for seeing the value and importance of this book. Your work has changed LIS and encouraged us to reach for excellence within the profession. Your feedback, understanding, and leadership throughout this process were stellar. We are honored to have this book in your *Series of Critical Race Studies and Multiculturalism in LIS*. We stand on your shoulders and hope to do you proud. We are exceedingly grateful to Rory Litwin and Lacey Torge for publishing this book under Litwin Books and Library Juice Press.

*Building Our Own* wouldn't exist without the thoughtful research of our contributors. We couldn't have done this without you. The critiques, narratives, and best practices you contributed to this book are thought-provoking and powerful. Sharing your stories has been the highlight of our careers, and we are honored that you shared your work in this book of ours. Your insights and expertise will shift the paradigm of how we think about BIPOC librarians and library workers and the work they do. We'd also like to thank all our peer reviewers: Aisha Conner-Gaten, Jessica Y. Dai, V. Dozier, Danielle Rapue, Mallary Rawls, and Lizeth Zepeda. Your care, time, and attention in reviewing this text made this book better and more insightful. Thank you to Dr. Kel Hughes Jones and Lizeth Zepeda for their excellent forewords and support throughout this project.

To our MCCC colleagues Damon T. Gray, Fran L. Lassiter, & Dianna Sand, and dear friends Aisha Conner-Gaten, V. Dozier, Nora Franco, Nancy Olmos, Aisha Damali Lockridge, Renée Elizabeth Neely, Mallary Rawls, Leticia Ramos, Preethi Rao, and Lizeth Zepeda, we humbly thank you for your humor and encouragement throughout the writing process.

To our families, especially our mothers Michele and Elvia, we wouldn't be here without you both. Your strength, kindness, and love carried us throughout this process! To Robert, thank you for your encouragement, thoughtfulness, and kindness throughout this process. To Vanessa Codorniu, Heather McGinniss, and Ilona Pamplona: for your motivation to push towards greatness and stand in our own power! To husbands like Elizandro, for your strength in moments of self-doubt. You are loved and admired. Appreciation to *Tía* (aunt) Qui, the homegirl we all need. *Los quiero un chingo*! Sending love to Clinton S. Anderson, Jr., a beloved grandfather who passed away as we wrote this book. We are wishing you peace on the other side. We miss you. We humbly send gratitude and much love for everything you've done for us.

Lastly, to all the BIPOC community college librarians/library workers and BIPOC LIS workers out there, thank you for your work! Your critiques, narratives, and practices matter. You matter. We see you and honor you. We compiled this book with the hope that you no longer must build your own and find support within the field without hardship.

# Foreword

*Dr. Kel Hughes Jones*

Growing up in a majority Black city, I never considered myself a "minority" as a Black girl. When I went to school, I saw plenty of students and teachers who looked like me. On Sundays, I attended a Black church and witnessed congregants with varying socioeconomic levels, who all seemed equal in the sight of God. Black wealth and leadership were not foreign to me; I saw Black people in power. It wasn't until I went away to college that I began to feel marginalized. Thankfully, my upbringing gave me a strong foundation in my heritage, allowing me to be secure in who I am as a Black woman.

Years later, I vividly remember attending my first professional staff meeting in an educational setting and realizing I was the only Black employee. I remember feeling isolated and alone, with fears of being misunderstood or discriminated against. I eventually transferred to another school, where I was not the only Black professional. Although I was not in the majority regarding race and experienced discrimination, I felt more at ease because I found myself amongst a (small) community of educators who looked like me. I could go to the breakroom and have a conversation with a colleague about a Black popular culture or vent after school about racist policies and practices. Over time, we eventually created an affinity group that met each semester off campus. Likewise, research has shown that affinity groups can help build community for and enhance the wellness of BIPOC (Black Indigenous and People of Color) librarians.[1] Support groups can give BIPOC librarians a means to be themselves and embrace their multidimensionality,

---

1   Francesca Marineo, Chelsea Heinbach, and Rosan Mitola. "Building a Culture of Collaboration and Shared Responsibility for Educational Equity Work through an Inclusive Teaching Community of Practice," *Collaborative Librarianship* 13, no. 1 (2022): 72.

particularly in majority-White educational settings.[2] While librarians of color excel in building community for others, they may lack the reciprocal support of community in their personal lives. For example, a community can come in "sister circles," or small groups composed of only Black women that cultivate bonds and provide emotional reprieve[3] that marginalized individuals often need. As the chapters in this book show us, community is essential for BIPOC students and librarians to thrive.

Within community and technical college systems, BIPOC students, faculty, and staff face what Gusa describes as a"White institutional presence"[4] or practices, policies, and school culture that further marginalize people of color. Furthermore, commuter students often arrive on campus with multiple identities and roles and succeed when presented with opportunities to participate in common/shared experiences with similar students.[5] Research has shown various ways to create welcoming climates for BIPOC individuals in higher education and academic libraries,[6] including communities of practice.[7] Communities of practice are more than groups of like-minded individuals working together. They are inviting, engaging collaborative spaces and efforts that usher improvement and change.[8]

In my experience, I've existed in these groups in various ways that helped honor my community, my identity, and my work. I have established and served on committees (with other BIPOC employees) that

---

2   Marineo, et. al., "Building a Culture of Collaboration," 72.

3   Marsha Foster Boyd, "WomanistCare: Some Reflections on the Pastoral Care and the Transformation of African American Women," in *Embracing the Spirit: Womanist Perspectives on Hope, Salvation and Transformation*, ed. Emilie M. Townes (Maryknoll, NY: Orbis, 1997), 198.

4   Diane Lynn Gusa, "White Institutional Presence: The Impact of Whiteness on Campus Climate," *Harvard Educational Review* 80, no. 4 (2010): 466; Bryan K. Hotchkins, Jon McNaughtan, and Hugo A. García, "Black Community Collegians Sense of Belonging as Connected to Enrollment Satisfaction," *Journal of Negro Education* 90, no. 1 (2021): 55.

5   Mariana Regalado, and Maura A. Smale. *Academic Libraries for Commuter Students: Research-Based Strategies* (Chicago: ALA Editions, 2018), 6-7.

6   Teresa Y. Neely and Kuang-Hwei Lee-Smeltzer. *Diversity Now: People, Collections, and Services in Academic Libraries: Selected Papers from the Big 12 Plus Libraries Consortium Diversity Conference.* (Haworth Information Press, 2002), 70; Stephen Weiner. "Accrediting bodies Must Require a Commitment to Diversity when Measuring a College's Quality." *The Chronicle of Higher Education*, October 1990.

7   Marineo, et. al., "Building a Culture of Collaboration," 63.

8   Felicia Darling. *Teachin' It!: Breakout Moves That Break Down Barriers for Community College Students* (Teachers College Press, 2019), 162.

have uplifted and honored Black culture and tradition in my educational community. I have been able to share my story with Black mentors who have guided me along the way. And finally, I have participated in formal/established affinity groups on campus where I have space to reflect on my personal and professional work. Similarly, this text gives us an example of building belonging through three sections: *Honoring Our Communities*, *Honoring Our Stories*, and *Honoring Our Labor*. Not only does each chapter provide a blueprint of different ways this can occur, but it also honors the voices of BIPOC librarians. So often, librarianship pushes BIPOC librarian voices to the margins,[9] and this book allows our voices and experiences to be centralized, amplified, and valued.

Part one, *Honoring Our Communities*, brings us three narratives from BIPOC, female librarians who describe how they work with colleagues on campus to build their community. In the narrative *Communities of Practice*, Oates describes her process of becoming a library administrator at academic libraries as a Black female librarian. She discusses the unique challenges of working at a research university compared to a community college. She learned to overcome isolation by creating ways to give herself, her library, and her position well-deserving recognition while finding community with a Black administrator on campus. Leftwich, Lassiter, Nnadi, and Hobdy further the conversation around honoring communities through a group dialogue around communities of practice in their chapter, *Unique Communities of Practice through Library Work*. The authors explore their identities as Black women and share the individual/ communal benefits of participating in a community of practice. In addition to sharing how they support and inspire each other, the scholars offer suggestions for establishing long-lasting communities of practice.

In *Breaking the Bamboo Library Ceiling*, three Asian American women, Porter, Koshi-Lim, and Ventura, reflect on their time in community and technical colleges. We are introduced to the term "bamboo ceiling" (like "glass ceiling"), which is specific to the problems Asian American women face when seeking promotion and within the profession.[10]

---

9  Rose L. Chou, and Annie Pho. *Pushing the Margins: Women of Color and Intersectionality in LIS* (Sacramento: Library Juice Press, 2018), 8.

10  Sylvia Ann Hewlett, "Breaking Through the Bamboo Ceiling," *Harvard Business Review*, August 3, 2011, https://hbr.org/2011/08/breaking-through-the-bamboo-ce.

The discussion group includes librarians and administrators describing the stereotypes and challenges they have faced in community and technical colleges. Themes revolve around support and community being a strength in the face of adversity and breaking through the bamboo ceiling.

After reading examples of those who have benefited from the community, we take research-based, self-reflective journeys in part two, *Honoring Our Stories*. Four librarians present chapters highlighting themes of realizing self-worth, creating belonging, and advocating for BIPOC student success. In two narratives, the exploration of self-worth includes *Testament of Perseverance: A Journey Through Tenure* by Simpson and *Accepting My Own Worth* by Romero. Both authors carefully describe the process of self-acceptance but through different means. Simpson focuses on prioritizing wellness and self-care as a Black female librarian, while Romero embraces her intersectional identities (Latina and mother) to break the imposter cycle. Kuo, an Asian American male librarian, addresses students' need for community in *Creating a Sense of Belonging*. He provides practical steps community college libraries can take to re-envision spaces for BIPOC students that extend beyond a quiet study space. In *Student Success and Equity in the Library*, Onwuchekwa furthers those steps by focusing on student diversity and equity support in library collections, funding, and outreach.

Finally, in *Honoring Our Labor*, librarians address attitudes, policies, and structures that impact BIPOC individuals on community college campuses. In *Racelighting*, Overduin uses her lived experience as a BIPOC librarian who faced microaggressions to explain how to combat systemic racism. Through powerful writing, she explores how she found her voice and regained her confidence in a system where she was marginalized. Rios-Alvarado addresses some of these same systems in *Learning from the Brown Body*, where she introduces Xicana feminism.[11] She poignantly pulls on her Xicana identity to show how to bring a pedagogy of care into the community college library. Inclusivity is another theme tackled by Ladejobi, who describes her onboarding process as a BIPOC librarian. In *And Now We Are Strangers to Each Other*, the author stresses the importance of creating a positive work

---

11    Ana Castillo, *Massacre of the Dreamers: Essays on Xicanisma*, (Albuquerque: University of New Mexico Press, 2014), 219–35.

environment for librarians of color and reflects on positive and destructive changes that occurred through the years at her institution. Her piece leaves one with a sense of wonder about what "could be" achieved if procedures were more equitable. In a three-part approach, the contributors to *Building Our Own* describe components of communities of practice and form a community for readers. Through lived experience and research, each chapter heightens one's awareness of pedagogy, beliefs, and systems that can enhance a community college library. Most importantly, BIPOC librarians throughout the book are encouraged to use their voices to usher in change in educational settings.

## *Bibliography*

Boyd, Marsha Foster. "WomanistCare: Some Reflections on the Pastoral Care and the Transformation of African American Women." In *Embracing the Spirit: Womanist Perspectives on Hope, Salvation and Transformation*, edited by Emilie M. Townes, 197-202. Maryknoll, NY: Orbis, 1997.

Castillo, Ana. *Massacre of the Dreamers: Essays on Xicanisma*. Albuquerque: University of New Mexico Press, 2014.

Chou, Rose L., and Annie Pho. *Pushing the Margins: Women of Color and Intersectionality in LIS*. Sacramento, CA: Library Juice Press, 2018.

Darling, Felicia. *Teachin' It!: Breakout Moves That Break Down Barriers for Community College Students*. New York: Teachers College Press, 2019.

Gusa, Diane Lynn. "White Institutional Presence: The Impact of Whiteness on Campus Climate." *Harvard Educational Review* 80, no. 4 (2010): 464–90. https://doi.org/10.17763/haer.80.4.p5j483825u110002.

Hewlett, Sylvia Ann. "Breaking Through the Bamboo Ceiling." Harvard Business Review, August 3, 2011. https://hbr.org/2011/08/breaking-through-the-bamboo-ce.

Hotchkins, Bryan K., Jon McNaughtan, and Hugo A. García. "Black Community Collegians' Sense of Belonging as Connected to Enrollment Satisfaction." *Journal of Negro Education* 90, no. 1 (2021): 55–70.

Marineo, Francesca, Heinbach, Chelsea, and Mitola, Rosan. "Building a Culture of Collaboration and Shared Responsibility for Educational Equity Work through an Inclusive Teaching Community of Practice." *Collaborative Librarianship* 13, no. 1 (2022):62-77. Accessed September 28, 2022. https://digitalcommons.du.edu/cgi/viewcontent.cgi?article=1486&context=collaborativelibrarianship.

Neely, Teresa Y., and Kuang-Hwei Lee-Smeltzer. *Diversity Now: People, Collections, and Services in Academic Libraries: Selected Papers from the Big 12 Plus Libraries Consortium Diversity Conference.* Haworth Information Press, 2002.

Regalado, Mariana, and Maura A. Smale. *Academic Libraries for Commuter Students: Research-Based Strategies.* Chicago: ALA Editions, 2018.

Weiner, Stephen. "Accrediting Bodies Must Require a Commitment to Diversity When Measuring a College's Quality." *The Chronicle of Higher Education,* October 1990.

# Foreword

*Lizeth Zepeda*

Community College was a space where my consciousness-raising and learning began. In high school, we're encouraged to strive for a four-year institution and not go to community college because we will get stuck, life will happen, and we will never transfer. There are various reasons why people decide to go to community college. I did not excel in my educational journey until I began my education in a community college. Before community college, I found no connection or inspiration to do my work. I started taking classes and met professors of color who taught curricula that excited me to learn and raised my consciousness. I could finally feel connected to something outside myself. My community college education gave me the foundation to grow and learn as a student. Still, I found the community college library a very white and intimidating space that was hard to navigate.

Now, as a librarian, I reflect on what I wish I had as a first-generation queer Chicana student to feel more welcome to use the space and ask for support. One of the most impactful experiences in a library I often think about when interacting with students was my first semester of community college. In my English 101 course, we wrote essays, were required to type them, and submit a physical copy every week. I was lucky to have a family desktop computer but no printing capabilities at home. I went to the library to print my essay, not realizing that because my old version of *Microsoft Word* was different from the one at the library when I pulled it up to print, it displayed characters instead of words I had written. I panicked and didn't know what to do, and I was so intimidated to ask for assistance from the library workers that I ended up not turning in my assignment or going to class. I felt so defeated. Moments like this that could make or break a student's experience in higher education. *Building Our Own: Critiques, Narratives, and*

*Practices from BIPOC Community College Workers in LIS* spoke to my younger self. The effort, time, and love BIPOC (Black Indigenous and People of Color) library workers in community colleges put into their work is inspirational—their work and visibility matter.

As I read *Building Our Own: Critiques, Narratives, and Practices from BIPOC Community College Workers in LIS*, a compilation by Amanda M. Leftwich and Eva M.L. Rios-Alvarado, I connected to the vulnerability, honesty, microaggressions, and burnout that happens to BIPOC library workers. This book is like nothing I have read before and shows a variety of ways in which we can tell valuable, fruitful stories and research. One example is Alyssa Jocson Porter, Jessica Koshi-Lum, & Gerie Ventura's chapter, where the authors interviewed each other about their experience as administrators and the mentorship needed for BIPOC librarians in these positions of power.

One of the most important things that struck me in this piece is how the authors center the importance of BIPOC visibility in and outside the library, but also a deep reflection of why they stay in these roles—showing what positive leadership is and is not. In Dr. Evangela Oates's chapter, positive leadership showcases an; she has an administrative position, values collaboration, and emphasizes support as an early librarian. This book describes stories, theories, and reflections as a profound love letter to BIPOC library workers' work for their students, staff, faculty, and fellow library community. *Building Our Own* names white supremacy and other powers of oppression that hinder the work of BIPOC library workers from doing their job and staying in the profession. One theme and connection these chapters speak to is the experiences of BIPOC in LIS (Library and Information Science) workers in community colleges. However, the authors in this book also state the very intentional and problematic structures that uphold white supremacy and only want BIPOC library workers for their labor and do not care about dehumanizing or burnout. Unfortunately, there are scenarios where administrators are toxic, as Terezita Overduin's chapter explains, an authentic and vulnerable experience and the impact they can have on BIPOC library workers. These chapters also provide practical step-by-step advice, reflections, and foresight about how the profession can successfully support faculty, staff, students, and librarians.

Many people take traditional or non-traditional routes to community college. Their time is precious, and therefore, community colleges need to be able to provide space, community, and empathy. As an academic librarian at four-year institutions, I have witnessed significant efforts focused on first-year students. The community college transfer students may have receive an orientation but automatically enroll in upper division or capstone courses, which was my experience as a student. Some universities provide classes for first-year students to get oriented to university life. When I began my role at the University of Tennessee in Knoxville, the library had a student success librarian and a curriculum focused on teaching information literacy and learning outcomes for first-year students. While at California State University, Monterey Bay, I participated in programming for the Common Read, where first academic institutions provide first-year students with the same book with an insightful theme and programming. The programming focus was on retaining first-year students and community building. However, the universities provide different community-building activities once they go further in their academic path (or commute or transfer in). The community college experience is different. Andrew Kuo's chapter mentions that there are often no official study spaces outside of the library or traditional programming in community college settings. Kuo says, "[in community college] campuses, the library's position as a study space is amplified as CCs do not have as many informal study spaces as other institutions of higher learning." Community college students commute to classes (which can happen in four-year commuter schools) and promptly go home or work. The community college library is where students will feel that sense of community. The work done by BIPOC librarians in community colleges within and outside the library building is intentional, inclusive, and crucial. As many authors in this book emphasize, these library interactions may be the only exchange students have with the campus community outside their professors.

The contributors of *Building Our Own* all focus on one common theme: students, faculty, and staff on campus need to respect BIPOC library workers in community college settings. This visibility breaks the barriers and institutions that white supremacy has created. One is the tenure process, as Shamika Jamalia Morris Simpson's chapter describes and reflects on how dehumanizing and traumatic working towards permanence can be, especially when you often must go beyond your job description to receive tenure. Another critical theme in this book is what happens when the BIPOC LIS workers get to be their whole selves to work and what masks they wear to avoid microaggressions. Some examples of this include but are not limited to boundaries for work-life balance, activist backgrounds, and ancestral wisdom, as mentioned in Eva M.L. Rios-Alvarado's chapter. Sally Romero's chapter describes her experience of not sharing about being a mother to avoid the microaggressions that come with people's assumptions about parenthood and what changed. As you engage with this book, you will recognize some authors writing about the COVID-19 global pandemic. The pandemic forced Romero to prioritize their own lives and sometimes take them out of their toxic work environments. *Building Our Own* reminds us that we cannot separate ourselves and our work from what is happening in the world and our lives. Moreover, more importantly, whatever BIPOC library workers are going through, they pull through and together to support the communities they serve. *Building Our Own* also allows us to fill a crucial gap in LIS literature and, more importantly, new ideas about where the research can go.

*Building Our Own* focuses on the specific cases in community colleges, and BIPOC LIS workers speak volumes about the LIS profession. These authors reimagine what research can look like when incorporating decolonial, BIPOC, practical, and reflective lenses. This book has taught me much and made me reflect on what it means to be a BIPOC librarian who was also a community college student. These authors' work intends to feel connected to the communities they serve. All library workers, even those outside community colleges, can benefit from the lessons, stories, and research involved in this work. One thing that makes *Building Our Own* so unique is that it reimagines and practices what librarianship can look like with a BIPOC lens through interviews and reflections. As Dele Chinwe Ladejobi's chapter reminds us, that hiring and retaining BIPOC librarians starts in the hiring and onboarding process and must constantly continue. This book speaks many truths and gives readers the tools to imagine a new place to fight for a more conscious world.

# Introduction

*Amanda M. Leftwich and Eva M.L. Rios-Alvarado*

Where are all the BIPOC (Black, Indigenous, and People of Color) from community colleges? This book was the brainchild of a conversation after the People of Color in Library & Information Science (POCinLIS) Summit at Loyola Marymount University in Los Angeles, California, held in 2018.[1] We knew each other colloquially, but at conferences, we noticed an absence of Black, Indigenous, and People of Color (BIPOC) community college librarians and workers. Library conferences are often grounds for networking and future research with colleagues nationwide. Frequently, library conferences are exclusionary to BIPOC community college librarians due to cost, timing, and lack of learning objectives that match collegewide goals.[2] If BIPOC community college librarians were often missing from those spaces, what does that mean for scholarly pursuits and the growth of the specialty? Organizations must not overlook the scholarship and voices of BIPOC community college (CC) librarians because of the unique nature of our work and the diverse community support. With this in mind, we sought to collect and understand the work of BIPOC community college library workers and the challenges and successes they face in the workplace.

We noticed a lack of understanding and awareness of the issues BIPOC community college library workers face outside of CCs. We had support from We Here and other designated BIPOC-only spaces, but the

---

1 "POCinLIS Summit," *Loyola Marymount University*, July 13, 2018, https://digitalcommons.lmu.edu/pocinlis/2018/.

2 Evangela Quinette Oates, "Marginalized Faculty at Marginalized Institutions: Counternarratives as Resistance in Exploring the Experiences of Black Librarians at Public, Two-Year Colleges," (PhD diss., University of Nebraska-Lincoln, 2020), 79.

focus remains on large research universities.[3] BIPOC CC library workers must have a place to express themselves, find community, create structures for solidarity, and find healing. From the outside, community colleges as institutions are inclusive spaces for students, not necessarily for BIPOC faculty or staff, especially not within LIS, because of the lack of support and structures from either group. Most of the literature focuses on student perspectives, including better accessibility needs for transportation to/from colleges, finances, mental health, and guidance for completing coursework.[4]

The absence of BIPOC narratives in community college literature is intrinsically rooted in how community colleges came into being. The very founding of these institutions involves a history of disenfranchisement and erasure. The Morrill Act of 1862, signed by President Lincoln, created land grants to provide access to higher education beyond secondary education for agricultural and technical education.[5] An updated version of the act in 1890 gave African Americans access to higher education as well (paving the way for Historically Black Colleges and Universities (HBCUs).[6] Access to federal funding paved the way for community colleges. However, the first community college, Joliet Junior College, didn't open until 1901 with the support of the president of the University of Chicago.[7] Other colleges existed as early as 1785 in Pennsylvania. However, they were funded at the state level and on year-term leases.[8] California had similar commitments and created the California Upward Extension Act, which authorized the creation of community colleges in the State in 1907.[9] Other States, following California's community colleges/junior colleges model, and opened

---

[3] We Here, accessed December 2, 2022, https://www.wehere.space/.

[4] Christine Wolff-Eisenberg and Bradlee, "Amplifying Student Voices: The Community College Libraries and Academic Support for Student Success Project," *Ithaka S+R*, August 13, 2018, https://doi.org/10.18665/sr.308086.

[5] George R. Boggs and Lawrence A. Galizio, "The Important History of Community Colleges," *Diverse: Issues in Higher Education* 38, no. 21 (2022), 33, https://www.diverseeducation.com/opinion/article/15288858/the-important-history-of-community-colleges.

[6] Boggs & Galizio, "The Important History of Community Colleges," 33.

[7] Boggs & Galizio, "The Important History of Community Colleges," 33; Richard L. Drury, "Community Colleges in America: A Historical Perspective," *Inquiry: The Journal of the Virginia Community Colleges* 8, no. 1 (2003): 1.

[8] Asa E. Martin, "Pennsylvania's Land Grant Under The Morrill Act of 1862," *Pennsylvania History: A Journal of Mid-Atlantic Studies* 9, no. 2 (April 1942): 87.

[9] Boggs & Galizio, "The Important History of Community Colleges," 33.

CCs in Texas, Illinois, Mississippi, Missouri, Iowa, Kansas, and Michigan.[10] In 1920, the American Association of Community Colleges (AAJC) aimed to support the development and sustainability of community colleges.[11] However, it was not until the Servicemen's Readjustment Act, also known as the GI Bill of Rights, passed in 1944, gave veterans scholarships to attend college, and the Truman Commission Report of 1947 which "called for the establishment of a network of public community colleges that would charge little or no tuition, provide cultural centers, serve the local areas in which they served, and offer a comprehensive curriculum.[12] The Commission, in essence, called for equality of opportunity for all and a massive expansion of higher education in America."[13] While the Morrill Acts of 1862 and 1890 gave an equitable start to education for farmers and Black (African American) students, it stole Indigenous land already settled within what would become community colleges and university campuses. Bryan McKinley Jones Brayboy and Amanda R. Tachine noted, "The Morrill Act was intentional and linked to systemic goals of eliminating Indigenous presence and replacing it with settlers."[14] This, coupled with accounting for the lack of Indigenous faculty and staff within community colleges, is troubling. Brayboy and Tachine explain, "erasure is still achieved by the lack of Indigenous students, staff, and faculty in institutions of higher education. There are too few Native students in "mainstream" institutions and even fewer staff and faculty."[15] Community colleges, and therefore, community college libraries, are not above reproach! The vocational awe, "the set of ideas, values, and assumptions librarians have about themselves and the profession that result in beliefs that libraries as institutions are inherently good and sacred, and therefore

---

10   Alice C. Andrews and James W. Fonseca, *Community Colleges in the United States: A Geographical Perspective* (Washington, DC.: Association of American Geographers, 1998), 5.

11   Drury, "Community Colleges in America: A Historical Perspective," 3.

12   Alice C. Andrews and James W. Fonseca, *Community Colleges in the United States: A Geographical Perspective*, 6.

13   Drury, "Community Colleges in America: A Historical Perspective," 5.

14   Bryan McKinley Jones Brayboy and Amanda R. Tachine, "Myths, Erasure, and Violence: The Immoral Triad of the Morrill Act," *Native American and Indigenous Studies* 8, no. 1 (Spring 2021): 140, https://www.muse.jhu.edu/article/784826.

15   Bryan McKinley Jones Brayboy and Amanda R. Tachine, "Myths, Erasure, and Violence", 141.

beyond critique,"[16] surrounding these institutions must be examined and discussed. Stigma or shame have no place in CCs, but we must evaluate our understanding of the history around them to create equitable processes and better systems for students and employees.

The ratio of diversity, equity, and retention for faculty to students at community colleges is problematic because it fosters issues of inequity and places of unchecked racism. Currently, there are 1,462 community colleges across the United States.[17] The percentages for BIPOC full-time faculty are small, with only "8% were Asian/Pacific Islander males, and 3% were Asian/Pacific Islander females. Black males, Black females, and Hispanic males accounted for 2% of full-time professors. The following groups each made up 1% or less of full-time professors: Hispanic females, American Indian/Alaska Native individuals, and individuals of Two or more races."[18] The ratio of BIPOC faculty/librarians is not reflective of the BIPOC student population, with 41% Hispanic or Latino/x students, 32% Black students, and 25% Asian students, respectively.[19] With these demographics at play, it is no wonder faculty of color report problems with isolation[20] and cultural taxation or "the obligation to show good citizenship toward the [academic] institution by serving its needs for ethnic representation on committees or to demonstrate knowledge and commitment to a cultural group, which may even bring accolades to the institution but which is not usually rewarded by the institution on whose behalf the service was performed."[21] These unrecognized requirements of BIPOC faculty in a

---

16  Fobazi Ettarh, "Vocational Awe and Librarianship: The Lies That We Tell Ourselves," *In the Library with the Lead Pipe* (January 10, 2018), https://www.inthelibrarywiththeleadpipe.org/2018/vocational-awe/.

17  "Community College Facts at a Glance", About Ed," U.S. Department of Education, Office of Career, Technical, and Adult Education, last modified February 10, 2017, https://www2.ed.gov/about/offices/list/ovae/pi/cclo/ccfacts.html.

18  U.S. Department of Education, National Center for Education Statistics, *The Condition of Education 2020 (NCES 2020-144)*, May 2022, 151, https://nces.ed.gov/pubs2020/2020144.pdf.

19  U.S. Department of Education, Office of Planning, Evaluation and Policy Development, *Advancing Diversity and Inclusion in Higher Education Key Data Highlights Focusing on Race and Ethnicity and Promising Practices*, November 2016, 28, https://www2.ed.gov/rschstat/research/pubs/advancing-diversity-inclusion.pdf.

20  Adalberto Aguirre, Jr., "The Personal Narrative as Academic Storytelling: A Chicano's Search for Presence and Voice in Academe," *International Journal of Qualitative Studies in Education* 18, no. 2 (2015): 154; Oates, "Marginalized," 112,161.

21  Amado M. Padilla, "Ethnic Minority Scholars, Research, and Mentoring: Current and Future Issues," *Educational Researcher* 23, no. 4 (1994): 26.

predominantly white profession leave them dissatisfied, especially library workers, moving them negatively towards the effects of burnout, low morale, workism, or " the belief that work is not only necessary to economic production, but also the centerpiece of one's identity and life's purpose; and the belief that any policy to promote human welfare must always encourage more work," traumatic work experiences (e.g., violent or aggressive behavior), and isolation.[22]

Librarianship must explore BIPOC community college library workers' lived experiences to create opportunities for positive changes. The limited research obscured serious problems with unpaid labor, workplace hostilities, and a poor retention rate of BIPOC community college librarians. A seminal text by Alyssa Jocson Porter, Sharon Spence-Wilcox, and Kimberly Tate-Malone surveyed women of color librarians working at community and technical colleges (CTCs) and emotional labor.[23] They explained the lack of literature on the subject, "emotional labor is an inevitable experience for CTC reference and instruction librarians, who must regulate the complicated emotions that arise for the sake of their students, colleagues, and themselves. While professional literature offers insights into emotional labor from multiple academic disciplines, there is seldom focus on the CTC settings and the intersectionality of gender and race."[24] Dr. Evangela Oates' dissertation is one of the few empirical research studies that explores gender and race in CCs.[25] LIS tends to group BIPOC LIS workers' experiences, focusing on the effects of racism on their work lives. Juleah Swanson, Azusa Tanaka, and Isabel Gonzalez-Smith's

---

22  Nathan M. Smith and Veneese C. Nelson, "Burnout: A Survey of Academic Reference Librarians," *College and Research Libraries* 44, no. 3 (1983): 248, https://doi.org/10.5860/crl_44_03_245; Barbara Wood, Ana Guimaraes, Christina Holm, Sherrill Hayes, and Kyle Brooks, "Academic Librarian Burnout: A Survey using the Copenhagen Burnout Inventory (CBI)," *Journal of Library Administration* 60, issue 5 (2020): 13, https://doi.org/10.1080/01930826.2020.1729622; Kaetrena Davis Kendrick and Ione T. Damasco, "Low Morale in Ethnic and Racial Minority Academic Librarians: An Experiential Study," *Library Trends* 68, no. 2 (2019): 181, doi:10.1353/lib.2019.0036; Derek Thompson, "Workism Is Making Americans Miserable," *The Atlantic*, February 25, 2019, https://www.theatlantic.com/ideas/archive/2019/02/religion-workism-making-americans-miserable/583441/; "Survey Data Visualizations," *Urban Library Trauma Study*, accessed December 13, 2022, https://urbanlibrariansunite.org/ults/#ults-survey; Adalberto Aguirre, Jr., "The Personal Narrative as Academic Storytelling," 26.

23  Alyssa Jocson Porter, Sharon Spence-Wilcox, and Kimberly Tate-Malone, "I, Too: Unmasking Emotional Labor of Women of Color Community College Librarians," in *Pushing the Margins Women of Color and Intersectionality*, eds. Rose L. Chou and Annie Pho (Sacramento: Library Juice Press, 2018), 273.

24  Alyssa Jocson Porter, Sharon Spence-Wilcox, and Kimberly Tate-Malone, "I, Too," 277.

25  Oates, *"Marginalized,"* 185.

important work on the lived experiences of academic librarians of color makes some references to community college librarians and focuses on the student population and perceptions of working at a two-year institution.[26] These gaps in the literature are not the fault of one author or survey but a springboard to more research into understanding the experiences of BIPOC community college librarians. In sharing our stories, we begin to shine a light on the problems within the field of education and aim to change them for the next generation of BIPOC community college librarians and library employees.

## Amanda M. Leftwich

As a junior in high school, my collegiate options seemed endless. Which school should I choose? Should I move away from my family or stay close to home? What major should I choose? What resources should I have to create a successful career? As a first-generation college student, I was unaware of how many decisions I needed to make! A local community college was behind my high school, and I frequently crossed paths with its students. As a result, I began to wonder if community college was the right choice for me. I didn't know what I wanted to do career-wise, and the idea of a large university made me nervous, particularly after attending a small Catholic high school. However, broaching the idea of a CC wasn't well-received by family and friends. My queries were met with many of the same stereotypes CC students experience today (e.g., CC students never finish college/transfer out, and it takes longer to complete the degree). This was the first time I experienced "ccstigma" — the stereotype that community colleges are lesser institutions and, therefore, not worth students attending or considering as an option within their educational journey.[27]

It is essential to discuss stigma because it outlines the scarcity of BIPOC CC librarians/library workers and their crucial roles in the institutions they support. Steve Robinson has called for an end to this stigma

---

26. Juleah Swanson, Azusa Tanaka, and Isabel Gonzalez-Smith, "Lived Experience of Academic Librarians of Color," *College and Research Libraries* 79, no. 7 (2018): 881, https://doi.org/10.5860/crl.79.7.876.

27. Jonathan Turk, "Erasing the Community College Stigma," last modified June 28, 2019, https://www.higheredtoday.org/2019/06/26/erasing-community-college-stigma/.

using the hashtag #EndCCStigma on social media platforms.[28] Robinson mentions, "The only way to change the inaccurate stereotypes is to address them directly. Sharing the hashtag is a framework for promoting these institutions and empowers those on the receiving end of negative comments. Community college stigma is not something that marketing alone can change. Rather, the campaign simultaneously highlights positive stories while directly calling out the stigma for what it is."[29] The high cost of college education makes this stigma more insidious, especially considering student career outcomes. The stigma also doesn't end with just students. Academic librarians and faculty have long faced "ccstigma." I have had and continue to have derisive assumptions made about my education. Frequently, I am asked why do I stay at a community college when there are "so many other options for work." People want to know if I do any *real* work during my workday. Many of these questions come from within the field— from colleagues, research institutions, and universities. My experience is not singular. Stigmatizing and ostracizing BIPOC from the profession means their labor and narratives will continue to exist in the shadows.

Supporting and collecting information on the lived experiences of community colleges is essential to our profession because of its role in BIPOC communities. Our work with students, ending stigma, and confronting community college history is vital to challenging the myths surrounding community colleges. Our students' needs are changing, and the role of faculty/staff must also change. As we ask this population to do more, we must do more to support them to avoid system collapses. The pandemic and post-pandemic eras continue to reveal that we must question everything we thought we knew before.

BIPOC community college librarians are not receiving the assistance for their labor assistance. As we collected stories of our colleagues' experiences, it became even more apparent how much labor BIPOC CC librarians and library workers do outside traditional librarian roles. To do our jobs effectively, library workers need to embody the skills

---

28  Steve Robinson, "From the President's Desk #EndCCStigma: Social Media as a Tool to Change Public Perception of 2-year Colleges," *New Directions for Community Colleges* 197 (2022): 142, https://doi.org/10.1002/cc.20503.

29  Steve Robinson, "From the president's desk #EndCCStigma: Social Media as a Tool to Change Public Perception of 2-year Colleges," *New Directions for Community Colleges*, 144.

of social workers,[30] leaders, teachers, volunteer therapists. Our diverse faces within the profession and support for their needs are at the bottom of the list. Library workers must do this because CCs refuse to invest in those student support roles. We're often in these roles because of the nature of our work and closeness with students. BIPOC CC librarians cannot and should not fill the gaps that CCs are either unable to pay for or unwilling to serve because of the critical nature of our work. We are professionals and must receive respect from our institutions and colleagues. Our Gen Z students and the pandemic revealed the shortsightedness of grind culture— "a culture of raw achievement where longer and longer hours are not just the norm, they are the metric for success."[31] As cultural workers move towards collective healing,[32] we must challenge this outdated narrative and how it has proliferated library work and its workers. Moreover, while we move in new, better, more productive directions, we must do more to showcase the sheer amount done in our libraries by these overburdened workers and the critical role it plays in making those institutions great.

BIPOC community college librarians matter. Receiving support for our work matters. *Building Our Own* highlights the fact that not only do BIPOC CC librarians exist, but the role of our work within the profession. However, it's crucial to validate these stories and look for sustainable solutions to their problems. The profession thrives when we all can share and amplify our work. Locally, library organizations should ensure all CC librarians receive monetary support to attend and present at conferences, like the People of Color in Library and Information Science Summit (POCinLIS Summit) and the ACRL (Association of College and Research Libraries conference — the very place that created the space for this book. CC library workers rarely receive leave time for professional development for research development and scholarly work for this essential population. However, being included in scholarship means scholars must have time to write away from the

---

30  Lynn Westbrook, "I'm Not a Social Worker: An Information Service Model for Working with Patrons in Crisis," *The Library Quarterly: Information, Community, Policy* 85, no. 1 (January 2015): 7, https://doi.org/10.1086/679023.

31  Lewis Nathaniel, "Grind Culture," last modified Nov 26, 2019, https://medium.com/@lewisibdp/grind-culture-e2aa2b84ab5c.

32  Alice Hahn, "A Collective Effort: Healing, Trauma, and Precarity in Public Librarianship," accessed December 13, 2022, https://aireuhl.github.io/portfolio/Collective%20Effort_Hahn.pdf.

reference desk. Nationally, support could result in lower costs or more scholarships for CC librarians; most CCs have no professional development funding outside the larger institutions. As you read through these narratives, ask yourself one question: whose stories are missing from LIS scholarship? Why aren't these stories being shared? The more we question, the more we can collect and share stories outside of the overrepresented narratives and shift the paradigm to highlight previously untold stories. Our intentions and inclusion practices must not exclude anyone based on where they work.

## Eva M.L. Rios-Alvarado

We are deeply passionate about telling our stories, to document how we work with students who empower us to be dedicated community college library educators. We set out to build our own. We constructed the idea to write this text some years back and began to recruit interesting and interested community college colleagues. Amanda, being the visionary she is, trusted me, and I trusted her to share our deepest and most critical thoughts about our work in the community colleges. Recently, we have experienced a significant trauma in learning and teaching due to the events of the COVID-19 pandemic.[33] Yes, learning has changed. Pandemic or not, community colleges and college libraries need moratoriums to bring in the praxis of a changing education. Has your library wholeheartedly confronted education within the COVID-19 pandemic context? Have we reality-checked ourselves to note this new generation has endured a moment of learning hardships that we now need to figure out?[34] Have we healed? We cannot lie to ourselves and say it will fix itself and everything will return to what it was. Do we even want to go back to what it was? Not me.

I first met Amanda when she presented her work on the "Wheel of Wellness"[35] for information workers at the POCinLIS Summit in Southern California. Her work as a healer in LIS gives me hope and calls to

---

33   Christopher Prokes and Jaqueline Housel, "Community College Students Perceptions of Remote Learning Shifts Due to COVID-19," *TechTrends* 65, no. 4 (July 2021): 586.

34   Eliza Fawcett, "The Pandemic Generation Goes to College. It Has Not Been Easy," *New York Times*, November 1, 2022, https://www.nytimes.com/2022/11/01/us/covid-college-students.html.

35   Amanda M. Leftwich, "Redefining the Wellness Wheel for Librarians of Color" (lightning round talk, People of Color in LIS Summit (POCinLIS Summit), Loyola Marymount University, Los Angeles, CA, July 13, 2018).

me as a person seeking healing. In retrospect, when Amanda invited me to join her, I felt the endeavor to co-edit a book about librarians of color in community colleges to be timely and needed. Never having worked on a project of its kind, I had little idea of how deeply I would devote myself to ensuring we got this done right. And with our project came personal growth, to work on an academic venture that allowed me to lovingly analyze and reflect on my community college work and that of colleagues around the nation. Our collaboration aspires to weave our librarian lives into the academic and personal realms in ways that value our feminist and womanist methods and thoughts. Within me, I feel a great privilege to share my humble experiences as a community college librarian from the Southwest, where my spatial realities and connections to education and libraries derive. I also feel an even more significant commitment to ensure community college voices and experiences from all over the nation are in this book to frame who we are in the community colleges at this moment and to share what is happening in the lives of information workers in our diverse and unique sector of education.

Previously, in my years developing into my librarian career, I had read books about librarians' lives and work experiences. To this day, the *Black Librarian in America*, edited by E.J. Josey,[36] is a vivid reminder of how librarians have been treated in our profession and society. These *testimonios* (testimonies) by Black librarians are gifts, and similarly, they are painful librarian genealogies, which form the historical and social context of our profession as information workers. Having a reference to written experiences by librarians before us, explaining their work in our profession, helped frame a context for the value of our stories as people of color in community college libraries. Thus, it was the work and lives of librarians of color, Black librarians, before us who dared document their experiences, which validated and inspired me to share mine. As community college library educators, we are part of a learning atmosphere different from four-year universities. As educators and students, our realities, lives, and stories are just as important to share. Our worlds are filled with life lessons and knowledge that will go unknown unless framed from our perspectives.

As educators and anyone alive now, I wish it were possible to stop the clock and heal. However, we are not in spaces of care for the most part

---

36   E.J. Josey, ed., *Black Librarian in America* (Metuchen: Scarecrow Press, 1970), vii-xvi.

within institutions. Encouraging care is excellent; however, when will our library jobs allow the time for care in our current academic and library production models for the benefit of ourselves and students? What would we do and demand if we could stop the clock and have a moment of truth? Our chapters clearly express and require the attention of what matters in our work. I am not interested in work focused on reform, *necesitamos libertad* (we need freedom)! So much of education is reformist, not addressing the pain and joy communities, students, and their families experience. As I have learned in my community and from learning from others, it is impossible to divide our needs as people from our needs as learners. In the words of Mestre Claudio, a Capoeira teacher from Brazil, who came to teach a week of Capoeira Angola workshops for Solsinmotion,[37] where I train Capoeira Angola in El Sereno, a Los Angeles *barrio* (neighborhood), a few years back at the Eastside Café: "you have to be willing to teach, and you have to be willing to learn." I live by these words in my daily educational practice. Furthermore, I would like all readers of this text to consider how you work and similarly acknowledge what you have or will learn from these fantastic chapters.

## About the book

This collection has common themes throughout the sections, including isolation, emotional and invisible labor, sexism, racism, lack of access to training/professional development awareness, self-care, communities of practice, and harmful systems. While these experiences and incidents are included in other essential works, no collection is dedicated solely to BIPOC LIS community college leaders, scholars, and educators. The contributors opted to tell their stories through interviews and reflective writing. Their approaches are familiar to the profession but have the potential to set a new standard for the CC field because there are so few narrative-focused collections in the field. All the chapters were peer-reviewed by BIPOC librarians of color, most of whom have either worked in or are alumni of a CC. The purpose of the peer review was to allow intentional feedback where we had cultural, institutional, and experiential gaps in knowledge. We acknowledge and recognize other gaps within the book, including the need for scholarly from Indigenous CC librarians. We hope future books about

---

37 "About," Solsinmotion, accessed November 16, 2022, https://solsinmotion.com.

community college libraries/librarians include more Native American and Indigenous perspectives, lenses, and experiences. This book aims to start a conversation about the lived experiences and stories of BIPOC CC librarians and examine the systems in which we work. There will always be more stories to share and more to learn.

The editors divided the book into sections: Section 1: Honoring Our Communities: Building Our Own Practices; Section 2: Honoring Our Stories: Frameworks, Identities, and Narratives; and Section 3: Honoring Our Labor: Reflections on Our Work. We have intentionally and carefully laid out these sections to provide the reader with a better understanding of our work and processes. Within these chapters, you'll find a common thread of experiences. Although community college librarians are not a monolith, similar experiences of how they approach their work and research are illustrated here. You'll often see the terminology of BIPOC and librarian/library workers throughout the book. The term, BIPOC "highlights the unique relationship to whiteness that Indigenous and Black (African Americans) people have, which shapes the experiences of and relationship to white supremacy for all people of color within a U.S. context. We unapologetically focus on and center relationships among BIPOC folks."[38] This framework provides an intentional understanding of who the authors and we are referring to within the chapters; no social identity is a catch-all; using the term, BIPOC assists with a clarification that we hope anchors authors' research and narratives. The terms librarian and library worker are used interchangeably throughout this collection. Although this collection mainly focuses on the narratives and experiences of librarians, we validate the work of our colleagues and their contributions to our work. We thank them for their often-unseen labor, energy, and time. We hope this collection will encourage others to focus on their work within the field.

When we started this book, we endeavored to tell our stories with thoughtful applications and experiences. We hope it inspires future authors to share their stories in ways that focus on educational liberation for library employees, communities, and libraries. As we edited the chapters, we were empowered to share the authors' stories and bring their inspiration and power to LIS scholarship. This book, *Building Our Own*, is a small but mighty compilation of the work of BIPOC CC librarians and library workers. It holds no punches in grounding our

---

38 "Our Mission," The BIPOC Project, accessed December 13, 2022, https://www.thebipocproject.org/.

work and centering our voices in solidarity. We may have had to build our own, but we hope to move beyond building our own structures. Our experiences and narratives matter. We see you. We hear you. We are rooting for you.

## Bibliography

Aguirre, Jr. Adalberto. "The Personal Narrative as Academic Storytelling: A Chicano's Search for Presence and Voice in Academe." *International Journal of Qualitative Studies in Education* 18, no. 2 (2005): 147–63. https://doi.org/10.1080/0951839042000333956.

Andrews Alice C., and James W. Fonseca. *Community Colleges in the United States: a Geographical Perspective.* Washington, DC.: Association of American Geographers, 1998.

The BIPOC Project. "Our Mission." Accessed December 13, 2022, https://www.thebipocproject.org/.

Brayboy, Bryan McKinley Jones, and Amanda R. Tachine. "Myths, Erasure, and Violence: The Immoral Triad of the Morrill Act." *Native American and Indigenous Studies* 8 no, 1, (Spring 2021): 139–1404. https://www.muse.jhu.edu/article/784826.

Boggs, George R., and Lawrence A. Galizio. "The Important History of Community Colleges." *Diverse Issues in Higher Education 38*, no. 21 (2022): 33–34. https://www.diverseeducation.com/opinion/article/15288858/the-important-history-of-community-colleges.

Drury, Richard L. "Community Colleges in America: A Historical Perspective." *Inquiry The Journal of the Virginia Community Colleges* 8, no. 1 (2003): 1–7.

Ettarh, Fobazi. "Vocational Awe and Librarianship: The Lies That We Tell Ourselves." *In the Library with the Lead Pipe* (January 10, 2018). https://www.inthelibrarywiththeleadpipe.org/2018/vocational-awe/.

Fawcett, Eliza. "The Pandemic Generation Goes to College. It Has Not Been Easy." *New York Times.* November 1, 2022. https://www.nytimes.com/2022/11/01/us/covid-college-students.html.

Hahn, Alice. "A Collective Effort: Healing, Trauma, and Precarity in Public Librarianship," accessed December 13, 2022, https://aireuhl.github.io/portfolio/Collective%20Effort_Hahn.pdf.

Jocson Porter Alyssa, Sharon Spence-Wilcox, and Kimberly Tate-Malone. "I, Too: Unmasking Emotional Labor of Women of Color Community College Librarians." in *Pushing the Margins Women of Color and Intersectionality*, edited by Rose L. Chou and Annie Pho, 273–300. Sacramento: Library Juice Press, 2018.

Josey, E.J. ed., *Black Librarian in America*. Metuchen: Scarecrow Press, 1970.

Kendrick, Kaetrena Davis, and Ione T. Damasco, "Low Morale in Ethnic and Racial Minority Academic Librarians: An Experiential Study." *Library Trends* 68, no. 2 (2019): 174–212. doi:10.1353/lib.2019.0036.

Leftwich, Amanda M. "Redefining the Wellness Wheel for Librarians of Color." Lightning round talk, People of Color in LIS Summit (POCinLIS Summit), Loyola Marymount University, Los Angeles, CA, July 13, 2018.

Nathaniel, Lewis. "Grind Culture." last modified Nov 26, 2019, https://medium.com/@lewisibdp/grind-culture-e2aa2b84ab5c.

Oates, Evangela Quinette. "Marginalized Faculty at Marginalized Institutions: Counternarratives as Resistance in Exploring the Experiences of Black Librarians at Public, Two-Year Colleges." PhD diss., University of Nebraska-Lincoln, Nebraska, 2020. ProQuest.

Padilla, Amado M. "Ethnic Minority Scholars, Research, and Mentoring: Current and Future Issues." *Educational Researcher* 23, no. 4: 24–27.

"POCinLIS Summit." *Loyola Marymount University*. July 13, 2018. https://digitalcommons.lmu.edu/pocinlis/2018/.

Prokes, Christopher, and Jaqueline Housel. "Community College Students Perceptions of Remote Learning Shifts Due to COVID-19." *TechTrends* 65, no. 4 (July 2021): 586–87. https://doi.org/10.1007/s11528-021-00587-8.

Robinson, Steve. "From the President's Desk #EndCCStigma: Social Media as a Tool to Change Public Perception of 2-year Colleges." *New Directions for Community Colleges* 197 (2022): 141–55. https://doi.org/10.1002/cc.20503.

Solsinmotion. "About. "Accessed November 16, 2022, https://solsinmotion.com.

Smith, Nathan M., and Veneese C. Nelson, "Burnout: A Survey of Academic Reference Librarians." *College and Research Libraries* 44, no. 3 (May 1983): 245–50. https://doi.org/10.5860/crl_44_03_245.

Swanson, Juleah, Azusa Tanaka, and Isabel Gonzalez-Smith. "Lived Experience of Academic Librarians of Color." *College and Research Libraries* 79, no. 7 (2018): 876–94. https://doi.org/10.5860/crl.79.7.876.

Thompson, Derek. "Workism Is Making Americans Miserable." *The Atlantic*, February 25, 2019. https://www.theatlantic.com/ideas/archive/2019/02/religion-workism-making-americans-miserable/583441/.

Turk, Jonathan. "Erasing the Community College Stigma." Last modified June 28, 2019. https://www.higheredtoday.org/2019/06/26/erasing-community-college-stigma/.

Urban Library Trauma Study. "Survey Data Visualizations." Accessed December 13, 2022, https://urbanlibrariansunite.org/ults/#ults-survey.

U.S. Department of Education, Office of Career, Technical, and Adult Education, "About Ed." Last modified February 10, 2017, https://www2.ed.gov/about/offices/list/ovae/pi/cclo/ccfacts.html.

U.S. Department of Education, National Center for Education Statistics. *The Condition of Education 2020 (NCES 2020-144)*. May 2020. https://nces.ed.gov/pubs2020/2020144.pdf.

U.S. Department of Education, Office of Planning, Evaluation and Policy Development. *Advancing Diversity and Inclusion in Higher Education Key Data Highlights Focusing on Race and Ethnicity and Promising Practices*. November 2016. https://www2.ed.gov/rschstat/research/pubs/advancing-diversity-inclusion.pdf.

We Here. Accessed December 2, 2022. https://www.wehere.space/.

Westbrook, Lynn. "I'm Not a Social Worker": An Information Service Model for Working with Patrons in Crisis." *The Library Quarterly: Information, Community, Policy* 85, no. 1 (January 2015): 6–25. https://doi.org/10.1086/679023.

Wolff-Eisenberg, Christine, and Braddlee. "Amplifying Student Voices: The Community College Libraries and Academic Support for Student Success Project." *Ithaka S+R*. Last Modified 13 August 2018. https://doi.org/10.18665/sr.308086.

Wood, Barbara, Ana Guimaraes, Christina Holm, Sherrill Hayes, and Kyle Brooks. "Academic Librarian Burnout: A Survey Using the Copenhagen Burnout Inventory (CBI)." *Journal of Library Administration* 60, issue 5 (2020): 512–31. https://doi.org/10.1080/01930826.2020.1729622.

**Honoring Our Communities**
Building Our Own Practices

# "Breaking the Bamboo Library Ceiling"
## Asian American Women's Path to Community & Technical College Library Administration

*Alyssa Jocson Porter, Jess Koshi-Lum, and Gerie Ventura*

## Introduction

In this transcribed interview, we—three Asian American[1] women leaders in community and technical colleges (CTC), two in library administration roles, and one faculty member who wonders if a similar role is in her own future—explore our career paths in library administration, the challenges we have faced because of our identities, and the scarcity of mentors who look like us.[2] We each, at times, have felt unseen or unheard while sitting in unfriendly spaces, and we wondered if other Asian American women share similar experiences. The phrase "bamboo ceiling," similar to the phrase "glass ceiling," has been used to describe the hardships particular to Asian American women wanting to seek promotion.[3] We recognize that the phrase "bamboo ceiling" is problematic as it does not capture the comprehensive experiences of Asian Americans in administrative roles. However, it is still a

---

1   Anna Purna Kambhampaty, "In 1968, These Activists Coined the Term 'Asian American'—And Helped Shape Decades of Advocacy," *Time*, May 22, 2020, https://time.com/5837805/asian-american-history.

2   Binh P Le, "Academic Library Leadership Race and Gender," *International Journal of Librarianship* 6, no. 1 (2021): 15. According to Le, "only a handful of Asian Americans hold the position of library director in over 3,500 U.S. academic libraries."

3   Sylvia Ann Hewlett, "Breaking Through the Bamboo Ceiling," *Harvard Business Review*, August 3, 2011, https://hbr.org/2011/08/breaking-through-the-bamboo-ce.

commonly used term in research on this topic. The imagery resonates with the challenges that we experienced as we moved into higher education leadership in community colleges, where we weren't seeing ourselves represented.

We chose the interview format for the ease of clearly conveying our stories and for its accessibility in language. Although we come from different backgrounds and experiences, we lead with a similar "heart talk" over "head talk" framework, as these topics of race and identity are emotional to discuss and easily identified in formal academic research. This interview took place over Zoom sessions on July 2 & 9, 2021. We've edited the interview transcript for length and clarity, added citations, and suggested resources to provide context to our conversation. We also offer tips at the end of this chapter for existing executive administrators to recruit and retain a more diverse workforce, and we hope we provide insight and inspire Asian Americans to pursue library leadership and administrative roles.

## The Interview

**Alyssa Jocson Porter**  *Let's start by introducing ourselves, our current roles and workplaces, and why we've gathered today.*

**Jocson Porter**  I'm Alyssa, a Filipina-American faculty librarian at Seattle Central College (SCC). I started as a reference assistant there in 2012, became adjunct faculty, then full-time tenure-track, and now I'm already thinking, "What's next," which is bizarre.

**Jess Koshi-Lum**  My name is Jess Koshi-Lum. I am a fifth-generation Japanese-Chinese American. I'm currently the associate dean of the library at Renton Technical College (RTC) in Renton, Washington, just south of Seattle. I came to RTC as a tenure-track faculty librarian, and I coordinated the information literacy instruction program. In my last year of the tenure process, I was appointed to be the interim associate dean of the library. A few months later, I applied for a permanent position and was hired. In my current role, I oversee library faculty and staff.

**Gerie Ventura**  I'm Gerie Ventura (also Filipino American), the library director at Highline College in Des Moines, Washington. I started at Highline as a work-study student in the library. My supervisor wasn't happy with her job, and she mentored me so I could do her job part-time when she resigned. I started working full-time in 1995 as a paraprofessional for 20 years. I realized I needed more education if I was going to "move up" or do anything different. So, I went to library school, and the stars aligned. I've been the library director for three-plus years at the same institution the whole time, which has its pluses and minuses.

**Jocson Porter** I've been thinking about how we're already under-represented as Asian Americans in the library profession and even less so in administrative roles.[4] When I started at SCC, Wai-Fong Lee was the library dean, and it was inspiring to see a library administrator who was Asian right away. When she retired soon after, though, I thought, "Wait, who else is there?" Also, I was recently talking to my dad about his 40+ year career as a mechanical engineer, and he revealed that he never pursued promotions because he didn't think his white colleagues would take him seriously. That blew my mind. There are times when I hang back at work myself because I doubt my leadership abilities. So, I wanted to talk to the current Asian American library admins I know—you two—about ideas like this.

**Koshi-Lum** Not too long ago, I was in Alyssa's position, where I was like, "Do I have leadership capabilities? Am I a leader?" It took a few people to encourage me to apply for leadership roles to realize I had leadership material. I want to share our stories, to talk about our barriers, but also talk about our commonalities and our sources of strength.

**Ventura** I'm excited that Alyssa's even considering joining us. I think we're all natural leaders; we just must get to the point where we realize it.

**Jocson Porter** What inspired y'all to become librarians and why, specifically in community & technical colleges?

**Koshi-Lum** As an undergraduate, I did a lot of retail. I spent much of my childhood on the islands of Maui and Oahu. When you're young in

---

4  U.S. Department of Labor, Bureau of Labor Statistics, 2021, "Labor Force Statistics from the Current Population Survey: Household Data Annual Averages, 11: Employed Persons by Detailed Occupation, Sex, Race, and Hispanic or Latino Ethnicity," https://www.bls.gov/cps/cpsaat11.htm. According to recent Bureau of Labor statistics, only 3.7 percent of librarians identified as Asian.

Hawai'i, you don't have a lot of career opportunities. You're either in hospitality, or you're in retail. I chose the retail route, and I started working as a makeup artist at Macy's and Nordstrom. I loved being able to help people feel like they are at their best. However, this got old after a while. We had to meet all these quotas, we had to sell all these credit cards, we had to upsell, and it began to feel more like a chore than something I enjoyed.

I wanted something different, so I applied for work-study jobs on campus. I got my start as a circulation assistant at the University of Hawai'i. Working there gave me the most joy because I met so many people from across the campus. When I graduated with my Bachelor of Arts, it was at the height of the recession. I couldn't find a job with an English degree, so I worked as a bank teller for a year. Once, I was working my normal shift as a teller, and a man pointed a gun at my face and robbed me. I remember being so scared and thinking, "I am getting paid $9 an hour to risk my life." Being short-cut financially inspired me to find a different career path. I remembered all the good times I had working at the library, and that's when I decided to return to school. I went to the University of Hawai'i to work on my Master's in Library and Information Science (MLIS) degree.

In my last year of the degree program, I landed a job as a technical services assistant at a local community college in Honolulu. A few months in, my director said, "You are a public services person. We will occasionally take you out of this area to get some public service experience. Go help the reference librarians and get some teaching experience." So, I got a lot of good professional experience at this college. During that time, I had been reflecting on how I'd been in Hawai'i for a good chunk of my life. I was feeling a sense of island fever. I needed to explore, take risks, go to new places, and learn about new cultures. My husband's a musician, and [so] we landed on moving to Seattle because we had known people from the Seattle area. I took an adjunct faculty librarian position at a community college in the Seattle area, and the rest was history. For the past ten years, I have been at a community or technical college. I love what I do. I love the ability to help students meet their goals and to see them get jobs that provide them with a living wage but also are meaningful to them. I can't imagine myself in any other place.

**Ventura** Libraries have always been in my life. I was that child who was taken to the closest public library by my father on the weekends, and we'd check out books and participate in the summer reading program; all of that. So, I always loved libraries. I thought that the librarians were kind and encouraging. I fell in love with the community college as an undecided library work-study student. When I say, "Let's focus on the students," I feel that at a deep level because I've seen the impact on my life. It seems that community colleges can be more agile and can implement innovative ways of serving our students as opposed to navigating the massive bureaucracy that universities have. After considering other careers like Nursing or English to Speakers of Other Languages (ESOL), I became a librarian because I realized that the career that I really wanted was right where I was already as a paraprofessional, the same environment where I have felt most comfortable since childhood: the library.

**Jocson Porter**   Gerie, your career path is such a special one. When I attended grad school, I was pursuing public librarianship. Still, I had been working at SCC in various departments for years already, and I realized I could thrive in a CTC library where there were many Black, Indigenous, and People of Color (BIPOC). These students also want to see faces like ours as their teachers and administrative leaders.[5]

**Ventura**   They want to see us, and [so] I try not to be that administrator locked in an office with the door shut. I am out on the floor each week. I know that for my student body—our percentage of students of color is so high—it's so important to me to be out there. I'll be at the front circulation desk or sometimes the reference desk or just walk around each floor. There seems to be an expectation at other colleges that the administrators are administrators, and they should just do administrative work and leave all that front-facing customer service to the paraprofessionals or the reference librarians. If I get "bogged down" with administrative work, I must tell myself to go out, get to know the students, know their names and say hi. So, they know me too.

**Koshi-Lum**   Like Gerie, I work at the service desk. We serve a student population primarily students of color, including many Asian

---

5   Alyssa Jocson Porter, Sharon Spence-Wilcox, and Kimberly Tate-Malone, "I, Too: Unmasking Emotional Labor of Women of Color Community College Librarians," in *Pushing the Margins: Women of Color and Intersectionality in LIS*, eds. Rose L. Chou and Annie Pho (Sacramento, CA: Library Juice Press, 2018): 290.

Americans, so it's essential for me to be there for them.[6] Not just for our students but for BIPOC faculty and staff, too. I think it's vital for them to see BIPOC in dean-level roles and within the division of Instruction. I need to be very visible to my community, and I wonder if that's an Asian leadership quality. Since we know what it is like to be one of the few [Asian American leaders], we want to make sure that we take care of our community. I sometimes feel that higher education can be very individualistic, and a lot of that stems from systems of whiteness. I think a lot of the best things about being an Asian American leader is our community outlook. We consider a lot about other people and their well-being. We sometimes think more about other people than we think about ourselves, and maybe it's an Asian American thing, but we're a communal group of people.

**Ventura**  Plus, how we incorporate lessons from our upbringing and our childhood and how we approach the world... I mean, can we generalize about being Asian American? Is it a collective thing? And here's the thing, we're still doing more work than usual. I mean, other deans and directors say, "I couldn't possibly do that. I don't have time." But I feel like this is propelled from my memories as a community college student. Representation does matter when you walk into a building and you see a black or brown person who's friendly and familiar. That's important. I'm trying to create a supportive environment that I did not have. The library was a punitive place when I was a student. I should mention that when I say other directors don't do certain tasks, I'm saying that the way that the library profession has created the leadership/power structure—it's all intentional.[7] I was a paraprofessional for 20 years, and nobody ever encouraged me to go into leadership even though I was asking a lot of questions and I was curious about things. The whole structure we're working to change is a white supremacist, a racist institution at its core,[8] which we don't dare name when we're in a room full of all-white colleagues because then they think, "Oh, I'm a bad person." How do you find the words to point these things out and point out

---

6   Johnny Hu, "Asian American Community College Presidents: An AsianCrit Analysis of their Approaches to Leadership," (PhD diss., University of Washington Tacoma, 2019), 12–13.

7   Lalitha Nataraj et al., "Nice White Meetings": Unpacking Absurd Library Bureaucracy through a Critical Race Theory Lens," *Canadian Journal of Academic Librarianship* 6 (2020): 6–7.

8   Kimberlé Crenshaw, et. al., *Introduction to Critical Race Theory: The Key Writings That Formed the Movement*, eds. Kimberlé Crenshaw, et al. (New York: New Press, 1995), xiii–xxxii.

the need for change? Or point out the need for hiring more people of color to those who are thinking, "You're trying to displace me"? It's a threat like we're trying to take their jobs away. It's hard even to start that conversation.

**Koshi-Lum**  Gerie, your comments made me reflect on how fortunate I was to have people like us and be represented in leadership positions and education growing up in Hawai'i. It made me think about how different it is growing up in Hawai'i versus growing up here [in Washington state], where you may not necessarily see yourself reflected in many places.

**Ventura**  That's a massive distinction for you. You should talk more about how diverse the faculty and student body are in Hawai'i.

**Koshi-Lum**  Absolutely. I worked at a community college in Honolulu. My library director was Japanese American, and most faculty librarians were Asian Americans and Pacific Islanders. Through my experiences working here, I got the idea that maybe I could be a leader, too, because I saw my boss, as an Asian American, just really doing excellent work while being extremely confident. I saw myself represented in so many ways, including in the community college system, where many faculty and staff are of Asian American and Pacific Islander descent. Growing up in Hawai'i spoiled me.

**Ventura**  I was born and raised in Tacoma, Washington, [so] I only met a Filipino American librarian once I was in my late 30s, at a conference for the Filipino American National Historical Society in Alaska. I've attended one American Library Association (ALA) annual conference on an Asian Pacific American Librarians Association (APALA)[9] library student scholarship. I remember being overwhelmed by how many black and brown librarians there were. That was when I realized there are so many BIPOC academic librarians on the East Coast and from California, but [definitely] not in Washington state.

**Koshi-Lum**  I am lucky to have mentors like you, Gerie. I don't think I would have been able to get into my current job or my tenure track job if you hadn't hired me [in the past] and mentored me.

---

9  "APALA = Asian Pacific American Librarians Association," About, Asian Pacific American Librarians Association, accessed December 30, 2021, https://www.apalaweb.org/about.

**Ventura**  I'm at that point in my life now where I feel like I need to build the next generation in addition to mentoring existing Asian American library workers. We need to find them, hire them, get them in the pipeline, get them in the system because I don't enjoy being one of the only Asian library deans or directors in the state. But that's dependent on hiring. The colleges are going to have to be seriously committed to wanting to increase diversity in their library staff, and I just don't see that happening. Human Resources and campus administrators put out a job posting, and then they say no people of color ever applied. But they're not trying very hard.

**Koshi-Lum**  We need to strive to do better. Administrators should research and advertise where librarians of color are [located].

**Jocson Porter**  We haven't yet mentioned that in the Washington State CTC system, in which we all currently work, out of a system of 34 colleges, there are how many Asian American library administrators?

**Ventura**  You're looking at them. It's just the two of us.

**Jocson Porter**  Why do you think this is?

**Koshi-Lum**  Community colleges have their own *ivory tower*, where academia can sometimes be exclusive in nature, and there are a lot of hoops and hurdles to get to a tenure-track job [to begin with].[10] When you're in a homogeneous society, this environment has the potential to create a culture of conformity, and that conformity runs thick. You can see it in our meetings and in other spaces in higher education, where it's thick with whiteness and it's centered on white feminism.[11] The farther away you deviate from being the norm (white female), the more likely you may be punished for who you are. One of my bosses in the past has mentioned this. She was a woman of color who grew up on the mainland and had said that to survive, she had to learn how to make her cultural differences less apparent. Now that she's in a position of authority, she recognizes that she can fight

---

10  Esther Care and Helyn Kim, "From Ivory Towers To The Classroom: How Can We Make Academic Research Useful In The Real World?," Brookings, January 30, 2018, https://www.brookings.edu/blog/education-plus-development/2018/01/30/from-ivory-towers-to-the-classroom-how-can-we-make-academic-research-useful-in-the-real-world/amp.

11  Nataraj et. al., "Nice White Meetings," 6–11.

for racial equity. If we hire stereotypical librarians, we won't be taken seriously. But if we can diversify, I think that's when people say, "Oh, look, this department is trying to make their staff reflective of our student population and be on the same page as everyone else."

**Ventura**  A few years ago, I had a light bulb click on while sitting in an interview session, and one of the librarians started talking about "fit"[12] after the interview. I finally realized what "fit" meant in library hiring: people who look like us [white people], people who are like us [white people]. I realized how important it was to design a hiring process that could fight against that. Now, Human Resources trains us on implicit bias. I don't know if it's helping enough.

**Jocson Porter**  *How would you describe your leadership styles?*

**Koshi-Lum**  I see myself as a servant leader.[13] I love working with individuals on my team to see how I can help their careers and learn what projects they would like to do to support the students. Based on the information I get from them, I want to see how I can support them in whatever they want to do. That might mean that they may want to leave the college for a different kind of position, and I must be okay with that. I love being able to remove barriers and connect my faculty and staff to opportunities that will help enrich their professional lives.

**Ventura**  For a very long time, I've been interested in servant leadership. Its principles align with the eight years of Catholic schooling that I went through in my younger years. I am still determining what my leadership style is right now. I am a micromanager, and I am constantly trying not to micromanage. I immediately want to solve everything. So, if somebody comes to me with a problem, instead of immediately trying to fix it, I listen and hear what they're not saying, and then I ask them how they think the issue might be resolved.

---

12  Sojourna Cunningham, Samantha Guss, and Jennifer Stout, "Challenging the 'Good Fit' Narrative: Creating Inclusive Recruitment Practices in Academic Libraries," ACRL Conference Proceedings, April 2019: 12–21, https://www.ala.org/acrl/sites/ala.org.acrl/files/content/conferences/confsandpreconfs/2019/ChallengingtheGoodFitNarrative.pdf.

13  Yvonne Nalani Meulemans and Talitha R. Matlin, "Are You Being Served? Embracing Servant Leadership, Trusting Library Staff, and Engendering Change," *Library Leadership & Management* 34, no. 1 (2019): 3, https://doi.org/10.5860/llm.v34i1.7399.

I empathize with all my library staff and remember my years as a work-study student and paraprofessional.

**Jocson Porter**  How do stereotypes, such as the Model Minority Myth,[14] undermine us as leaders, potential leaders, and folks trying to get hired or stay in their jobs? How do you see those stereotypes come into your own experiences?

**Koshi-Lum**  When I was a tenure-track faculty member, one of the patterns that I saw on my student evaluations was, "Jess is really articulate" or "Jess has an opinion, and I like it." After a few comments about me having an opinion, I began to wonder, "Why are they freaking out about me having an opinion? Would they say this about a white person? Are they assuming I am quiet and submissive and won't say anything?" I saw this as a theme throughout my tenure experience. If something's not going right personnel-wise, I will try to be straightforward and mention it to my staff and try to help them improve. For example, I had an employee in the past who stopped doing their work. I was like, "I am here for you. How can I help you be on time with your work?" and, "I noticed that there's this pattern where you are not doing the work I have asked you to do." In saying that, this person was not happy with me having an opinion and holding her accountable. As an administrator, I can be approachable. So, some individuals see me as a friend, and they may be like, "She's so lenient. She's so nice. She's not going to say anything." I could use the gentlest approach, but there have been folks who do not like it when a woman of color holds them accountable to high standards.

**Ventura**  I have only felt comfortable in my director role in the past two years, so there was some imposter syndrome[15] stuff and doubting my ability to be a natural leader. As I was trying to get my footing as library director, I've been too "Asian quiet" and deferential in many ways. I'm trying to assert myself more on campus and in one-on-one meetings with staff. I've been reminded by colleagues in other disciplines of the concept of colonial mentality, where perhaps

---

14  Hu, "Asian American," 13–16.

15  Ruchika Tulshyan and Jodi-Ann Burey, "Stop Telling Women They Have Imposter Syndrome," *Harvard Business Review*, February 11, 2021, https://hbr.org/2021/02/stop-telling-women-they-have-imposter-syndrome.

some of the feelings of doubt or inadequacy can be attributed to internalized oppression.[16] I was thinking about how Jess and I are supported by our Vice Presidents and how that helps. If we weren't, all of this would be hard. Just being a woman in leadership, it's challenging. As Asian women, what we also deal with is challenging white supremacy and racism.

**Koshi-Lum**  Yes, I think there's another layer for us. The Pacific Northwest attitude can feel passive-aggressive. When I moved here, I learned the general community does not like direct speaking styles. In a previous role, I remember describing to my older white female coworker a situation where I thought I was on the receiving end of racism. I straight-up called it racism, but this coworker told me, "Well, I don't know if that's racism... Even one of our white male colleagues deals with this." She was uncomfortable with my directness and my openly talking about racism.

**Ventura**  The people that think they're woke just don't get it. I was in a leadership meeting once, and a white female librarian said to me, "Well, I can't tell my colleagues that they're being racist to their face," and I immediately looked at her and said, "Unless they are." She just didn't have a response. When I get these windows of insight, I realize, wow, white fragility[17] is genuinely something we must work against. When I finally went from acting to associate to library director, I did hold back for more than a year in significant meetings where there were lots of people from campus. I didn't talk much because I decided it was my learning time. I wanted to understand the group dynamics for that committee or that group on campus, and I [kind of] waited for some way to interject the library point of view. Only recently have I [really] been more vocal in big meetings. I guess that's filed under "campus politics," but I am constantly trying to figure out what aspect of my library services I can apply to a conversation. Lately, I've been talking more, and then I'll say, "I normally don't say very much." Then somebody said last week, "Gerie, you don't [really] talk very often, but when you do, we all listen to you." That was surprising to hear. I'm going to make it a personal goal of

---

16  University of Washington's Indigenous Wellness Research Institute, "Internalized Oppression Presentation by EJ David," News & Events, 2016, http://iwri.org/internalized-oppression-presentation-by-ej-david.

17  Robin DiAngelo, *White Fragility: Why It's So Hard For White People To Talk About Racism* (Boston, MA: Beacon Press, 2018).

mine to speak more in big meetings and to advocate in meetings in ways that maybe I didn't before. It's a personal, professional development thing for me.

**Koshi-Lum**  Some of the challenges I have faced have been centered on the intersection of being relatively young for a dean and being an Asian American female. I just turned 34. I am one of the younger deans on campus. If a person doesn't know me, they generally think that I am a student. I honestly must dress up more formally and make sure I wear my name tag so that people know that I work there as a dean. At a previous institution, one of my white colleagues, who was in a North Face jacket and jeans, asked, "Why are you dressed up so much all the time? You have so many dresses." I thought to myself that I must dress up because I wouldn't get the same amount of respect if I dressed as casually as this [particular] colleague and others. To be taken seriously, I try to dress up, look tidy, and take up space. While there are some challenges in being a younger leader, as I get older, they will judge me for being "too old." I need to be comfortable with this discomfort, represent it in significant ways, and not be afraid to take up space.

**Jocson Porter**  Like Jess, I also dress up at work for similar reasons. When I explain this to others, I get frustrated when I'm told, "It's a compliment to be mistaken for being young" or "You'll miss the attention when you get older." I want to be respected and taken seriously now. I don't want to wait until later.

**Koshi-Lum**  Yes, I have learned that even when I get treated that way by a student, I still must act in the best interest of my students. I must find a way to navigate through that process, but it's going to be happening whether I want it to or not. I can't change my students' minds, but I can certainly control how I behave and lead.

**Ventura**  At the base of it all, we're women—and then layer on top that we're Asian American women—and others feel like they can interact with us in a condescending or subservient way. Sometimes, I find myself listening in a meeting and watching the loudest men dominate the conversation, depending on who's facilitating.

**Koshi-Lum**  Even by the people we think should be our brothers, like men of color. It's the most hurtful when it comes from them.

**Ventura**  It's a constant presence of patriarchy and a constant push against the white supremacy structure that undergirds the entire workplace dynamic. I'm just naming that left and right every time I get into this conversation. Like, can we just point out that this is systemic and it's not just me trying to "assert myself"? It's systemic. This is heavy.

**Jocson Porter**   I recently read a posting by Kayonne Christy, a Black-Caribbean feminist scholar, asking, "Is it imposter syndrome, or is it white supremacy?"[18] and that was a revelation to me. Maybe shifting the burden from me to the system is what I need so I can live!

**Ventura**   I wish I had known this stuff like 20 years ago. It made me feel less insecure.

**Koshi-Lum**   One of the things I heard from my Social Justice Leadership Institute[19] training the other day was that you are never alone, even if you're the only one [of your race or ethnicity] in a particular setting. When you come into a room, and you're the only Asian American leader there, you bring your ancestors with you. You bring anyone who has helped pave the way for you to be there. That's inspiring, too.

**Ventura**   It's comforting and empowering. It's deep, deep, deep. And on your darkest days, you must draw on them.

**Jocson Porter**   *When you're having a tough day, what or who do you reach out to?*

**Ventura**   I surround myself with art and quotes and things to pump me up on random days. I have mentors throughout the campus and the [Washington State CTC] system. Nationally, I've met amazing people at conferences, and we keep in touch via social media or email. I don't necessarily reach out all the time, though.

**Koshi-Lum**   I've been lucky to have mentors and peers on campus here who are very supportive of the work that I do. It's been so inspiring to have met Asian American administrators through our state affinity group. We've had good conversations about what it means to be an Asian American leader. Nowadays, it's vital for me to find

---

18   Kayonne Christy (@KSChristy1), "Is it Imposter Syndrome or is it White Supremacy? Is it Imposter Syndrome or is it Misogyny? Shifting the Locus [sic] of Blame from Myself to the Structure...," Twitter, July 6, 2021, 2:17PM, https://twitter.com/KSChristy1/status/1412415377309679622?s=20.

19   Debi Jenkins (presentation, Social Justice Leadership Institute, Seattle, WA July 2021).

dean-level or administrative-level mentors because I still navigate the transition from being a faculty member to an administrator. But personally, it's been my mom. I don't know what I would do without her. And certainly, my friends and my community, especially my Hawai'i community, have been the ones that have uplifted me. And Gerie's amazing.

**Ventura**   I have a vast Filipino-American community worldwide, and we lift each other. The faculty and staff of color on campus are tight. It's just important to keep people around you that keep you grounded. The leadership structure at my college has changed a lot in the last few years, and the upper administration needs to do a better job explaining this new structure. Withholding this information like a secret seems part of the system, keeping BIPOC faculty and staff out. We, BIPOC, couldn't do this without our support network. If you don't have people of color staff and faculty groups, create them—recognizing that this requires additional emotional labor, though.

**Koshi-Lum**   Our campus [RTC] is very proud of our relatively high amount of faculty and staff of color compared to other colleges in the [Washington State CTC] system, but there's still a lot of work to do. This was a long time coming, and it has been helpful to have a progressive executive leadership to help support these efforts to diversify our campus. However, there can sometimes be a lack of diversity in executive leadership roles in general. Because of this, it was important for us to create a Faculty and Staff of Color Network, where we could all come together, share professional development opportunities, and develop our opportunities for each other. For example, we hosted a session featuring our former Vice President of Instruction, and he was able to share his story, from working in the farms in Washington to joining executive leadership ranks. Stories like these are powerful for those who are thinking that they may be interested in leadership, so we've created professional development opportunities featuring our very own folks on campus, where they tell their stories and talk about their career paths.

**Jocson Porter**   *What makes you stay despite all the challenges we've discussed?*

**Ventura**   I'm an "ideas person;" [I'm] constantly discovering new projects or initiatives we can try. That's why I've stayed because I have that latitude now as director. I'm having a lot of fun because I can mention an idea to a librarian or other library staff, and sometimes, they run with it. When I mentioned that Pierce College, another Washington State community college, was doing online story times for their staff during the COVID-19 [pandemic], our newest librarian going through the tenure process jumped on it and immediately started implementing it. A few months later, we had a whole series on YouTube, and we've had different departments on campus, and student groups reach out to us wanting to read stories. I stay because it's super fun. Also, I get energy and motivation from our students, and I just want to help them succeed, whatever that means for them. If the position I'm in removes me from these interactions, then I'm not interested in just sitting in meetings. I want to work actively with the library staff to make things happen. Good things. Good trouble.[20]

**Koshi-Lum**   If you are interested in administration, it helps if you're a big "ideas person" and you like to introduce ideas to your team, let them run with it, and see what they can come up with. That's what keeps me in this field. When I was a faculty member, I was active on campus and was on a lot of committees and councils. I thought I knew much about what was happening on campus because I was an active contributor. But that changed once I became an administrator. As an administrator, you are often one of the first folks on the campus to know about certain things, and you have a good grasp of what's happening campus-wide. You can learn so much more about politics, about who's beefing with whom, and you become intimate with nuances of the financial situation. My brain exploded when I became a dean because you are privy to more information!

## Recommendations

Based on this interview, we have identified some recommendations for Asian American library workers who might be interested in entering (CTC) library administration:

- Take on challenging positions, tasks, and projects even if you do not feel "qualified." It's through these "risky" projects that you can learn and grow a lot.

---

20  Jay Reeves, "John Lewis' Legacy Shaped in 1965 on 'Bloody Sunday,'" *AP News*, July 17, 2020, https://apnews.com/article/us-news-ap-top-news-voting-selma-voting-rights-eda3ffe8fbf-cf7727270e67bba1c9566.

- Seek training or learning opportunities in grant and budget management, which are essential skills in administration. In a faculty or other staff position, you may need more time to get budgeting experience, depending on what is feasible based on your collective bargaining agreement. Still, there are other ways to gain these skills. For example, you could be the treasurer of a library organization to get the experience of planning and implementing a budget.
- Set up informational interviews with library administrators, especially Asian Americans and other BIPOC, to ask about their experiences and career paths.
- Connect with groups such as APALA and We Here,[21] nationwide networks (with some local chapters) where you can grow your Asian American and BIPOC professional circles. Getting involved in their committees and planning groups is helpful to gain experience and skills to prepare for administrative responsibilities. Additionally, having support systems can make the transition into a new position go more smoothly.

Additionally, our recommendations for library administrators are:

- Implement inclusive screening and hiring practices to attract and hire Asian American and other BIPOC applicants.[22] For example, make sure to advertise to ALA's National Associations of Librarians of Color (formerly the ethnic affiliate groups): American Indian Library Association (AILA), Asian Pacific American Librarians Association (APALA), Black Caucus of the American Library Association (BCALA), Chinese American Librarians Association (CALA), and REFORMA: The National Association to Promote Library and Information Services to Latinos and the Spanish Speaking. Encourage other (library) administrators to do the same.
- Encourage Asian Americans and other BIPOC library workers to take on projects and tasks that interest them and provide opportunities for them to learn and grow. If they show interest and qualities that would make them effective administrators, be a resource for them.

---

21  "About Us," We Here, accessed December 30, 2021, https://www.wehere.space/about.

22  Jess Koshi-Lum, "Faculty Diversity Toolkit for Library Leaders," Renton Technical College Library, accessed January 3, 2022, https://libguides.rtc.edu/facultydiversity.

- Mentor and introduce Asian American and other BIPOC library workers to other library administrators.

## Conclusion

This interview allowed us to reflect on our experiences surviving and thriving in CTC library administration, to consider our next steps, and to share our lived experiences. A few months after this interview, after 13 years of working within academic library settings, Jess accepted a library administrator position in a California public library system. While applying for dean-level jobs in other community college systems, her colleague said she would have to "look more mature and style herself more formally to be accepted as someone who could be a dean in the interview setting." While this was initially disheartening to her, it signaled that she needed to work in a place that accepted her wholly. Jess accepted the public library administrative position based on her interview experience. The public library interview panel was warm and welcoming, while the interviews for dean positions felt more rigid and exclusive. This experience served as a reminder that while community colleges tend to occupy their own space in higher education, these spaces are not exempt from the racism, elitism, and sexism that exist within academia.

Jess and Gerie were the first Asian American (and BIPOC in general) persons to hold library administrative positions at their respective campuses and did not want to be the last. Gerie is trying to find someone to mentor, particularly someone to replace her someday. Alyssa is content in her current position as a faculty librarian; after this interview, she is still considering a career path in CTC library administration, though perhaps in 10–15 years when she's ready for a new challenge. Meanwhile, her professional development focus includes improving both leadership and administrative skills.

As we look to nurture the next Asian American CTC library leaders and administrators, we should strive to ask ourselves: How can we create spaces of inclusive excellence in our libraries? When we talk about diversity, equity, and inclusion, we aim to truly live our values, from how we conduct our hiring processes to supporting others in their own pathways to leadership. We want to contribute to the emerging conversations about Asian American women breaking through that bamboo library ceiling and building community as we grow our numbers. It's so crucial for future Asian American library administrators to know that they're needed, they are wanted, and that they deserve to be in the positions they are in or aspire to hold.

## Bibliography

"APALA = Asian Pacific American Librarians Association." About, Asian Pacific American Librarians Association. Accessed December 30, 2021. https://www.apalaweb.org/about.

Care, Esther, and Helyn Kim. "From Ivory Towers To The Classroom: How Can We Make Academic Research Useful In The Real World?" *Brookings*, January 30, 2018. https://www.brookings.edu/blog/education-plus-development/2018/01/30/from-ivory-towers-to-the-classroom-how-can-we-make-academic-research-useful-in-the-real-world/amp.

Christy, Kayonne (@KSChristy1). "Is it Imposter Syndrome or is it White Supremacy? Is it Imposter Syndrome or is it Misogyny? Shifting the Locus [sic] of Blame from Myself to the Structure…" Twitter. July 6, 2021, 2:17PM. https://twitter.com/KSChristy1/status/1412415377309679622?s=20.

Crenshaw, Kimberlé, Neil T. Gotanda, Gary Peller, and Kendall Thomas. Introduction to *Critical Race Theory: The Key Writings That Formed the Movement*. Edited by Kimberlé Crenshaw, Neil T. Gotanda, Gary Peller, and Kendall Thomas, xIII–xxxii. New York: New Press, 1995.

Cunningham, Sojourna, Samantha Guss, and Jennifer Stout. "Challenging the 'Good Fit' Narrative: Creating Inclusive Recruitment Practices in Academic Libraries." *ACRL Conference Proceedings*, April 2019: 12–21. https://www.ala.org/acrl/sites/ala.org.acrl/files/content/conferences/confsandpreconfs/2019/ChallengingtheGoodFitNarrative.pdf.

DiAngelo, Robin. *White Fragility: Why It's So Hard For White People To Talk About Racism*. Boston, MA: Beacon Press, 2018.

Hewlett, Sylvia Ann. "Breaking Through the Bamboo Ceiling." *Harvard Business Review*, August 3, 2011. https://hbr.org/2011/08/breaking-through-the-bamboo-ce.

Hu, Johnny. "Asian American Community College Presidents: An AsianCrit Analysis of their Approaches to Leadership." PhD diss., University of Washington Tacoma, 2019, 1–96.

Jenkins, Debi. Presentation at the Social Justice Leadership Institute, Seattle, WA, 2021.

Jocson Porter, Alyssa, Sharon Spence-Wilcox, and Kimberly Tate-Malone. "I, Too: Unmasking Emotional Labor of Women of Color Community College Librarians." In *Pushing the Margins: Women of Color and Intersectionality in LIS*. Edited by Rose L. Chou and Annie Pho, 273–300. Sacramento, CA: Library Juice Press, 2018.

Kambhampaty, Anna Purna. "In 1968, These Activists Coined the Term 'Asian American'—And Helped Shape Decades of Advocacy." *Time*, May 22, 2020. https://time.com/5837805/asian-american-history.

Koshi-Lum, Jess. "Faculty Diversity Toolkit for Library Leaders." Renton Technical College Library, Accessed January 3, 2022. https://libguides.rtc.edu/facultydiversity.

Le, Binh P. "Academic Library Leadership Race and Gender." *International Journal of Librarianship* 6, no. 1 (2021): 13–26.

Meulemans, Yvonne Nalani, and Talitha R. Matlin. "Are You Being Served? Embracing Servant Leadership, Trusting Library Staff, and Engendering Change." *Library Leadership & Management* 34, no. 1 (2019): 1–12. https://doi.org/10.5860/llm.v34i1.7399.

Nataraj, Lalitha, Holly Hampton, Talitha R. Matlin, and Yvonne Nalani Meulemans. ""Nice White Meetings": Unpacking Absurd Library Bureaucracy through a Critical Race Theory Lens." *Canadian Journal of Academic Librarianship* 6, (2020): 1–15. https://doi.org/10.33137/cjal-rcbu.v6.34340.

Reeves, Jay. "John Lewis' Legacy Shaped in 1965 on 'Bloody Sunday.'" *AP News*, July 17, 2020. https://apnews.com/article/us-news-ap-top-news-voting-selma-voting-rights-eda3ffe8fbfcf7727270e67bba1c9566.

Tulshyan, Ruchika and Jodi-Ann Burey. "Stop Telling Women They Have Imposter Syndrome." *Harvard Business Review*, February 11, 2021. https://hbr.org/2021/02/stop-telling-women-they-have-imposter-syndrome.

University of Washington's Indigenous Wellness Research Institute. ""Internalized Oppression" Presentation by EJ David." News & Events. 2016. http://iwri.org/internalized-oppression-presentation-by-ej-david.

U.S. Department of Labor, Bureau of Labor Statistics. 2021. "Labor Force Statistics from the Current Population Survey: Household Data Annual Averages, 11: Employed persons by detailed occupation, sex, race, and Hispanic or Latino ethnicity." https://www.bls.gov/cps/cpsaat11.htm.

We Here. "About Us." Accessed December 30, 2021. https://www.wehere.space/about.

# Communities of Practice
Responsibility and Opportunities for Shared Praxis in Community College Libraries

*Evangela Q. Oates*

## Introduction

My tenure in community college libraries started in September 2014 when I accepted Director of the Library role at a public, two-year college. Before becoming an administrator, all my professional experiences in academic libraries were in public services at comprehensive (four-year; Master's) colleges and research (doctoral; R1) universities. Even though I received varying levels of funding for professional development at each institution, I was fortunate as I was able to attend at least one national conference during the academic year. I was even more fortunate as my conference attendance was not limited to those in which I was a presenter or speaker. My participation and access to broader professional networks received support from each institution, and these experiences gave me greater confidence in my capabilities and facilitated my growth as a librarian.

My selection and participation in the Emerging Leaders Program[1] of the American Library Association (ALA) was a valuable introduction to building relationships with librarians. The opportunity to meet and network with librarians who were navigating the newness of

---

1   "ALA Emerging Leaders Program," American Library Association, last modified April 29, 2022, https://www.ala.org/educationcareers/leadership/emergingleaders.

librarianship was refreshing and helped me to gauge the climate, expectations, and resources of other libraries. I also participated in the program track of the Immersion Program by the Association of College & Research Libraries (ACRL).[2] As the Information Literacy Coordinator for my campus, I was charged with articulating the need to embed information literacy competencies in the curriculum. The week-long institute was intense, but I left with language and strategies for engaging stakeholders in conversations about critical thinking in the research process.

My involvement in these national programs was in the earlier part of my career, and I am thankful for them. They helped me see myself and my capacity beyond the needs of my campus and the profession. In reflection, it was good that I started my career at a research university. There, I learned that financial resources are just as crucial to professional growth as mentorship. My Black woman scholar supervisor supported my development and implored me to seek opportunities external to our organization. She also taught me that advocating for myself was necessary as I, a Black woman, did not share the social capital valued by my White colleagues.

My values live in a social capital that honors the collective power of a community formed by Black people outside of the gaze and influence of whiteness to support, inform, affirm, and nurture each other.[3] Mutual aid, church groups, women's clubs, and other community groups have often been the mechanism by which Black forms of capital are actualized[4] and are a part of the Black experience, including mine. Tara Yosso shared how the community cultural wealth of people of color often manifests differently than forms of capital valued by Whites, as it rejects the deficit lens propagated by deficit scholars and white supremacy.[5] As in the corporate environment, the values of academe are evident by what it prioritizes.

---

2   "Immersion Program," Association of College & Research Libraries (ACRL), last modified September 25, 2020, https://www.ala.org/acrl/conferences/immersion.

3   Caitlyn Garcia and Cynthia Godsoe, "Divest, Invest, & Mutual Aid," *Columbia Journal of Race and Law* 12, no. 1 (2022): 9.

4   Dorothy E. Roberts, "Black Club Women and Child Welfare: Lessons for Modern Reform," *Florida State University Law Review* 32, no. 3 (2005): 959.

5   Tara J. Yosso, "Whose Culture Has Capital?: A Critical Race Theory Discussion of Community Cultural Wealth," *Race Ethnicity and Education* 8, no. 1 (2005): 82.

I recognize that at least one of the aforementioned programs (Immersion) requires substantial support from one's institution in the form of funding and a written commitment from the organization. Given the prohibitive nature of such programs, community college librarians must establish their own Communities of Practice (COP). In my quest for more budgetary and leadership experience, I applied for administrator positions at four-year universities and two-year colleges. I mainly looked at directorship positions, but I wasn't sure I would make it to the interview phase of the selection process. Although I had seen the rapid ascent of some White colleagues to director-level positions in academic libraries, I knew that I would likely face more scrutiny. Still, I applied for positions that seemed attainable and some that were a long shot. To my surprise, I was offered two interviews: from a four-year for-profit college and a public, two-year college (community college). I eventually accepted the position at the community college. I did not think I would be hired as I had turned down the position based on the salary. I did not think the institution would hire me as I had turned down the position based on the salary. Thankfully, the institution met my previous counteroffer more favorably, and negotiations went smoothly. Soon after, I left a position I [really] enjoyed to get the administrative experience I desired.

As a community college library administrator, I immediately recognized the differences in support for professional conferences, particularly for national conferences. My funding was much more constrained—even as an administrator— and my networking opportunities were limited to system-wide meetings (for Directors and Deans), which I, alone, could attend. While this was tolerable for me, it also meant that funding would be even more restrictive for my professional and paraprofessional staff. Through conversations with other community college librarians, I discovered they also had minimal funding for national conferences and felt they missed out on developing relationships with other librarians due to the lack of money and support.

Never in my career was I as restricted in professional development as my stint as an administrator in a community college library. As a director, I assumed I would get the chance to manage budgets and develop as a leader to advance in my career. Even though I knew community colleges were marginalized, I viewed them as just another higher education sector. I did not anticipate the differences in professional development would be so pronounced, especially given the sector's assertion of being teaching colleges. Community colleges vary greatly based on size, demographics, location, and other characteristics.

Given those differences, one should read this chapter as a call to action in which they may find similarities with their own experiences and institutions.

In addition to understanding the complexities and differences in two-year colleges and that my experiences do not represent the institutional type as a whole, my recommendation for praxis focuses on the gendered and racialized experiences of my career in librarianship and the results from empirical research inspired by those experiences.[6] Black librarians make up 5.4% of academic librarians,[7] a small percentage of the profession that does not capture the racial composition by institutional type. This chapter explores my experiences as an administrator in a community college library and how those experiences shaped my understanding of how community college librarians navigate professional growth. My call for action is the establishment of communities of practice to counter professional isolation, which the racialized and gendered environments of academe can exacerbate.

## Recognition of the Problem

As the Director of the Library, I soon realized that I had to adjust my expectations for conference attendance. The administration told me that two system-wide meetings would require my attendance and that the college would cover the costs; however, it was clear that funding outside these meetings would be unlikely. As the library director, my membership in the system-wide library organization was automatic, and I served as the sole representative from my campus. Only after attending the first meeting did I understand why it was so crucial for me to participate. Discussions of our products, services, and policies are negotiated and selected at these meetings. To better understand the organization and its membership, I volunteered to serve as an officer and, ultimately, on the executive board. While this was a deliberate way to ensure that our library had great resources and competitive pricing, my professional networks were limited to the goals, benefits, and priorities of the institution. In the grand scheme, my work was

---

6   Evangela Quinette Oates, "Marginalized Faculty at Marginalized Institutions: Counternarratives as Resistance in Exploring the Experiences of Black Librarians at Public, Two-Year Colleges," (PhD diss., University of Nebraska-Lincoln, 2020), 185.

7   American Library Association, "Diversity Counts," 2012, accessed August 12, 2022, http://www.ala.org/aboutala/sites/ala.org.aboutala/files/content/diversity/diversitycounts/diversitycountstables2012.pdf.

productive as it yielded the intended results (electronic collections, package deals, consortia agreements, etc.) for the faculty, staff, and students at the college alone.

My interest in learning more intimately about the work of community college librarians took a backseat. For instance, my public services librarian started and cultivated a graphic novel and anime collection, which birthed several student organizations. Given my intention to support him, I needed to connect him with other community college librarians with similar interests. Sure, there were research libraries with such collections and examples of student engagement and learning. Still, there was no one I could point to as a potential collaborator or resource. I assumed my lack of professional network in community colleges was due to my employment exclusively at comprehensive and research libraries. When I attended national conferences, I did not remember meeting librarians who worked at two-year colleges. Why? Did I not ask? Where were community college librarians and their voices in the profession?

## Isolation in the Profession

Professional isolation is a phenomenon found throughout the literature for educators. In education and librarianship, professional isolation seems to be acute,[8] especially for Black women educators[9] who are often responsible for creating their networks without departmental support.[10] Additionally, they contend with inconsistent professional

---

8   Mee-Len Hom, "Invisible Presence: An Asian American Librarian's Experience," in *In Our Own Voices: The Changing Face of Librarianship*, ed. Teresa Y. Neely and Khafre K. Abif (Lanham, Md.: Scarecrow Press, 1996), 159; Laura O'Grady, "Lonely at the Top: Is Professional Isolation Suffocating Our Library Directors?," *Public Libraries* 57, no. 5 (2018): 7; Dorothea Salo, "Can We Block the Pipeline Out?," *Library Journal* 139, no. 6 (April 1, 2014): 16.

9   Amelia N. Gibson, "Civility and Structural Precarity for Faculty of Color in LIS," *Journal of Education for Library and Information Science* 60, no. 3 (July 2019): 219, https://doi.org/10.3138/jelis.2019-0006; J. Camille Hall, Joyce E. Everett, and Johnnie Hamilton-Mason, "Black Women Talk about Workplace Stress and How They Cope," *Journal of Black Studies* 43, no. 2 (March 2012): 220, https://doi.org/10.1177/0021934711413272; Kimberly A. Griffin, "Voices of the 'Othermothers': Reconsidering Black Professors' Relationships with Black Students as a Form of Social Exchange," *The Journal of Negro Education* 82, no. 2 (2013): 169, https://doi.org/10.7709/jnegroeducation.82.2.0169; Teresa Y. Neely, "The Jackie Robinson of Library Science: Twenty Years Later," in *In Our Own Voices, Redux: The Faces of Librarianship Today*, ed. Teresa Y. Neely and Jorge R. Lopez-McKnight (Lanham, Maryland: Rowman & Littlefield, 2018), 74.

10  Oates, "Marginalized," 68.

development funding,[11] lack of preparation, and an overwhelmingly White and gendered profession.[12]

For Black, Indigenous, and People of Color (BIPOC), I would argue that professional isolation is distinct from social isolation due to how each group perceives their work and whether one's social life has a place in their work. For instance, although I have purchased food for staff to eat, I do not expect that a relationship exists beyond our respective roles. I view it as a way to show appreciation for their contributions to the organization. The food is available for them to take at their leisure without any expectation. Conversely, Black educators often report professional isolation in the form of exclusion from informal gatherings with their White colleagues.[13] As noted by Oates, their exclusion only presents a problem because, as Black educators believe, it is during these gatherings that decisions about the organization and department (and their work) occur.[14] In this way, not only are they not involved in decision-making, but they are also cut off from knowing about essential processes, policies, opportunities, and initiatives. This is a crucial point to understand as professional isolation goes beyond one's desire—if they have any desire at all—to be socially integrated.

In my case, working at a rural community college with perpetual financial deficits produced compounded feelings of isolation and stagnation. Oddly enough, I was relieved of this reality when I began conducting my research studies. Through the coursework in my doctoral program, I started to seek answers to many of the questions I had since I began working at the community college. Curiosity about my circumstances, a gap in research on community college libraries, and what I perceived as lacking collaboration between community college librarians led me to my dissertation topic. Knowing so little about my peers, their experiences, and their work brought me closer to them in ways I did not anticipate. Through my study, I learned how the narrators (participants) worked in libraries as undergraduates. They all had

---

11  Oates, "Marginalized," 79.

12  Trevar Riley-Reid, "Breaking down Barriers: Making It Easier for Academic Librarians of Color to Stay," *Journal of Academic Librarianship* 43, no. 5 (September 2017): 393.

13  Brandoyn Jones, Eunjin Hwang, and Rebecca M Bustamante, "African American Female Professors' Strategies for Successful Attainment Of Tenure And Promotion At Predominately White Institutions: It Can Happen," *Education, Citizenship, and Social Justice* 10, no. 2 (July 2015): 141.

14  Oates, "Marginalized," 161.

worked in libraries at four-year or research universities as students and staff. Most profoundly, I learned that poor management, hostile environments, lack of advocacy, and persistent dysfunction intensified their feelings and reality of isolation.[15]

In relation, my narrators (participants) and I embarked on a journey to reflect on our experiences, and through their stories, I saw similarities in their experiences and the need to create our network of professionals. The need for a community of practice was also used in the design of the study as I wanted my work to demonstrate both how these relationships could organically form out of mutual interests as practitioners, the possibilities of creating partnerships for the dissemination of scholarship, and a way to extend *service* beyond the traditional avenues and organizations.

## What is a Community of Practice?

The term community of practice (CoP) is often informally used to describe people with shared interests in the community who share their knowledge to learn, improve, and solve problems based on practice. More formally, in *Communities of Practice: An Introduction*, Wenger-Trayner defined a community of practice as having three essential elements: the domain, the community, and the practice. Identity and collective interests make up the domain.[16] The community comprises members who see themselves concerning each other based on their interest in the domain; they "engage in joint activities and discussions, help each other, and share information."[17] Lastly, the community membership comprises practitioners (the practice). This collective effort based on shared interests by the membership may include practices such as reusing assets, coordination, synergy, documenting projects, visiting other practitioners' programs, discussing development, mapping knowledge, and identifying gaps.[18] These are just a few

---

15  Oates, "Marginalized," 97, 112.

16  Etienne Wenger-Trayner and Beverly Wenger-Trayner, "Communities of Practice: A Brief Introduction," (June 2015), 2.

17  Wenger-Trayner, "Communities," 2. https://www.wenger-trayner.com/wp-content/uploads/2022/06/15-06-Brief-introduction-to-communities-of-practice.pdf.

18  Wenger-Trayner, 3.

activities in which the practices of these communities can be seen, and many of them are used by librarians in all types of libraries.[19]

While community college librarians may have well-established communities of practice, their work is almost invisible to the broader profession as there is minimal scholarship or other writings on their work.[20] Therefore, I encourage librarians at two-year colleges to write about their experiences, challenges, successes, and accomplishments as a responsibility to the sector. Consider submitting your work to higher education journals (community college focus) and those from the profession. I recommend the *Association of College & Research Libraries*, *Community College Journal of Research and Practice*, *Community College Review*, *Public Services Quarterly*, and the *Journal of Applied Research in Community College*.

## Responsibility and Opportunities for Communities of Practice (CoP)

While I wholeheartedly encourage librarians at four-year colleges, research universities, and community college scholars to research community college libraries, librarians at two-year colleges must become significant contributors to the writings and visibility of their sector. The work of academic libraries is mostly the same but varies across sectors. In this way, communities of practice should address the most salient issues of practice (tenure, retention, promotion, open educational resources (OERs)) in academic librarianship.

Smith and Lee reported some exciting results from a CoP that focused on OERs.[21] Members of the CoP found that "a distributed leadership, some administrative support, and being open to new members and

---

19  Christina H Gola and Lisa Martin, "Creating an Emotional Intelligence Community of Practice: A Case Study for Academic Libraries," *Journal of Library Administration* 60, no. 7 (2020): 756; Francia Kissel et al., "Bridging the Gaps: Collaboration in a Faculty and Librarian Community of Practice on Information Literacy," in *Information Literacy: Research and Collaboration across Disciplines*, ed. Barbara J. D'Angelo et al. (Fort Collins: University Press of Colorado, 2016), 415; Eboni A Johnson and Shaunda Vasudev, "I Cannot Be the Only One: Creating a Community of Practice for Outreach Librarians," *Public Services Quarterly* 16, no. 2 (2020): 126.

20  Jennifer Arnold, "The Community College Conundrum: Workforce Issues in Community College Libraries," *Library Trends* 59, no. 1–2 (2010): 220; Oates, "Marginalized," 135.

21  Brenda Smith and Leva Lee, "Librarians and OER: Cultivating a Community of Practice to Be More Effective Advocates," *Journal of Library & Information Services in Distance Learning* 11, no. 1–2 (2017): 120.

new ideas are keys to sustaining an active group."[22] Additionally, the collaborative nature of the CoP and the sharing of tools reduced the duplication of labor. The findings attributed distributed leadership as being an asset to CoP and are helpful to those who have concerns about the management of the group as well as how to keep the momentum going. This suggestion could also encourage library professionals who are used to hierarchical models (top-down leadership) to take a more active role in the administration of the CoP.

Community college librarians must also expand the conversation on academic libraries by focusing on all areas of their work but emphasizing what is unique to their sector. The tenure and promotion processes would be another ideal area for a CoP. Although the tenure process at community colleges is generally less laborious than research libraries (ex, publish or peril), one still must navigate the explicit and implicit expectations of their department and the institution. In cases where librarians are faculty or staff—or when the process for librarians is unclear—a CoP could improve morale, provide guidance, and link librarians with someone who could serve as an external reviewer.

A pilot study on the tenure and promotion process of Black faculty at a community college found that their tenure and promotion processes lacked mentorship, did not provide a formal, written protocol, and heavily relied on the support of Faculty of Color (FOC) during the process.[23] In *We Here, Speaking our Truth,* the authors showed how the issues of whiteness and neutrality influence the retention of LOC, particularly in early-career positions, which shape so much of one's trajectory in librarianship.[24] *We Here* createed spaces for the LOC community in which mentorship flourishes from organic and genuine relationships aimed at nurturing the whole person.[25] Community college librarians need intentional collaboration for professional development, advancement, and collegiality.

---

22  Smith and Lee, "Librarians and OER," 120.

23  Evangela Q. Oates, "Tenure and Promotion Experiences of Black Faculty at a Public, Two-Year Institution in the North: A Case Study," (Poster, 43rd Annual Association for the Study of Higher Education Conference, Tampa, Florida, November 2018).

24  Jennifer Brown, Jennifer A. Ferretti, Sofia Leung, and Marisa L. Mendez- Brady, "We Here: Speaking Our Truth," *Library Trends* 67, no. 1 (2018): 168.

25  Brown, Ferretti, Leung, and Mendez-Brady, "We Here," 175.

A CoP may start formally or informally based on the needs and objectives of the community. In *Bridging the Gaps: Collaboration in a Faculty and Librarian Community of Practice on Information Literacy,* the authors wrote about using CoP for faculty-librarian collaborations on information literacy.[26] While there were the expected tensions between faculty and librarians (curriculum, authority, etc.), the CoP allowed for deeper conversations about students' knowledge of the research process and plans for shared analysis and dissemination of the findings from student surveys.[27]

In *Using Digital Environments to Design Inclusive and Sustainable Communities of Practice in Academic Libraries,* Carroll and Mallon reported on another campus initiative, a miniature Community of Practice (Mini CoP).[28] Using a participatory leadership frame, their study focused on two roles within the CoP: Community Coordinator and Community Facilitator. The Community Coordinators were responsible for recruitment and management, while the Community Facilitators scheduled meetings for the Mini CoP. Members of the Mini CoP (3-5 members), which included the facilitator, reported they "felt a sense of ownership in their community, and felt accountable to show up to meetings on time and prepared."[29] Perhaps your department is large and would benefit from Mini CoP. On the other hand, if you are part of a small department, distributed leadership roles might be necessary to share tasks and responsibilities. By creating your CoP through informal or formal organizations or networks, you might find that specific models of CoP may work better for your purposes.

## Recommendations

The expansion of the conversation must also include the lived experiences of BIPOC librarians. While researching the state of librarianship for community college Librarians of Color (LOC), I was saddened but not surprised by the lack of investigation into their experiences.

---

26  Kissel et. al., "Bridging," 411.

27  Kissel et. al., 421.

28  Alexander J. Carroll and Melissa N. Mallon, "Using Digital Environments to Design Inclusive and Sustainable Communities of Practice in Academic Libraries," *The Journal of Academic Librarianship* 47, no. 5 (September 2021): 3.

29  Carroll and Mallon, "Using Digital," 5.

Besides works from Oates[30], Agbim[31], Porter, Spence-Wilcox, and Tate-Malone[32], I found no other writings from Black and Women of Color (WOC) whose work looked at their racialized experiences. Indeed, there are more stories to be told and shared with the larger community. CoPs are valuable in helping BIPOC librarians come together to enact changes not only at their campuses but as a collective effort to change policy, start initiatives, and conduct their research on their lived experiences. There is strength in numbers, and where one may not have the time, skills, professional support, and tools to publish (journal, book chapter, blog), members of their CoP may have the talent to organize and manage such projects.

Academic journals are good outlets to share one's work within the profession, but they are not the only medium to consider. If one desires to share their practices widely, consider blogging to connect to a broader audience. Blogs allow one to disseminate findings to laypersons as well as library professionals. Multiple members of the CoP could be responsible for managing the blog, vlog, or podcast. *LibVoices*, a podcast hosted via Anchor and other platforms, broadcasts interviews with LoC about their individual and collective work, projects, and scholarship.[33] Social media is another excellent way to elicit engagement, particularly X (formerly Twitter), as it has many academicians who use the platform. Hashtags *#WeHere*, *#WOCinLIB*, *#LibraryTwitter*, and *#AcademicTwitter* provide discourse, knowledge, and ideas for educators and library professionals. Reposts and hashtags are great ways to maximize the visibility of your tweets and track posts and discussions on the topic.

Lastly, I recommend collaborating with teaching faculty and administrators.[34] Leading faculty could be great partners in your CoP, especially

---

30  Evangela Q. Oates, "Battered but Not Broken: A Composite of the Experiences of Black Librarians at Public, 2-Year Colleges—Dissertation of the Year," *Community College Review* 51, no. 2 (April 2023): 151.

31  Ngozi P. Agbim, "The Role of a Black Chief Librarian in the Urban Community College Library," in *The Black Librarian in America Revisited*, ed. E. J. Josey (Metuchen: Scarecrow Press, 1994), 171.

32  Alyssa J. Porter, Sharon Spence-Wilcox, and Kimberly Tate-Malone, "I, Too: Unmasking Emotional Labor of Women of Color Community College Librarians," in *Pushing the Margins: Women of Color and Intersectionality in LIS*, ed. Rose L. Chou and Annie Pho, Series on Critical Race Studies and Multiculturalism in LIS, no. 3 (Sacramento: Library Juice Press, 2018), 273.

33  LibVoices is a podcast that seeks to amplify the voices of librarians of Color. It is co-hosted by librarians Jamia Williams and Jamillah R. Gabriel. https://anchor.fm/libvoices.

34  Kissel et al., "Bridging the Gaps," 419.

those who are strong proponents of library services and are involved in collaborative projects (research instruction, collections, OERs, etc.). Combining your expertise and professional development funding may provide resources for software, equipment, and other tools needed for your projects. If your institution has a grant-writing office, determine which grants may be available to support your CoP. Administrators may be more open to financial support CoP if other funding contributes to the project. While I have not received funding for a CoP, I have been able to leverage financial support for professional development when I received travel grants or other fellowships through external organizations.

## Conclusion

I write knowing the task at hand is heavy. Even now, my recommendations may seem impossible for specific individuals. However, during this global health crisis, age of disinformation, and the doubling-down on fascist and white supremacist policies, the need for more support, acknowledgment of trauma, and a critical look at the impact of professional isolation will require more compassion and collaboration. As it is, I am not convinced, nor have I seen evidence from national library organizations of their intent to address ongoing issues of equity and incivility for community college librarians. As evident in the work of our pioneers[35], it will be the responsibility of small, committed groups to bring the profession forward, and with this chapter, I charge you to take your seat at the table or, if needed, build your own.

### *Bibliography*

Agbim, Ngozi P. "The Role of a Black Chief Librarian in the Urban Community College Library." In *The Black Librarian in America Revisited*, edited by E. J. Josey, 171–80. Metuchen: Scarecrow Press, 1994.

Almeida, Nora. "Interrogating the Collective: #Critlib and the Problem of Community." In *The Politics of Theory and the Practice of Critical Librarianship*, edited by Karen P. Nicholson and Maura Seale, 237–57. Sacramento: Library Juice Press, 2017.

---

35  Oates, "Battered but Not Broken," 149.

American Library Association. "ALA Emerging Leaders Program." last modified April 29, 2022. https://www.ala.org/educationcareers/leadership/emergingleaders.

American Library Association. "Diversity Counts 2012." Accessed December 22, 2021. http://www.ala.org/aboutala/sites/ala.org.aboutala/files/content/diversity/diversitycounts/diversitycountstables2012.pdf.

Association of College & Research Libraries (ACRL). "Immersion Program." last modified September 25, 2020. https://www.ala.org/acrl/conferences/immersion.

Brown, Jennifer, Jennifer A. Ferretti, Sofia Leung, and Marisa L. Mendez-Brady. "We Here: Speaking Our Truth." *Library Trends* 67, no. 1 (2018): 163–81.

Bugg, Kimberley. "The Perceptions of People of Color in Academic Libraries Concerning the Relationship between Retention and Advancement as Middle Managers." *Journal of Library Administration* 56, no. 4 (May 18, 2016): 428–43. https://doi:10.1080/01930826.2015.1105076.

Carroll, Alexander J., and Melissa N. Mallon. "Using Digital Environments to Design Inclusive and Sustainable Communities of Practice in Academic Libraries." *The Journal of Academic Librarianship* 47, no. 5 (September 2021): 102380. https://doi.org/10.1016/j.acalib.2021.102380.

Clendon, Jill. "Nurse Educators: What Really Matters to Patients?" *Kai Tiaki: Nursing New Zealand* 22, no. 1 (2016): 38.

Garcia, Caitlyn, and Cynthia Godsoe. "Divest, Invest, & Mutual Aid." *Columbia Journal of Race and Law* 12, no. 1 (June 30, 2022): 1–28. https://doi.org/10.52214/cjrl.v12i1.9922.

Gibson, Amelia N. "Civility and Structural Precarity for Faculty of Color in Lis." *Journal of Education for Library and Information Science* 60, no. 3 (July 2019): 215–22. https://doi:10.3138/jelis.2019-0006.

Griffin, Karin L. "Pursuing Tenure and Promotion in the Academy: A Librarian's Cautionary Tale." *Negro Educational Review* 64, no. 1–4 (2013): 77–96.

Gola, Christina H, and Lisa Martin. "Creating an Emotional Intelligence Community of Practice: A Case Study for Academic Libraries." *Journal of Library Administration* 60, no. 7 (2020): 752–61.

Grantland, Jacqueline. "Rural Counselors' Use of Technology to Address Professional Isolation." PhD diss., Walden University, Minnesota, 2020. ProQuest.

Hall, J. Camille, Joyce E. Everett, and Johnnie Hamilton-Mason. "Black Women Talk about Workplace Stress and How They Cope." *Journal of Black Studies* 43, no. 2 (March 2012): 207–26. https://doi:10.1177/0021934711413272.

Hill, Renee F. "The Danger of an Untold Story: Excerpts from My Life as a Black Academic." *Journal of Education for Library and Information Science* 60, no. 3 (July 2019): 208–14. doi:10.3138/jelis.2019-0008.

Hom, Mee-Len. "Invisible Presence: An Asian American Librarian's Experience." In *In Our Own Voices: The Changing Face of Librarianship*, edited by Teresa Y Neely and Khafre K Abif, 155–63. Lanham: Scarecrow Press, 1996.

Jensen, Kristi, and Quill West. "Open Educational Resources and the Higher Education Environment: A Leadership Opportunity for Libraries." *College & Research Libraries News* 76, no. 4 (April 1, 2015): 215–18. https://doi:10.5860/crln.76.4.9298.

Johnson, Eboni A, and Shaunda Vasudev. "I Cannot Be the Only One: Creating a Community of Practice for Outreach Librarians." *Public Services Quarterly* 16, no. 2 (2020): 124–29.

Jones, Brandolyn, Eunjin Hwang, and Rebecca M Bustamante. "African American Female Professors' Strategies for Successful Attainment of Tenure and Promotion at Predominately White Institutions: It Can Happen." *Education, Citizenship and Social Justice* 10, no. 2 (July 2015): 133–51. https://doi.org/10.1177/1746197915583934.

Kissel, Francia, Melvin R. Wininger, Scott R. Weeden, Patricia A. Wittberg, Randall S. Halverson, Meagan Lacy, and Rhonda K. Huisman. *Bridging the Gaps: Collaboration in a Faculty and Librarian Community of Practice on Information Literacy*. Fort Collins: University Press of Colorado, 2016.

Oates, Evangela Q. "Tenure and Promotion Experiences of Black Faculty at a Public, Two-Year Institution in the North: A Case Study." Poster presented at the 43rd Annual Association for the Study of Higher Education Conference, Tampa, Florida, November 2018.

Oates, Evangela Quinette. "Marginalized Faculty at Marginalized Institutions: Counternarratives as Resistance in Exploring the Experiences of Black Librarians at Public, Two-Year Colleges." PhD diss., University of Nebraska-Lincoln, Nebraska, 2020. ProQuest.

Oates, Evangela Q. "Battered but Not Broken: A Composite of the Experiences of Black Librarians at Public, 2-Year Colleges—Dissertation of the Year." *Community College Review* 51, no. 2 (February 22, 2023): 147–72. https://doi.org/10.1177/00915521221145313.

Okamoto, Karen. "Making Higher Education More Affordable, One Course Reading at a Time: Academic Libraries as Key Advocates for Open Access Textbooks and Educational Resources." *Public Services Quarterly* 9, no. 4 (October 2013): 267–83. https://doi:10.1080/15228959.2013.842397.

Porter, Alyssa J., Sharon Spence-Wilcox, and Kimberly Tate-Malone. "I, Too: Unmasking Emotional Labor of Women of Color Community College Librarians." In *Pushing the Margins: Women of Color and Intersectionality in LIS*, edited by Rose L. Chou and Annie Pho, 273–300. Series on Critical Race Studies and Multiculturalism in LIS, no. 3. Sacramento, CA: Library Juice Press, 2018.

Riley-Reid, Trevar. "Breaking down Barriers: Making It Easier for Academic Librarians of Color to Stay." *Journal of Academic Librarianship* 43, no. 5 (September 2017): 392–96. https://doi:10.1016/j.acalib.2017.06.017.

Roberts, Dorothy E. "Black Club Women and Child Welfare: Lessons for Modern Reform" *Florida State University Law Review* 32, no. 3 (Spring 2005): 957–72.

Salo, Dorothea. "Can We Block the Pipeline Out?" *Library Journal* 139, no. 6 (April 1, 2014): 16–16.

Smith, Brenda, and Leva Lee. "Librarians and OER: Cultivating a Community of Practice to Be More Effective Advocates." *Journal of Library & Information Services in Distance Learning* 11, no. 1–2 (2017): 106–22.

Trust, Torrey, Jeffrey Paul Carpenter, and Daniel G Krutka. "Leading by Learning: Exploring the Professional Learning Networks of Instructional Leaders." *Educational Media International* 55, no. 2 (2018): 137–52.

VanHandel, Leigh, ed. "Challenges and Opportunities of Teaching Music Theory at Community Colleges." In *The Routledge Companion to Music Theory Pedagogy*, 357–65. New York: Routledge, Taylor & Francis Group, 2020.

Wagner-Bennett, McKenzie Taylor. "Professional Learning Communities: Perceptions of Rural Missouri Educators Plc's Ability to Enhance Collaboration and Eliminate Teacher Isolation." PhD diss., William Woods University, Missouri, 2020. ProQuest.

Wenger-Trayner, Etienne, and Beverly Wenger-Trayner. "Communities of Practice: A Brief Introduction," (June 2015), 1–8. https://www.wenger-trayner.com/wp-content/uploads/2022/06/15-06-Brief-introduction-to-communities-of-practice.pdf.

Yosso, Tara J. "Whose Culture Has Capital? A Critical Race Theory Discussion of Community Cultural Wealth." *Race Ethnicity and Education* 8, no. 1 (2005): 69–91. https://doi.org/10.1080/1361332052000341006.

# Unique Communities of Practice through Library Work
## A Dialogue on Building Connections at a Community College

Amanda M. Leftwich, Fran L. Lassiter, Stephanie Nnadi, and Adriene Hobdy

## Introduction

Black women faculty only account for 3% of the full-time faculty at postsecondary institutions,[1] while Black and Latino students are enrolled at 41% and 32% at community colleges, respectively.[2] Faculty of color often fill roles often unnoticed by tenure committees, such as being diversity representatives on hiring committees and all-college / institutional committees, mentors to students of color, and advisors on race/diversity within the institution at large.[3] This phenomenon is known as cultural tax, a term coined by Amado Padilla, "the obligation to show good citizenship toward the [academic] institution by serving its needs for ethnic representation on committees or to demonstrate knowledge and commitment to a cultural group, which may even bring

---

1   U.S. Department of Education, National Center for Education Statistics, The Condition of Education 2020 (NCES 2020-144), May 2022, 151, https://nces.ed.gov/pubs2020/2020144.pdf.

2   U.S. Department of Education, Office of Planning, Evaluation and Policy Development, Advancing Diversity and Inclusion in Higher Education Key Data Highlights Focusing on Race and Ethnicity and Promising Practices, November 2016, 28, https://www2.ed.gov/rschstat/research/pubs/advancing-diversity-inclusion.pdf.

3   Judy A. Loveless-Morris and Latoya S. Reid, "Learning communities: Opportunities for the retention of faculty of color," Learning Communities: Research & Practice 6, no. 1 (2018): 2, https://washingtoncenter.evergreen.edu/lcrpjournal/vol6/iss1/6.

accolades to the institution but which is not usually rewarded by the institution on whose behalf the service was performed."[4] These issues, tied with instances of racism and sexism,[5] isolation, and silencing,[6] all affect the emotional and physical well-being of women of color faculty, especially Black women. When focusing solely on faculty diversification rather than retention, everyone suffers within the unchanged system. A handful of faculty members cannot dismantle systems without the proper roles (administrative, e.g., dean, director, or chair) or support from the institution with funding. Holistic and informative methods, even at the departmental level, can assist in genuine retention efforts. Forming communities of practice (CoP) can assist in building authentic connections within a homogenous workplace.

CoPs cannot replace the systemic failings of workplaces; however, they can act as a center for sharing lived experiences and counter-storytelling, discussing self-care, and effective mentorship.[7] These groups encourage workers to build networks, innovate, and collaborate to foster effective change.[8] Although the concept of CoPs isn't new, its framework and how to utilize ideas formulated in the workplace have amplified with increased attention within the last decade. How does an organization support a group of underrepresented workers to find common ground and generate ideas? First, institutions and people interested in creating communities of practice must have a foundational understanding of the concept and its importance in the workplace.

---

4   Amado M. Padilla, "Ethnic Minority Scholars, Research, and Mentoring: Current and Future Issues," *Educational Researcher* 23, no. 4 (1994): 26.

5   Bryan McKinley Jones Brayboy, "The Implementation of Diversity in Predominantly White Colleges and Universities," *Journal of Black Studies* 34, no. 1 (2003): 76.

6   Adalberto Aguirre, Jr., "The Personal Narrative as Academic Storytelling: A Chicano's Search for Presence and Voice in Academe," *International Journal of Qualitative Studies in Education*, 18, no. 2 (2015): 154.

7   Angel M. Jones, "Letters to Their Attackers: Using Counterstorytelling to Share how Black Women Respond to Racial Microaggressions at a Historically White Institution," *International Journal of Qualitative Studies in Education* (2021): 5; Jennifer L. Richardson, "Healing Circles as Black Feminist Pedagogical Interventions," In *Black Women's Liberatory Pedagogies Resistance, Transformation, and Healing Within and Beyond the Academy*, eds. Olivia N. Perlow, Durene I. Wheeler, Sharon L. Bethea, and BarBara M. Scott (Palgrave Macmillan, 2018), 288; T. Elon Dancy II to Gaetane Jean-Marie, "Faculty of Color in Higher Education: Exploring the Intersections of Identity, Impostorship, and Internalized Racism," *Mentoring & Tutoring: Partnership in Learning*, 22, no. 4 (2014): 364.

8   Thomas Garvan, Ronan Carbery, and Eamonn Murphy, "Managing Intentionally Created Communities of Practice for Knowledge Sourcing Across Organisational Boundaries: Insights on the Role of the CoP Manager," *The Learning Organization* 14, no. 1 (2007): 35, https://doi.org/10.1108/09696470710718339.

Communities of practice are a "group of people who share the concern, a set of problems, or a passion about a topic, and who deepen their knowledge and expertise in this area by interacting on an ongoing basis."[9] Through consistent CoP meetings and idea-sharing sessions, the community can thrive by offering supportive healing spaces and promoting authenticity.[10] As the practice grows, so does active participation, building and fostering a sense of belonging and shared knowledge. For faculty of color, this cannot only act as a retention tool but as a healing space. As Wegner, McDermott, and Snyder explain,

> These people don't necessarily work together daily, but they meet because they find value in their interactions. As they spend time together, they typically share information, insight, and advice. They help each other solve problems. They discuss their situations, their aspirations, and their needs. They ponder common issues, explore ideas, and act as sounding boards. They may create tools, standards, generic designs, manuals, and other documents—or they may simply develop a tacit understanding that they share. However, they accumulate knowledge, they become informally bound by the value that they find in learning together. This value is not merely instrumental for their work. It also accrues in the personal satisfaction of knowing colleagues who understand each other's perspectives and of belonging to an interesting group of people. Over time, they develop a unique perspective on their topic as well as a body of common knowledge, practices, and approaches. They also develop personal relationships and established ways of interacting.[11]

What role do libraries have to play in communities of practice? Librarians of color in higher education are underrepresented in librarianship. The data shows that 86% of academic librarians are White, while only 5.4% are African American, 4.8% Asian American/Pacific Islander, 2.6% Latino, and 2% Indigenous.[12] This highlights the importance of connections and relationship building with faculty of color within the institution. Also, the goals of librarianship include information

---

9  Etienne Wenger, Richard McDermott, and Williams C. Snyder, *A Guide to Managing Knowledge Cultivating Communities of Practice* (Boston: Harvard Business School Press, 2002), 4.

10  Richardson, "Healing Circles," 284; Dancy II & Gaetane, "Faculty of Color in Higher Education," 366.

11  Wenger, McDermott, and Snyder, *A Guide to Managing Knowledge*, 4.

12  "Diversity Counts," American Library Association, 2012. https://www.ala.org/aboutala/offices/diversity/diversitycounts/divcounts.

gathering and sharing, which naturally leans into the concepts and principles of communities of practice.

The Association of College and Research of Libraries (ACRL) Framework for Information Literacy for Higher Education (hereafter ACRL Framework) notes the importance of scholarship as a conversation.[13] The ACRL Framework states, "Communities of scholars, researchers, or professionals engage in sustained discourse with new insights and discoveries occurring over time because of varied perspectives and interpretations. Research in scholarly and professional fields is a discursive practice in which ideas are formulated, debated, and weighed against one another over extended periods of time."[14] The ACRL Framework guides librarians and library workers to view information as a concept that needs to be shared to evolve. As Kim explains, libraries have unique resources to support institution-wide projects, such as: "online access to all resources and services, face-to-face instruction, sponsored training, and forums…listserv, blog[s], chat reference services, and online handouts to facilitate communication of the CoP."[15]

However, institutions cannot force collaboration, which must be rooted in trust and mutual respect. As with any relationship, CoPs thrive where understanding, support, and honesty live. Wegner notes three critical characteristics of any CoP, including mutual engagement, negotiation of a joint enterprise, and shared repertoire.[16] These characteristics not only give CoPs purpose but determine how members will interact with one another.[17] Members of CoPs must understand what they are working towards, why it matters to them, and how they will implement their ideas in the short or long term.

---

13 "Framework for Information Literacy for Higher Education," Association for College & Research Libraries (ACRL), 2015/2016, https://www.ala.org/acrl/standards/ilframework.

14 "Framework."

15 Jong-Ae Kim, "Integrating Communities of Practice into Library Services," *Collaborative Librarianship* 7, no. 2 (2015): 49.

16 Etienne Wenger, *Communities of Practice: Learning, Meaning and Identity* (Cambridge: Cambridge University Press, 1998), 73.

17 Joel O. Iverson and Robert D. McPhee, "Knowledge Management in Communities of Practice Being True to the Communicative Character of Knowledge," *Management Communication Quarterly* 16, no. 2 (2002): 261.

## Interview with Our Community of Practice

This chapter explores the importance of CoPs through shared narratives, including advantages and challenges. It provides reflection questions for strategic relationship building through a transcribed interview with Montgomery County Community College's (MCCC) community of practice with Amanda M. Leftwich, M.S.L.S, Fran L. Lassiter, Ph.D., Stephanie Nnadi, Ph.D., and Adriene Hobdy, Ed.D. Each member is in different departments, including the Libraries, English, Biology, and Human Resources (H.R.), though with the shared experience of being one of the few Black women faculty or administrators in their areas. This community of practice is formed organically through the needs of the individuals in practice, as the college lacks a formal structure for collaborative work across the campus community, creating the need for employee-led communities of practice. The practice members have produced book chapters, national and local presentations, college-wide and library events/programs, and grants. Sharing their narratives will assist in empowering others with limited resources and support for creating collaborative groups, no matter their structure or rank.

**Question 1** *What does the community of practice (CoP) framework mean to you? Why is it important?*

**Dr. Stephanie Nnadi** To me, it's having a way of executing initiatives that are important to us as opposed to just talking about them and throwing things out there. There's a pathway to seeing something come to fruition. Also, it's essential to have a network you can rely on to find support. Communities of practice are necessary to any institution.

**Dr. Adriene Hobdy** I echo that. It is the bridge, especially in higher education [higher ed] institutions, when things can be very siloed. It's a way to connect people across departments, cultures, and many different things to bring them together to work together and learn from each other.

**Dr. Fran L. Lassiter** I agree with both of my colleagues here. And with me, it can be very isolating within your department or your division. These communities of practice allow you to get outside of that sort of limited framework and limited exposure, interacting with people and exposing you to a variety of people that otherwise you may not have ever had an opportunity to engage with. So, it's essential, mainly, maybe in a community college because of so much of what we do. We're so busy doing so many things it allows us to engage with people.

**Amanda M. Leftwich** It allows you to grow, learn, change, and get that feedback that sometimes you can't get when working with people in the same department. Sometimes, especially for our librarians, we must get outside of working only with librarians. We know how librarians think. That's fine. But getting to work, especially at a community college with so many different departments, is helpful because then you get to see what's happening on campus. That's the one reason why it's essential.

**Question 2** *As Black women in faculty and administrative roles, how has this framework supported you as individuals? What did you hope to gain or learn by participating in a CoP?*

**Hobdy** it's been imperative for me professionally because it's important to understand all aspects of the institution, especially as an administrator. It's critical to understand what all the administrative units and the academic departments do, the stakeholders, and if you are coming from a particular area. I work in H.R. If I'm coming from an H.R. background and coming into higher ed, which is very common, then you may need help understanding the industry that you're in. You know H.R., but you need to understand higher ed. Communities of practice have opened the door for us to understand better the work that we support and are servicing.

**Nnadi** I agree with Adriene, and I also would like to add that in being part of a community of practice, there's a sense of urgency that you now share about the work that you are passionate about. You know this work is going to impact your community positively. It's nice to be with like-minded colleagues and have support to move that work forward quickly and make an impact.

**Lassiter** I'm just speaking as a faculty member, at least with the community of practice, it exposes them to administrators in ways that I may not have ever had an opportunity to be exposed to, so that's also essential.

**Leftwich** I think when you're working in a profession that is predominantly White or predominantly homogenous, it's important to remember that you're not alone. And communities of practice can help you do that. You realize that you can work with other Black faculty or Black administrators and that they are there to support you and help you. And they can be your cheerleaders when you're trying to go up against some obstacles that come along with working at a predominantly white institution.

**Lassiter** If I could continue to expand on that, that's very true. For many of us, we are the only people of color within our department. And so, these communities of practice do provide a support system that otherwise we would not have within our departments.

**Question 3** *How did joining a CoP change your work or interactions with the libraries and institutions?*

**Lassiter** I'll jump in. With me, I work much more closely with the library than ever before. I've developed a closer relationship with library personnel, and I have a clearer sense of what they have available to me, not just on a professional level but also on a personal level in terms of any research that I want to do. And so that's how it's been beneficial.

**Nnadi** And, Fran, I'd like to echo that because it's not until I've been part of this community of practice that librarians have been in my classroom. I have learned the value of having a librarian come to my classes and offer many resources for my students. It's been an enormous benefit. And the other thing is I now also promote library events because it's beneficial for students to see the work that we're doing. So yes, bringing the immense resources that the libraries have into my classroom greatly extends the benefits of libraries to my students.

**Hobdy** I agree. I add, though, communities of practice, when it's done over time and not a sporadic thing, it's intentional and consistent. Because of the relationships that are built within the community, it opens the door to trust. That opens the door for brainstorming and creative thinking, and as an administrator, we had never partnered with the libraries. That was always a part of the academic side of things. And so, just being a part of this community opened the door for us to partner with and better support faculty members as students going through the doctoral process and students currently conducting research, or our employees are conducting research at their institutions using our students and our processes. That is not something we would have been able to do if we didn't have this community established where we could interact and think through things. The other piece at the institution is retention. It's retention, personally, for me. It has motivated me to stay at this institution longer than I would have.

**Lassiter**  I must agree wholeheartedly with you on that, Adriene. The community of practices does fill a support system that, otherwise, it's hard sometimes to be the only person in your department, and no one necessarily understands or shares the same sort of values or perspectives as you. That is what the community of practice does. In terms of working specifically with the library, I've always advocated for promoting research to and for our students. Still, because I have developed such a close relationship with Amanda, it makes it so much easier to introduce my students to her as someone they, too, can trust. So, it's been a win-win situation for all of us.

**Question 4**  *Why do you think CoPs, especially in partnership with libraries, are essential? Has your opinion of library work or libraries shifted through this practice?*

**Hobdy**  I think so, especially at a community college because it's not necessarily a research institution. Sometimes, the library is like a stepchild. No offense, Amanda, but we get it all the time: administrators are the stepchildren, too.

Everyone laughs.

**Hobdy**  Because of the communities of practice, we realize that libraries have also kept up with the times. There are parts. There are innovative pieces to research, writing, library resources, how we consume library resources, and all that has changed. Because we have a partnership and are part of an open and engaged community, we now understand how to better interact with modern libraries. Even though we're not a research institution, we still promote that amongst our students, staff, and faculty.

**Lassiter**  And in terms of the resources that our institution has, I am incredibly impressed as a community college. They (MCCC Libraries) have many resources that some four-year institutions still need. And so, our students are introduced to the skills they will need if they go to a four-year institution, especially if it's a research institution, which many of them do end up going to. So, it's a great proving ground for them, a foundation regarding what they must do in their future academic careers.

**Nnadi**  Also, I'll say this, and this is something that I try to get across to my students. The librarians are there to help you, support you, save you time, and show you how to do things efficiently and effectively. It's not just for students but for faculty as well. That's an important take-home message. It's not something negative like, oh, "now I have to bring a librarian to my classroom." We should be excited to bring librarians into our classroom because they navigate resources and systems that will take us much, much longer. So, yes, it is helpful and a good resource for our students.

**Question 5**  *What are some of the advantages of this type of work and practice?*

**Nnadi**  Strength in numbers is where I would start. Having to launch a program alone can be daunting. Who do I call? Or who do I connect with? Just having a network and not having to bear the challenges yourself. It makes it much easier to have support, especially if you're the only person of color in your department or division or whatever the case may be. Having those numbers to get that important work done that we're trying to do.

**Lassiter**  I like the idea of diversity, and by diversity, I'm talking about people from different backgrounds, people from different training. And that's what is most effective and beneficial regarding what communities of practices can offer all of us.

**Hobdy**  I will just add the creativity that comes out of it. I can't express that enough. From just the group and the community that has formed, so many beautiful ideas have come out of it, and we've seen them come to fruition in support.

**Leftwich**  It's good to get out of groupthink! When you're working with people in the same department who have the same ideas, and we come from the same educational background, for the most part. We're all on the same track, but when you go into a community of practice, you're not necessarily thinking the same [thing}, but want to generate ideas. It's great to say, I'm thinking about this, what do you think? And not to hear "And not, oh, well, we've always done it this other way, so we can't do that." That's what I like about our community of practice: I can say something off the wall, and everyone says, "Let's go for it! Let's do it!"

**Question 6**  *What are the biggest challenges with this type of work and practice?*

**Nnadi**  Time. Right? A lot of us are very passionate and very excited about our ideas, collaborating, and bringing new programs and new initiatives to our college community. However, you know, we have very full professional and personal lives, and just prioritizing can be very challenging.

**Lassiter**  I agree. I don't know that I could add anything more than I agree.

**Hobdy**  I would agree. Yeah. The follow-through and commitment, and you have to have people willing to participate and keep reviving it as it goes along.

**Leftwich**  I think it's easy to say, "Oh, we have this one idea," and then never return to it again. I think it's hard to keep the momentum going with another idea, topic, or something else you want to keep going. I guess the way to counteract that is not always to have a project surround it, maybe an idea with multiple steps that you can keep going with yearly.

**Question 7**  *What collaborations have developed through the community of practice?*

**Nnadi**  I worked very closely with you, Amanda, on getting our speaker series off the ground, Prof Talks. This is an example of me having this idea and mentioning it to people. I remember our first conversation and the excitement on your face and then that synergy. You were like, "Listen. You've got this part. I've got this part. I have these ideas, and we will make it happen." Within a few weeks, our speaker series was ready to go. This is a perfect example of how having that community of practice rapidly builds momentum, and ideas are executed, not just talked about.

**Lassiter**   I have a similar story; Amanda and I were working together on a grant for a poetry event. And from this collaboration, we came up with three exciting ideas. Unfortunately, COVID-19, among other things, changed and altered our plans. However, because we were committed to this, we found a way to still pull it off with varying degrees of success. And that is again because you have people willing to put in the time and put in the effort, and that's how you get to have successful events like this.

I don't know that had it not been with Amanda, I wouldn't have been able to pull this off because she has the same passion and commitment to these projects. There are other things that Amanda and I have worked on. On a personal note, because of the collaborative work that I have done with Amanda, it's also encouraged me to do some other work with other individuals. You know, so it works, really it just expands. And that's one of the great things about this whole thing about the community of practices.

**Hobdy**   Yeah. For us, it's the doctoral support group. As you all know, we have a rich tuition reimbursement policy, which we were tracking through to completion. So, we had a lot of people who leveraged the benefit, but they needed to complete it, or it was taking a significant amount of time for them to complete it. Well, you know, financially, that's not good for them. It's not good for morale. We also want our faculty to be doctorally prepared. The more credentials they have, the more courses they can teach. I'm just being transparent. I'm not trying to sign you up for anything. And then, for our administrators, there are specific qualifications for positions. People want to get promoted and advance, and they want to speak, and so do faculty. Anything we could do to support completion is what we were trying to do. We saw an uptick in completion, but the program took off once Amanda came on board, and the program started to take off once we partnered with the library. That came about because of a conversation that Amanda and I had with some other people across campus, but Amanda stuck in there with us. We have seen more people publish. We have seen more people present. We've also been able to present this program at other institutions and conferences. It's been beneficial because it's expanded the portfolio for many people, participants, and us as event organizers.

**Nnadi**  The other thing I want to mention is take-home message, once Amanda got involved, [laughter] all our programs took off. But, Amanda, you also gave, at least I can say this for Prof Talks, our speaker series, which tells the stories of different individuals in different fields; you gave our speaker series a home. There's a place where it lives, where people can see our work.[18] We can revisit what we've done and where it's going. So, I thought that was important.

**Leftwich**  It's been excellent working and learning from all of you. Like you've all said, books, chapters, grants, anything you can think of, we've completed these projects during COVID-19! Which was insane to me, but somehow, we got it done. That shows that communities of practice can work no matter where you are. We haven't seen each other in over a year, but we got all of this done. Adriene and I got a presentation done. We were the only community college that got to present. Those types of things make me feel great!

**Question 8**  *Do you feel the CoP framework is sustainable in the long term?*

**Lassiter**  It is. However, people must be realistic about what they will work on. It is indeed sustainable, especially if you have individuals committed to putting in the time and have the time to do the work, but yeah, it is sustainable.

**Nnadi**  I agree. You know, and to add to that, communities of practice are based on respect. So, we respect each other's experiences. We respect each other as people, of course, the work we're doing, and our expertise. If that respect is there, those relationships grow. When it's not there, those relationships are strained. Because we have that respect and we are like-minded individuals, this is sustainable. This will work in the long term.

**Hobdy**  I agree. You know, I think our community of practice sort of formed organically. There are some benefits to that. What would it be like if it was a little bit more structured and much more intentional? Which would be better? Still, in sustainability theory, when you're looking at development, you do think about adding structure

---

18  Amanda M. Leftwich and Stephanie Nnadi, "Prof Talks," Your Library, Montgomery County Community College, https://library.mc3.edu/about/eventsandworkshops#s-lg-box-24421062.

to things that you want to be sustainable over time. You lose something when you do that. You lose the organic piece of natural connections and natural interests. Which is better? I don't know. It depends on the environment and the purpose of the community of practice. But that is something worth exploring. Is there any value in putting some structure around it so that it is intentional and has the support to thrive?

**Leftwich** There have been studies on both, whether you do it organically or structured. And if it is structured, who's the manager of it? What's the time limit? I think it's sustainable if the people in the CoP are interested in it, as we've all said. If there's no interest, there's no point because it won't work. You can't force someone to be in a community of practice. It just won't work. If there is interest and people are honest about what they can do within the group, then it can be sustainable for as long as you like.

**Question 9** *How have you grown throughout this process, professionally or individually?*

**Lassiter** Both. Professionally, I'm more energized in teaching, coming up with ideas and research. I'm more energized and writing, something I had not done in a while. I put it aside. So professionally, yes. I mean to develop friendships, relationships, and connections with individuals. So yeah, it has been beneficial for me, personally and professionally, for the reasons I outlined.

**Hobdy** Absolutely! I came from being a full-time faculty (member). I missed the research. Now, I'm only an adjunct, and I missed the classrooms. I missed being the teacher. I missed all that coming over to the business side of the house. This allowed me to stick my toe back over there for a moment. It gives me the best of both worlds. I liked that because I got to engage with people in all areas. I had yet to gain experience in [any] sort of student services, student administration, or enrollment management. But through these communities [of practice], I've gained some knowledge and learned about some of the cycles and things that they experienced. That gets my wheels going about what that looks like in other areas. How can we start to innovate and be creative in those spaces? But that's one of the big things professionally. And individually, it's the retention piece. It helped me to stay at MCCC.

**Lassiter**   Whatever works.

**Nnadi**   I feel very grateful and very humbled. You know, I get to work with intelligent, dedicated, compassionate, purposeful colleagues who have all our best interests at heart—and I learned how generous our community is with their time and resources. That's also one of the reasons I'm at MCCC.

**Leftwich**   Professionally, it's helped me understand the importance of how the library fits in all these other places, not just on the faculty side and student support sides. How we can help anyone grow, and how many resources do we have compared to these other departments? A lot of departments believe that the libraries don't have anything. Well, we have a website that no one controls but us. That means we can put anything up that we want to if it's not obscene or anything else. We can use the LibGuides for things that you all want to do. Individually, it did help me stay at MCCC; I would not have survived otherwise. It's exciting to go from a temporary job to being the only person [Black woman] in that space and trying to figure out your place. This community of practice helped me focus on what I could offer to the libraries and the campus community. These are the things that other people are working on that I can help with. That's how it helped me individually.

**Question 10**   *What advice do you have for others looking to cultivate this practice within their institutions?*

**Nnadi**   The simplest way to start is to talk to each other. It seems so simple, but Amanda, I know you and I have talked about this and Fran and Adriene, and you've touched on this today, too: our "bubbles," I always talk about my "biology bubble." You get siloed. You get stuck, and you're going through things day-to-day, which can be okay, but just telling everyone what you're passionate about. Also, sometimes people need help. Maybe there's already an initiative, and you can add to that. It doesn't have to be that you start this whole thing from scratch. You don't have to reinvent the wheel. Sometimes, you can collaborate very quickly.

**Hobdy**   I agree with that. The starting point is to set up a space where people can get to know each other, talk, and share their interests. And it will happen organically.

**Lassiter**  I think the other thing is that you must be willing to take risks regardless of what your idea is, regardless of how far-fetched it may sound, put it out there, and trust that those individuals who are around you can help you shape it into something that does make sense and will be beneficial. If we demonstrate a willingness to take risks, we will impart that same kind of enthusiasm to our students and colleagues. If nothing else, this project will show the great benefits of having a librarian who is actively involved in every aspect of the college's mission and what it does and fulfills its final obligation to the students and the community.

**Leftwich**  All that is amazing and on point, per usual. You must be willing to not be in the same place that you were. Communities of practice, yes, we're thinking of the same ideas, but you must be willing to share them and be "open" to hearing somebody else's thoughts based on where they work. I think one thing, especially since this book is for librarians, is that librarians really must get out of only working with librarians, only working with people who are in or are under the umbrella of Library and Information Science (LIS).

## Reflections for Your Community of Practice

Developing a community of practice not only takes intentionality but also commitment to the group. Collaboration, trust, and understanding take time to build. One must be open to possibilities and change for communities of practice to thrive. This doesn't mean you shouldn't have goals or outcomes for your communities, but rather be amenable and welcome changes based on the practice's needs. Make a note of changes and refer to the group when necessary. It will take time to learn the ebbs and flows of the group, but effective relationship-building is worthwhile in the long run. As you begin your communities of practice, reflect on the following questions. Feel free to add your questions as your practice grows.

1. Why do you want to create a community of practice?
2. What are you hoping to gain or learn from creating a community of practice?
3. What are you hoping to learn about yourself during this process?

4. Will this community of practice be goal-oriented with a project in mind or emotional-support focused? How will you determine whether either is successful?

5. How will you ensure honest conversations and mutual engagement within the practice?

6. How long (or short) do you hope the practice will last?

7. How often will your community of practice meet (e.g., bi-weekly, monthly, yearly)?

8. What are some barriers your community of practice might face (e.g., lack of support from your institution or department, lack of commitment, sustainability, etc.)?

9. Who will be invited to join your practice? Is it open to anyone wanting to participate within your department or institution-wide? How will you ensure people who wish to participate can join the practice?

10. How will you share what you've learned from your community of practice with your departments, institutions, and outside communities?

## Conclusion

As the enrollment of Black and Latino students increases at community colleges across the nation, the responsibilities of and expectations for faculty of color increase exponentially. In addition to contractual obligations, faculty of color fall into the phenomenon of cultural tax[19] that further strains their personal well-being and professional development, especially among Black female faculty. For many Black female faculty, their role as educators is often supplanted by the college's need for "student nurturers" under the guise of "student mentors." Unquestionably, a faculty member's role as a student mentor is critical to the success of BIPOC students; however, this additional responsibility can limit the faculty member's ability to create and implement new initiatives for the college. More importantly, it can significantly impact the mental health and wellness of faculty who are already strained by the professional obligations of the institution. The

---

19  Amado M. Padilla, "Ethnic Minority Scholars, Research, and Mentoring" 26.

collaborative approach central to Communities of Practice (CoP) creates a support system that benefits faculty members, who, in turn, develop a sense of belonging and inclusion that may be absent in their current institution's environment. Although administration overlooks support for BIPOC faculty, care for BIPOC faculty within higher education can help them better serve and support their students and institutions.

Retaining committed faculty and administrators at any institution is crucial to the institution's future success and viability. This is especially important in promoting diversity and equity and creating institutions that attract and retain BIPOC faculty and administrative positions. Because CoPs foster an environment of mutual engagement, employees are likelier to remain at the institution because of a robust and collegial atmosphere. The idea of mutual engagement is fundamental in a successful CoP. Whether a research institution or community college, the library is pivotal as the conduit that links administrators, faculty, and students. For administrators and faculty, librarians can assist in identifying grants and essential resources across various disciplines. This is not to suggest that only libraries can and should be the central focus of a CoP; however, it is necessary to create a centralized system for accessing and disseminating information and materials to foster an environment of mutual engagement within the group. Including a library's existing resources (and, in some cases, underused) in a CoP is one way to achieve these goals. While concepts like equity and diversity are echoed frequently in the workplace, executing either (or both) is often hampered by a lack of trust and community necessary to foster true diversity and equity. Thus, an intentional focus on CoPs is an essential tool to create networks that thrive and expand, embrace purpose-driven and practical innovations, and promote collaborations that foster retention and creativity. Whether using embedded librarians in a course, creating speaker's bureaus for the college community, presenting workshops for faculty members in a terminal degree program, or writing grants for community-driven activities, the interviewees at MCCC have highlighted the benefits of building these connections. As we navigate the uncertainty of a post-Covid world in higher ed, including CoPs, can and should be a starting point to create networks from existing sources that can make a more open and engaged community.

## Bibliography

Aguirre, Jr., Adalberto. "The Personal Narrative as Academic Storytelling: A Chicano's Search for Presence and Voice in Academe." *International Journal of Qualitative Studies in Education* 18, no. 2 (2005): 147–63. https://doi.org/10.1080/0951839042000333956.

American Library Association, "Diversity Counts." 2012. Accessed July 12, 2021. https://www.ala.org/aboutala/offices/diversity/diversitycounts/divcounts.

Association of College & Research Libraries. [ACRL]. "Framework for Information Literacy for Higher Education." 2015/2016. Accessed July 12, 2021. https://www.ala.org/acrl/standards/ilframework.

Brayboy, Bryan McKinley Jones. "The Implementation of Diversity in Predominantly White Colleges and Universities." *Journal of Black Studies* 34, no. 1 (2003): 72–86. http://www.jstor.org/stable/3180858.

Dancy II, T. Elon, and Gaetane Jean-Marie. "Faculty of Color in Higher Education: Exploring the Intersections of Identity, Impostorship, and Internalized Racism." *Mentoring & Tutoring: Partnership in Learning*, 22, no. 4 (2014): 354–72. http://dx.doi.org/10.1080/13611267.2014.945736.

Garvan, Thomas, Ronan Carbery, and Eamonn Murphy. "Managing Intentionally Created Communities of Practice for Knowledge Sourcing Across Organisational Boundaries: Insights on the Role of the CoP Manager." *The Learning Organization* 14, no 1. (2007): 35–49. https://doi.org/10.1108/09696470710718339.

Iverson, Joel O., and McPhee, Robert D. "Knowledge Management in Communities of Practice Being True to the Communicative Character of Knowledge." *Management Communication Quarterly* 16, no. 2 (2002): 259–66. https://doi.org/10.1177/089331802237239.

Jones, Angel M. "Letters to Their Attackers: Using Counterstorytelling to Share how Black Women Respond to Racial Microaggressions at a Historically White Institution." *International Journal of Qualitative Studies in Education* (2021): 1–13.

Kim, Jong-Ae. "Integrating Communities of Practice into Library Services." *Collaborative Librarianship* 7, no. 2 (2015): 47–55. https://digitalcommons.du.edu/collaborativelibrarianship/vol7/iss2/2.

Leftwich, Amanda M. and Stephanie Nnadi, "Prof Talks," Your Library, Montgomery County Community College, https://library.mc3.edu/about/eventsandworkshops#s-lg-box-24421062.

Loveless-Morris, Judy A., and Latoya S. Reid. "Learning Communities: Opportunities for the Retention of Faculty of Color." *Learning Communities: Research & Practice* 6, no. 1 (2018): 1–4. https://washington-center.evergreen.edu/lcrpjournal/vol6/iss1/6.

Padilla, Amado M. "Ethnic Minority Scholars, Research, and Mentoring: Current and Future Issues." *Educational Researcher* 23, no. 4: 24–27.

Richardson, Jennifer L. "Healing Circles as Black Feminist Pedagogical Interventions," In *Black Women's Liberatory Pedagogies Resistance, Transformation, and Healing Within and Beyond the Academy*, eds. Olivia N. Perlow, Durene I. Wheeler, Sharon L. Bethea, and Barbara M. Scott, 281–94. Palgrave Macmillan: 2018.

U.S. Department of Education, National Center for Education Statistics. *The Condition of Education 2020 (NCES 2020-144)*. May 2020. https://nces.ed.gov/pubs2020/2020144.pdf.

U.S. Department of Education, Office of Planning, Evaluation and Policy Development. *Advancing Diversity and Inclusion in Higher Education Key Data Highlights Focusing on Race and Ethnicity and Promising Practices*. November 2016. https://www2.ed.gov/rschstat/research/pubs/advancing-diversity-inclusion.pdf

Wenger, Etienne. *Communities of Practice: Learning, Meaning and Identity*. Cambridge: Cambridge University Press, 1998.

Wenger, Etienne, McDermott, Richard, and Williams C. Snyder. *A Guide to Knowledge Management Cultivating Communities of Practice*. Boston: Harvard Business School Press, 2002.

**Honoring Our Stories**
Frameworks, Identities, and Narratives

# Accepting My Own Worth
## Reflecting and Healing from "Imposter Experience" as a Latina Librarian in Academia

Sally Najera Romero

*Reflective practice aims to integrate the scattered parts of ourselves that can interrupt our personal potential and, at the same time, stifle our potential to help others…[it] shows us to ourselves, reveals and brings to light those aspects of our professional lives that are best dealt with once they have been articulated.*

Michelle Reale[1]

## Introduction: Reflection as Healing

My reflection on my imposter experiences is on my terms—my emotions, how I view my worlds, my thoughts about my experiences, and my perceptions and values. As other scholars of color have done before me, I intentionally use scholarly space to push against white-centered norms that call for a distanced point of view by holding space for reflective healing. Through counter-storytelling and challenging dominant narratives and ideologies, I incorporate appropriate insights

---

1. Michelle Reale, *Becoming a Reflective Librarian and Teacher: Strategies for Mindful Academic Practice* (Chicago: ALA Editions, 2017), 120.

from scholarly literature and narratives to support my experiences.[2] To highlight my imposter experiences, defined in the latter portion of this chapter, I reflect on my identities, specifically as a Latina and mother. I explore the absence of a sense of belonging and identify my imposter experience as internalized racism as opposed to a personal issue. Through reflection and being true to who I am, I acknowledge that within these marginalized experiences, I still hold privilege as an able-bodied, heterosexual, cisgender woman.

This chapter recognizes the hardships of imposter experience as a Latina librarian and, at its core, empowers Black, Indigenous, and People of Color (BIPOC) librarians who face or have faced similar hardships to overturn the imposter phenomenon and accept and own our worth. Imposter experience, also referred to as imposter syndrome, at its root, is the struggle with feeling insecure and like a fraud for gaining attention or praise for one's accomplishments and successes. However, I argue that my negative feeling of self-worth was not a deficit on my part but rather on the institutional structures and limitations. This chapter introduces my Latina upbringing, reflects on my experiences as a woman of color in the field as well as a mother, and highlights how systemic oppression during my early career overshadowed the capability to fully come to terms with the fact that my professional successes, attributed to my professional competencies, including expertise, experience, and skill set, are due to my perseverance and virtues.

Ultimately, this professional reflection aims to give light and validation to Latina librarians and possibly other BIPOC librarians experiencing a similar phenomenon. My experiences will never be identical to anyone, even those who identify as Latina librarians. Still, I hope to hold a space to document my journey and add another voice to the collection of ever-growing narratives of people of color in libraries. Before writing this autoethnography, where the researcher is also the subject of inquiry,[3] I never imagined writing about myself, especially in personally vulnerable areas. Reflective writing is transformative and empowering and recognizes personal experience and knowledge as

---

2   Angel M. Jones, "Letters to Their Attackers: Using Counterstorytelling to Share How Black Women Respond to Racial Microaggressions at a Historically White Institution," *International Journal of Qualitative Studies in Education* (2021): 5, https://doi.org/10.1080/09518398.2021.1942292.

3   Anne-Marie Deitering, "Why Autoethnographic?," in *The Self as Subject: Autoethnographic Research into Identity, Culture and Academic Librarianship*, ed. Anne-Marie Deitering, (Chicago: ACRL Publications, 2017), 2.

valuable resources for teaching and learning.⁴ I hope this piece offers readers community and a sense of belonging, encouraging us to find the power and strength to heal from our imposter experiences—for we all deserve to see our self-worth.

## We Are Working People

I am the daughter of Mexican immigrants and a first-generation U.S. citizen. I can't move forward with this reflection without acknowledging my beloved parents and their sacrifices in the hope of a better future for me and my siblings. My parents sacrificed leaving their Yucateco life behind to give themselves and my family a life of possibilities. Most of my work ethic has been instilled in me by my parents. My parents worked long hours and showed up daily to provide for the family. As a starting place to understand the lives and culture of Mexican immigrants, Ashley-Marie Vollmer Hanna and Debora Marie Ortega identify, in their study, four themes that reflect the values of Mexican immigrants as well as their ability to persevere through the barriers and hardships they face: (1) 'We are working people'; (2) 'I am not an animal' (experiencing racism, prejudice, and discrimination); (3) fear; and (4) internal strength (perseverance, *luchar*, [fight] and *salir adelante* [get ahead]).⁵

I started working in public libraries at seventeen to save for college tuition. Starting at an entry-level position in libraries, I climbed the positional ladder over time. I took on a full-time paraprofessional position while going to graduate school and then, after graduation, worked at my first professional part-time community college librarian position. It is necessary to note that my transition from position to position within libraries was never, internally or externally, linear. Like my parents, I worked long hours daily, sometimes holding up two positions at a time to *salir adelante (get ahead)*. Despite my experience in public libraries at all levels, performing tasks that librarians did every day, such as reference, outreach, and collection development, I felt tremendous self-doubt in my abilities as I transitioned to academia as

---

4   Tracey T. Flores, "Breaking Stereotypes and Boundaries: Latina Adolescent Girls and Their Parents Writing Their Worlds," *Voices from the Middle* 25, no. 3 (2018): 24, https://www.academia.edu/36223905.

5   Ashley-Marie Vollmer Hanna and Debora Marie Ortega, "Salir Adelante (Perseverance): Lessons from the Mexican Immigrant Experience," *Journal of Social Work* 16, no. 1 (2016): 53, https://doi.org/10.1177/1468017314560301.

a librarian. All I could see was that I had no academic experience, and as a recent graduate, I wouldn't hold merit to the position. It took incredible time and support to build confidence in my capabilities, especially during my transition from part-time community college librarian to tenure-track community college librarian.

Years later, as I reflect on my career journey, including various librarian positions, I understand, through no fault of their own, how the barriers and hardships my parents faced founded my working conditions. I internalized the "we are working people" perception and was willing to be of service, with the notion that working harder would one day give me a better future, even though I felt unfit. I also had so much fear—not the fear my parents endured as immigrants, but fear of being a phony and, most intensely, the fear of not being enough. At heart, my perseverance, also learned by my parents, gave me the strength to face challenges and obstacles. She never knew it, but ultimately, the thing that kept me going, as a Latina, were my mother's words of encouragement along the way—*échale ganas* (give it all you got) and *tú sí puedes, mija* (you can do it, daughter).

## Latina as a Fraction of the Profession

I am my mother's daughter, a Chicana, a Latina. Delgado Bernal explains, "Most Chicanas lead lives with significantly different opportunity structures than men (including Chicano males) and White women- and our experiences are intertwined with issues of immigration, migration, generational status, bilingualism, limited English proficiency, and the contradictions of Catholicism."[6] Not to mention, Casanova points out that "children of immigrants must negotiate multiple cultures during their identity development and acculturation processes" and the "development of their identities depends highly on social mirroring and self-evaluation of the perceptions" of others.[7] Shamefully, from childhood to adulthood, and in fear of being outcasted by my peers, and people in general, I found acculturation occurred two ways for me: "ethnic flight (completely merging into American culture

---

6   Dolores Delgado Bernal, "Using a Chicana Feminist Epistemology in Educational Research," *Harvard Educational Review* 68 (1998): 561, https://doi.org/10.17763/haer.68.4.5wv1034973g22q48.

7   Saskias Casanova, "The Stigmatization and Resilience of a Female Indigenous Mexican Immigrant," *Hispanic Journal of Behavioral Sciences* 34, no. 3 (2012): 377, https://doi.org/10.1177/0739986312449584.

and denying Latino culture) or transcultural identity (interacting and transitioning between the American and Latino culture)."[8] Even more heart-breaking, as a Latina woman, throughout my career journey, I felt a constant battle between my identity and place in the whiteness of academia and academic libraries. Medina and Luna acknowledge that "Latina women have sometimes had to make the difficult choice of forsaking their past, their cultural identity, their language, and their indigenous roots for access and mobility in the academy."[9] Not only that, Brown et al. state that BIPOC librarians must learn about "not only the organizational culture but also the white 'professional' culture, all to 'fit' within our institution's boundaries of whiteness."[10]

Working in community colleges offered me different opportunities and experiences. One of my most deep-rooted experiences is that students can relate to me. Students can see themselves in me. Locally, over 69% of California community college students are people of diverse ethnic backgrounds, and roughly 53% are female.[11] Nationally, according to the American Association of Community Colleges, in the fall of 2020, 50% of Hispanic students represented community college undergraduates.[12] However, when I looked around the campus, I did not see myself represented in the faculty. Nearly 60% of community college faculty statewide are white (see Fig. 1).[13] Within every community college district in the state, the percentage of Latino students exceeds that of Latino faculty, sometimes by more than 50%.[14]

With a small percentage of faculty of color on campus, it's been difficult as a BIPOC faculty to truly feel a sense of belonging among my

---

8   Casanova, "The Stigmatization and Resilience," 377.

9   Catherine Medina and Gaye Luna, "Narratives from Latina Professors in Higher Education," *Anthropology & Education Quarterly* 31, no. 1 (2000): 47–66, https://doi.org/10.1525/aeq.2000.31.1.47.

10  Jennifer Brown, Jennifer A Ferretti, Sofia Leung, and Marisa Méndez-Brady, "We Here: Speaking Our Truth," *Library Trends* 67, no. 1 (2018): 170, https://doi.org/10.1353/lib.2018.0031.

11  "California Community Colleges Facts and Figures," Foundation for California Community Colleges, accessed August 12, 2021, https://foundationccc.org/About-Us/About-the-Colleges/Facts-and-Figures.

12  "Fast Facts 2022," American Association of Community Colleges, March 2022, https://www.aacc.nche.edu/research-trends/fast-facts/.

13  Thomas Peele and Daniel J. Willis, "California's Failure to Diversify Community College Faculty Tied to Arcane State Law," EdSource, last modified March 1, 2021. https://edsource.org/2021/californias-failure-to-diversify-community-college-faculty-tied-to-arcane-state-law/648977.

14  Peele and Willis, "California's Failure to Diversify Community College Faculty."

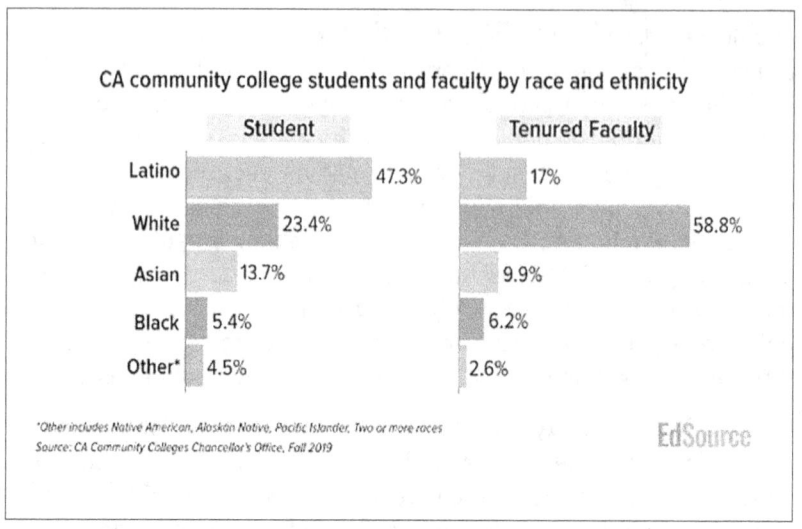

**Figure 1** CA Community College Students and Faculty by Race and Ethnicity.

peers. Even when I see a large population of students who look like me, due to the lack of faculty representation, I still feel self-doubt about my capacity as a faculty member. My experience with being confused as a student by a faculty colleague supports Brown et. al. claim that "many women of color are mistaken for students on campus, and then treated as though they are inexperienced or lack expertise."[15]

Specifically, in academic community college libraries, I have been one of the few, if not only, BIPOC librarian(s) on the roster. In truth, I concur with Brown et. al. declaration that "the only time we ever see other librarians of color is if we create spaces for ourselves."[16] According to the Department of Professional Employees's Library Professionals, "the librarian profession suffers from a persistent lack of racial and ethnic diversity that has not changed significantly over the past 15 years."[17] A deeper examination of the diversity of librarians shows that in the United States, BIPOC librarians make up only a fraction of the profession,

---

15  Jennifer Brown, et. al., "We Here," 170.

16  Jennifer Brown, et. al., "We Here," 169.

17  "Library Professionals: Facts and Figures 2021 Fact Sheet," Department for Professional Employees, AFL-CIO, accessed January 20, 2022, https://www.dpeaflcio.org/factsheets/library-professionals-facts-and-figures.

"Over 83 percent of librarians being white in 2020. More precisely, just 9.5 percent of librarians identified as Black or African American, 9.9 percent as Hispanic or Latino (of any race), and 3.5 percent as Asian-American or Pacific Islander. Librarians are slightly less diverse than the total workforce of people in education, training, and library occupations, which is 82 percent white. Black and African American professionals made up 10 percent of the education workforce, while Hispanic and Asian professionals represented 10.9 percent and 4.9 percent of the education workforce, respectively. Women represented 82.2 percent of graduates in Master of Library Science (MLS) programs in 2018–2019. However, Black women only accounted for 4.5 percent of all MLS graduates, while Hispanic and Asian/Pacific Islander women made up 7.8 and 2.5 percent of the 2019 class, respectively."[18]

With the meager number of Latina/o librarians nationwide, it is comprehensible to feel an absence of belonging in the profession. Unfortunately, as Nataraj et. al. denotes, "to survive and thrive in librarianship, BIPOC must remove, or at the very least downplay, all markers of intersectional identities in order to embrace a paradigm of whiteness."[19] To add more salt to the wound, comparing faculty race and ethnicity to librarian race and ethnicity, we see how librarianship is even less diverse in faculty representation than the overall faculty of color on campus.

## Hidden Motherhood in Librarianship

Motherhood has played a vital role in my identity. It is personal, challenging, sacred, and ever-changing. In short, motherhood is an evolving journey. For much of my librarian career, I've held my motherhood close to my chest and away from the institution and colleagues. As a young, early-career librarian, I was always perceived as childless since I avoided mentioning my young children. My lack of trust and experiences of microaggressions, "brief, everyday exchanges that send

---

18 "Library Professionals: Facts and Figures 2021 Fact Sheet", pt. 4.

19 Lalitha Nataraj, Holly Hampton, Talitha R. Matlin, and Yvonne Nalani Meulemans, "'Nice White Meetings': Unpacking Absurd Library Bureaucracy through a Critical Race Theory Lens," *Canadian Journal of Academic Librarianship*, 6 (December 2020): 9, https://doi.org/10.33137/cjal-rcbu.v6.34340.

denigrating messages,"[20] held me from sharing my motherhood when I entered academia. I encountered many microaggressions as a young mother towards the end of my paraprofessional journey, with the most personal attacks being a colleague asking if they needed to get me *another* present after announcing a pregnancy 15 months after giving birth and Human Resources telling me they've never processed back-to-back pregnancy leaves. In an exit interview, a male administrator told me that academic libraries require hard work and different expectations (because he came from academia). The latter example supports my experience outlined by Pitt et al. in how "assaults on [women's] professional competence are explicit reminders of how others see our worth."[21] More directly, Williams calls to attention how "women's successful performances tend to be more closely scrutinized and then assessed by stricter standards than men's."[22] These harrowing experiences during my early years of motherhood left me feeling inept and doubting my abilities, which carried over to my work in academic librarianship.

Gallin-Parisi signalizes that "the literature about motherhood and academia focuses on the traditional academic faculty (i.e., the teaching professor) and largely excludes the academic librarian who is also a mother."[23] In addition, Gallin-Parisi distinguishes that "library faculty are different as our schedules, flexibility, demands, required hours on-campus, and autonomy are distinct from most faculty colleagues outside the library."[24] Eva, Lê, and Sheriff highlight that "the lack of existing literature on the topic of motherhood and librarianship is

---

20 Iain A. Smith and Amanda Griffiths, "Microaggressions, Everyday Discrimination, Workplace Incivilities, and Other Subtle Slights at Work: A Meta-Synthesis," *Human Resource Development Review* (2022): 3, https://doi.org/10.1177/15344843221098756.

21 Jenelle S. Pitt, et. al., "Black Women in Academia: The Invisible Life," in *Racial Battle Fatigue: Insights from the Front Lines of Social Justice Advocacy*, ed. Jennifer L. Martin (Santa Barbara, CA: Praeger, 2015), 210.

22 Joan C. Williams, "The Glass Ceiling and the Maternal Wall in Academia," *New Directions for Higher Education* no. 130 (2005): 93, http://dx.doi.org/10.1002/he.181.

23 Alexandra Gallin-Parisi, "It's a Marathon, Not a Sprint, and Other Lessons for Supporting Librarianship and Motherhood," *Library Leadership & Management* 31, no. 4 (2017): 3, https://doi.org/10.5860/llm.v31i4.7213.

24 Alexandra Gallin-Parisi, "An Academic Librarian–Mother in Six Stories," *In the Library with the Lead Pipe* (May 2018), http://www.inthelibrarywiththeleadpipe.org/2018/academic-librarian-mother.

stark."[25] Even more, the authors acknowledge in their study that "BIPOC academic librarians of all genders who are mothers face many additional challenges," after not including race in their analysis. I recall in an informal conversation about scheduling, as a part-time librarian at a community college, a lead made the confessional, irritated comment, "It's really hard to schedule people with children for coverage." She had no idea I was a mother. She inferred that working parents and guardians are perceived as unable to give 100% of themselves to the job. Gallin-Parisi relates that "issues such as the flexibility stigma and bias avoidance are realities to many women (and men) with families trying to survive within universities and colleges."[26]

As I entered the academic world, I quickly noticed how "the topic of academic mothers too often remains both silent and invisible."[27] In my experience, motherhood is non-existent among librarian colleagues. I was highly aware of the stereotypes and assumptions of people with children in the workforce, especially those of working mothers. In Odenweller and Rittenour's study on stereotypes of working mothers, their findings evidence an oppressive way of thinking about mothers.[28] I vividly recall a library department chair confronting another mother-librarian about missing a last-minute meeting on a day she was scheduled off to take care of her child. The department chair asked my colleague, "What is more important, your job or your daughter?" Although these words were not directed at me, my heart sank. I felt gut-punched because her comment indirectly impacted me. I stood there, shocked. How can anyone ask such an insensitive question and openly display bias against mothers? William identifies that the "maternal wall bias is triggered at any point when maternity becomes salient," such as when a woman seeks a modified schedule.[29] Consequently, the author suggests that "women may experience benevolent as well as

---

25  Nicole Eva, Mê-Linh Lê, and John Sheriff, "Less Money, Less Children, and Less Prestige: Differences Between Male and Female Academic Librarians," *The Journal of Academic Librarianship* 47, no. 5 (2021), https://doi.org/10.1016/j.acalib.2021.102392.

26  Alexandra Gallin-Parisi, "It's a Marathon, Not a Sprint," 2.

27  Laura J. Beard, "'Which June?' What Baby?: The Continued Invisibility of Maternity in Academia," in *Academic Motherhood in a Post-Second Wave Context: Challenges, Strategies and Possibilities*, ed. D. Lynn O-Brien Hallstein & Andrea O'Reilly, (Ontario: Demeter Press, 2012), 144.

28  Kelly G. Odenweller and Christine E. Rittenour, "Stereotypes of Stay-at-Home and Working Mothers," *Southern Communication Journal* 82, no. 2 (2017): 68, https://doi.org/10.1080/1041794X.2017.1287214.

29  Williams, "The Glass Ceiling," 97.

hostile prescriptive stereotyping."[30] When I think of mothers in academia, I regularly reflect on that day, on that specific incident. I reflect on the challenges and barriers mothers must endure but, at the same time, build resilience to survive.

However, even with the effort of building resilience, all these negative experiences end up causing working mothers to feel inadequate.[31] Feeling stereotyped and perceived as not dependable was enough for me to hide a large part of my identity completely: my motherhood. More specifically, as Pitt et al. reveal, "women of color engage in shifting as a way of surviving the structures embedded in academia that largely privilege white male profiles and career paths."[32] In my early career, I have purposefully forsaken my intersectional identities to fit within the academy. Instead of being proud of my culture and motherhood, I found myself feeling a sense of inadequacy and phoniness since I was not being true to myself or others. As painful as it has been to articulate the hardships and challenges of motherhood in academia and to heal properly, I agree with Eva, Lê, and Sheriff's sentiment that "it is important to be truthful about obstacles or hardship to bring about changes and attention. By being more vocal and open about our personal experiences, and by adding to the literature on this understudied topic, we can advise and mentor and bring formerly under-discussed issues to light."[33]

## Recognizing Imposter Experience

Throughout my early career journey, I had difficulty grasping the feelings of inadequacy, self-doubt, and never being enough. As many commonly know it, imposter syndrome (IS) is a familiar workplace experience and, apparently, one that I carried with me through my early career journey. Imposter syndrome, at its original foundation, is the struggle with feeling insecure and like a fraud for gaining attention or praise for one's accomplishments and successes. Faulkner further reveals that "the experience is expressed in the forms of generalized

---

30  Williams, 97.

31  "4 Working-Mom Stereotypes That Need to Go," PayScale, last modified July 5, 2016. https://www.payscale.com/career-news/2016/07/working-mom-stereotypes.

32  Jenelle S. Pitt, et. al., "Black Women in Academia," 209.

33  Nicole Eva, Mê-Linh Lê, and John Sheriff, "Less Money, Less Children, and Less Prestige,".

anxiety and stress, low self-confidence, and even depression and job burnout as sufferers self-impose impossible standards of achievement and then fail to live up to their own expectations."[34] The term imposter syndrome was coined by Pauline Rose Clance and Suzane Ament Imes in 1978. Even further, T. Elon Darcy II and Gaetane Jean-Marie identify in their research the following subcategories of imposter experience in faculty of color:

- Feeling like a fake, or the belief that one does not deserve their success or professional position.
- attributing success to luck or other external reasons and not to one's internal abilities.
- discounting success or the tendency to downplay or disregard the achievement of success.[35]

Because the term imposter syndrome "doesn't fit the clinical criteria for a psychological syndrome, defined as a cluster of symptoms that causes intense distress or interferes with a person's ability to function,"[36] for this article, imposter experience is called imposter syndrome. The reason for this distinction is that it's crucial to acknowledge early on that the term "syndrome" implies the deficit that causes the phenomenon is about the person experiencing it instead of the racist systemic structures bearing the responsibility for creating an imposter experience. In reflection, Pauline Rose Clance shared, "If I could do it all over again, I would call it the imposter experience because it's not a syndrome or a complex or a mental illness; it's something almost everyone experiences."[37] Therefore, as a means to heal, I intentionally refer to this phenomenon as an imposter experience because I have concluded that my negative feeling of self-worth was not a deficit on my part but rather on the institutional structures.

---

34  Ashley E. Faulkner, "Reflections on the Impostor Phenomenon as a Newly Qualified Academic Librarian," *New Review of Academic Librarianship* 21, no. 3 (2015): 266, https://doi:10.1080/13614533.2015.1070185.

35  T. Elon Dancy and Gaetane Jean-Marie, "Faculty of Color in Higher Education: Exploring the Intersections of Identity, Impostorship, and Internalized Racism," *Mentoring & Tutoring: Partnership in Learning* 22, no. 4 (2014): 355, http://dx.doi.org/10.1080/13611267.2014.945736.

36  L. V. Anderson, "Feeling Like an Impostor Is Not a Syndrome," *Slate Magazine*, (April 12, 2016), https://slate.com/business/2016/04/is-impostor-syndrome-real-and-does-it-affect-women-more-than-men.html.

37  L. V. Anderson, "Feeling Like an Impostor Is Not a Syndrome," para. 4.

## Imposter Experience in Libraries

Anecdotally, there has yet to be an organization where I have worked where librarians or personnel have not shared their fears and anxieties about their position or profession. Lacey and Parlette-Stewart note that Library and Information Science (LIS) scholarship on imposter experience is profound and documented throughout research.[38] Furthermore, the authors distinguish that "librarians set high goals for themselves, which, when overworked, are not easily achieved…this leads to further feelings of doubt regarding one's abilities, and amplifies the feeling of imposter experience in our roles."[39] Clark, Vardeman, and Barba's study found that one in eight librarians report above-average imposter experience, with feelings most noticeable in librarians within their first three years of professional experience.[40] In a profession with just over 83% of librarians identified as white in 2020.[41] Brown et al. bring to light that "it is worth noting how rare it is for white librarians and scholars to state their whiteness anywhere in their writing or presentations openly, or as part of the methodology or limitations of the research they conduct."[42]

As crucial as imposter experience and many other studies are to librarianship, it is hard to ignore that it still centers around whiteness since it lacks data collection without an equity lens that considers race and ethnicity as part of the data collection methodology. Current research on LIS imposter experience overshadows the concept that BIPOC librarians may feel the imposter phenomenon harder. In support of this concept, scholars T. Elon Dancy II and Gaetane Jean-Marie observed "that people of color internalizing racism, by believing White people are superior, may self-question one's abilities"[43] a byproduct of imposter experience. In addition, Moore identifies how scholars Kerry

---

38 Sajni Lacey and Melanie Parlette-Stewart, "Jumping Into the Deep: Imposter Syndrome, Defining Success and the New Librarian," Partnership: *The Canadian Journal of Library and Information Practice and Research* 12, no. 1 (2017): 2, https://doi.org/10.21083/partnership.v12i1.3979.

39 Lacey and Parlette-Stewart, "Jumping Into the Deep," 2.

40 Melanie Clark, Kimberly Vardeman, and Shelley Barba, "Perceived Inadequacy: A Study of the Imposter Phenomenon among College and Research Librarians," *College & Research Libraries* 75, no. 3 (2017): 255; 259–60, https://doi.org/https://doi.org/10.5860/crl12-423.

41 "Library Professionals: Facts and Figures 2021 Fact Sheet" pt. 4.

42 Jennifer Brown, et. al., "We Here," 166.

43 Dancy II and Jean-Marie, "Faculty of Color in Higher Education," 358.

Anne Rockquemore and Tracey Laszloffy "argue that there is a fundamental difference in the experiences of Black and white tenure-track faculty because of the disparate positions they occupy in the larger social order."[44]

Almost the entirety of the research on imposter experience and librarians fails to address the added barriers faced by librarians of color before mentioning race and ethnicity, echoing Kendrick and Damasco's revelation that the LIS field and space are overwhelmingly White.[45] More importantly, we need to start seeing the imposter experience not as a personal issue but as a systemic oppression. As library professionals, we need to stop suggesting that fear and anxiety are normalized and expected emotions to have in the workplace and within our profession "and instead examine how these narratives are the result of institutions deflecting the need for change."[46] Dancy and Jean-Marie declare how "college faculty of color experience impostor-ship is understudied."[47] More specifically to LIS, according to Gonzalez-Smith, Swanson, and Tanakawe, there is a lack of a multidimensional view of the experiences of academic librarians of color.[48] Since the librarian profession suffers from a persistent lack of racial and ethnic diversity that has not changed significantly over the past 15 years,[49] it's easy to see how this also impacts racial and ethnic diversity in LIS scholarship and research. Concerning imposter experience, we should continuously, in an equity-minded lens, where we recognize cultural relevance and call attention to patterns of biases, ask ourselves, how does diversity impact the academic librarian's sense of self and, more specifically, how do academic librarians of color perceive themselves

---

44  Mignon R Moore, "Women of Color in the Academy: Navigating Multiple Intersections and Multiple Hierarchies," *Social Problems* 64, no. 2 (2017): 201, https://doi.org/10.1093/socpro/spx009.

45  Kaetrena Davis Kendrick and Ione T. Damasco, "Low Morale in Ethnic and Racial Minority Academic Librarians: An Experiential Study," *Library Trends* 68, no. 2 (2019): 207, https://muse.jhu.edu/article/746745.

46  Nicola Andrews, "It's Not Imposter Syndrome: Resisting Self-Doubt as Normal for Library Workers," *In the Library with the Lead Pipe* (June 2020), https://www.inthelibrarywiththeleadpipe.org/2020/its-not-imposter-syndrome/.

47  Dancy II and Jean-Marie, "Faculty of Color in Higher Education," 355.

48  Isabel Gonzalez Smith, Juleah Swanson, and Azusa Tanaka, "Unpacking Identity: Racial, Ethnic, and Professional Identity and Academic Librarians of Color," In *The Librarian Stereotype: Deconstructing Perceptions and Presentations of Information Work*, ed. Nicole Pagowsky and Miriam Rigby, (Chicago: Association of College and Research Libraries, 2014), 149.

49  "Library Professionals: Facts and Figures 2021 Fact Sheet," pt. 4.

in a predominantly white profession, and how can we interpret these perceptions to understand their experiences better?[50] To combat this systemic oppression, Jones expresses that "our scholarship must include the voices, stories, and experiences of marginalized people who are too often silenced by dominant groups."[51]

## Imposter Experience as/and Internalized Racism

Until recently, I always attributed my feeling of "not being enough" as simply coincidental to belonging to a racially marginalized group. However, it's evident from my lived experiences and those of other BIPOCs, according to Dancy and Jean-Marie, that "imposter experience aligns with the internalized racism concept, particularly around superfluous questions of one's abilities or merit."[52] During my first interview for a tenure-track position, in a one-on-one, I was surprisingly asked to speak Spanish and demonstrate my fluency for a position that did not list such requirements in their job description. Initially, I was shocked, but I followed the directions and spoke Spanish to be compliant and seen as a favorable candidate. It's not until recently, reflecting on the incident, that I acknowledge it was essentially linguistic bias. Although I believe the employer intended to give me an "opportunity" to demonstrate my worth in the position, it's essential to keep in mind Ro's point that "not every type of linguistic discrimination is intentional; many people who think they're being inclusive don't understand that their inherent biases are pushing them to make judgments they don't even know they're making."[53] It's also important to address that although I grew up in a Spanish-speaking household, the author makes the related observation that linguistic stereotyping applies even when BIPOC individuals are, in fact, native speakers of English.[54]

With my intersectional identities mentioned earlier, I struggled with using Spanish to fit into the whiteness of academia early in my career.

---

50 Isabel Gonzalez-Smith, Juleah Swanson, and Azusa Tanaka, "Unpacking Identity," 151.

51 Jones, "Letters to Their Attackers," 8.

52 Dancy II and Jean-Marie, "Faculty of Color in Higher Education," 359.

53 Christine Ro, "The Pervasive Problem of 'Linguistic Racism,'" Worklife, last modified June 3, 2021, https://www.bbc.com/worklife/article/20210528-the-pervasive-problem-of-linguistic-racism.

54 Christine Ro, "The Pervasive Problem of 'Linguistic Racism,'" para. 9.

Bernal highlights, "Bilingualism is often seen as un-American and is considered a deficit and an obstacle to learning."[55] While having a private conversation with a library staff colleague, I was told by a non-Spanish speaking librarian how rude it was for me to talk in a language she didn't understand. This was contradictory since I was the librarian who asked to help anyone who spoke Spanish. How is it fair for me to use my bilingualism for the benefit of the institution yet find it unacceptable to use it personally amongst other BIPOC staff? Machado reflects on how "Spanish is viewed mostly through a lens of suspicion and disdain" and recalls that "there is no pride in Spanish/English bilingualism."[56] As a result, and in my self-doubt, I was always conscious of my multilingualism and how it's merited. While I should be proud to speak, read, and write in another language, the system makes me feel ashamed.

As established earlier, there is a lack of BIPOC librarians in academic libraries. In my first tenure-track librarian position, there were no BIPOC librarians in managerial, administrative, or leadership roles. As the only BIPOC librarian, I was constantly told, "This is how 'we' do it," or "This is how we've always done it," when I questioned the process, motivation, and intent to duties, responsibilities, and workload. Every instance left me thinking, who is "we"? I also noticed that library paraprofessional staff, in my experience, most of whom were people of color, would also receive the same, if not harsher, response when discussing similar conversations. Again, it's easy to say that these are all mere coincidences. But it holds value to consider that it may not be a coincidence after all, but oppression that, over time, leads to self-destruction and feeling of not belonging and, worse, of not being enough.

It doesn't have to stay this way; Brown et al. recommend that "if we are to overcome the isolation that mars our experience, the LIS profession must be critically examined starting from the shared acknowledgment that our values, systems, policies, education, and institutions are based on whiteness."[57] The authors continue by advocating that

---

55  Dolores Delgado Bernal, "Using a Chicana Feminist Epistemology in Educational Research," 562.

56  Amanda Machado, "How the U.S. Taught Me That My Spanish Was Shameful," *NBC News*, Last modified March 26, 2019, https://www.nbcnews.com/think/opinion/how-u-s-taught-me-spanish-was-shameful-ncna986746.

57  Jennifer Brown, et. al., "We Here," 178.

"librarianship needs to meaningfully address systems of structural oppression in order to actualize diversity and inclusion initiatives at large."[58] Nataraj et. al., points out that "continuing to adopt institutionalized white-washed practices without specifically naming and addressing the white supremacy that is built into their foundations will prevent libraries from ever being the inclusive, diverse, and equitable spaces they purportedly wish to become-leading to decisions or outcomes that fail students, staff, faculty and the communities we serve."[59] From my lived experiences as a woman of color, I no longer accept these historically oppressive structures and, in turn, declare that LIS should intentionally work to dismantle inequitable practices in the field. Librarianship and those in the field must intentionally make space and efforts for cultural relevance, diversity, and inclusion.

## Accepting and Owning My Worth

I reflect on healing and offering solidarity with other librarians of color who may feel any sense of imposter experience. As a Latina librarian, I have accepted that everything I have done thus far is of merit. So, this, my success, is mine. I had to believe in myself because, historically, institutions have not. There has seldom been a time when institutions or organizations I have worked for intentionally stopped to reflect on their practices and how they adversely affect their BIPOC employees and their sense of belonging and worth. To all the BIPOC librarians out there, ever feeling a single ounce of self-doubt and accepting it as an imposter experience– it is not you.

It took me many years to come out of the "assembly line" and look at the ways systemic oppression has played a role in my insecurities and self-doubt. There are more days than not where I want to give in. Where I ask, is the fight even worth it? If I do what has "always been done," I will still have a job and paycheck. But I can no longer live that way. I can no longer accept institutionalized oppression. I must take back the institution's power over how I feel about myself. I must hold my institution accountable.

We must hold our institutions, administration, and leadership accountable. In Clark et al., a study observed that "library organizations

---

58  Jennifer Brown, et. al., 163.

59  Lalitha Nataraj, et. al., "'Nice White Meetings,'" 11.

may not necessarily cause imposter feelings; however, survey respondents perceived that the culture fosters those feelings."[60] Lacey and Parlette-Stewart claim that "collegial support, encouragement, constructive feedback, and formal and informal mentorship opportunities can go a long way to combat imposter experience."[61] Suppose you happen to be at an institution that isn't adjusting white-centric practices to provide meaningful, culturally competent spaces. In that case, BIPOC employees deserve to start and continue to speak their truth and own their worth. Andrews declares that "we must never underestimate the power of changing ourselves, of committing to be a force for liberation, light, wellness, justice, and right action wherever we go."[62] I will no longer hide my identities but proudly display them on my sleeve. I am worthy of my degree, my position, and this profession.

## Moving Forward

I humbly write this chapter not solely to criticize and scrutinize a systemic oppressive structure to validate my internal struggle with accepting my worth of work and skills but to heal genuinely and wholeheartedly. For many years, I felt inside my heart and soul that this imposter experience was a "me" problem. With support from colleagues, BIPOC groups and communities, professional development, and honest reflection, I accepted that I am worthy. With dedication and hard work, I have merited the position I find myself in. Position and title should never be confused with talent, skills, and ability.

For those attempting to break the imposter experience cycle, here are a few things I've done over the years to accept my worth:

- Create a support group:

    My support group comprises BIPOC colleagues who have a genuine interest in my success and family and friends who support my passion and work. I have individuals in this group who help with specific areas of my life and work. A crucial one for me is the "no" people. I speak to this group when I overcommit or need

---

60   Clark, Vardeman, and Barba, "Perceived Inadequacy," 264.
61   Sajni Lacey and Melanie Parlette-Stewart, "Jumping Into the Deep," 3.
62   Nicola Andrews, "It's Not Imposter Syndrome," para. 57.

that confidence boost to say 'no' to things that will ultimately not benefit me.

- Participate in BIPOC community spaces:

I've curated a collection of helpful communities sharing similar experiences as a BIPOC educator. I've surrounded myself with individuals with similar identities to avoid the feeling of isolation. It wasn't until joining/following groups that I realized there were more BIPOC experiences like mine. Groups and individuals, such as *Mindfulinlis, We Here, WeAllGrow Latina, Poderistas,* and *Academic Mujeres,* to name a few, have provided the most sense of belonging because at least one of my identities is at the forefront of their spaces.[63]

- Surround yourself with words/images of affirmation:

My personal space surrounds me with words and images of affirmation. If I see it regularly, it'll manifest inside of me. In most of my workspaces, whiteness is the norm. Even my office was all white walls. I quickly put up empowering quotes and images that represent me. As my first affirmation to you- repeat this to yourself—I am worthy today. I was worthy yesterday. I will be worthy tomorrow.

## Conclusion

Writing this reflection while exploring my intersectional identities as a Latina and mother in academic libraries was hard. After giving myself to this profession day after day, I've come to realize that my feelings of self-doubt and never feeling enough, known as imposter experiences, are not a deficit on my part but internalized racism- a byproduct of systemic institutional oppression. As much as I'd liked to forget they existed, I can't and shouldn't. Instead, through true reflective healing and articulating the experiences, I can move forward and help others. I write to confront injustices, reflect on past experiences, make sense

---

[63] mindfulinlis (@mindfulinlis), 2023, Instagram, https://instagram.com/mindfulinlis?igshid=YmMyMTA2M2Y=; We here® (@wehere.space), 2023, Instagram,https://instagram.com/wehere.space?igshid=YmMyMTA2M2Y=; WeAllGrow Latina® (@weallgrowlatina), 2023, Instagram, https://instagram.com/weallgrowlatina?igshid=YmMyMTA2M2Y=; Poderistas® Latinas in Poder (@poderistas),2023, Instagram, https://instagram.com/poderistas?igshid=YmMyMTA2M2Y=; Dr. Mara Nohemi Lopez (@academicmujeres), 2023, Instagram, https://instagram.com/academicmujeres?igshid=YmMyMTA2M2Y=.

of my journey, heal, look to the future, and let the world know that Latina Librarians, with all their barriers and challenges, exist. Since the totality of the research on imposter experience and librarians fails to address the added barriers faced by librarians of color, this reflection aims to give light and validation to the underwhelming low account of BIPOC librarian voices experiencing a similar imposter phenomenon. This reflection offers the hope that more BIPOC librarians have the power and strength to heal from our imposter experiences by finding community, a sense of belonging, and self-worth.

## Bibliography

American Association of Community Colleges. "Fast Facts 2022." March 2022. https://www.aacc.nche.edu/research-trends/fast-facts/.

Anderson, L. V. "Feeling Like an Impostor Is Not a Syndrome." *Slate Magazine*, (April 12, 2016). https://slate.com/business/2016/04/is-impostor-syndrome-real-and-does-it-affect-women-more-than-men.html.

Andrews, Nicola. "It's Not Imposter Syndrome: Resisting Self-Doubt as Normal for Library Workers." *In the Library with the Lead Pipe* (June 2020). https://www.inthelibrarywiththeleadpipe.org/2020/its-not-imposter-syndrome/.

Beard, Laura J. "'Which June?' What Baby?: The Continued Invisibility of Maternity in Academia." In *Academic Motherhood in a Post-Second Wave Context: Challenges, Strategies and Possibilities*, edited by D. Lynn O-Brien Hallstein & Andrea O'Reilly, 143–55. Ontario: Demeter Press, 2012.

Bernal, Dolores Delgado. "Using a Chicana Feminist Epistemology in Educational Research." *Harvard Educational Review* 68 (1998): 555–83. https://doi.org/10.17763/haer.68.4.5wv1034973g22q48.

Brown, Jennifer, Jennifer A Ferretti, Sofia Leung, and Marisa Méndez-Brady. "We Here: Speaking Our Truth." *Library Trends* 67, no. 1 (2018): 163–81. https://doi.org/10.1353/lib.2018.0031.

Casanova, Saskias. "The Stigmatization and Resilience of a Female Indigenous Mexican Immigrant." *Hispanic Journal of Behavioral Sciences* 34, no. 3 (2012): 375–403. https://doi.org/10.1177/0739986312449584.

Clark, Melanie, Kimberly Vardeman, and Shelley Barba. "Perceived Inadequacy: A Study of the Imposter Phenomenon among College and Research Librarians." *College & Research Libraries* 75, no. 3 (2017): 255–71. https://doi.org/https://doi.org/10.5860/crl12-423.

Dancy II, T. Elon, and Gaetane Jean-Marie. "Faculty of Color in Higher Education: Exploring the Intersections of Identity, Impostorship, and Internalized

Racism." *Mentoring & Tutoring: Partnership in Learning* 22, no. 4 (2014): 354–72, http://dx.doi.org/10.1080/13611267.2014.945736.

Deitering, Anne-Marie. Why Autoethnographic?" in *The Self as Subject: Autoethnographic Research into Identity, Culture and Academic Librarianship*, edited by Anne-Marie Deitering, 1–22. Chicago: ACRL Publications, 2017.

Department for Professional Employees, AFL-CIO. "Library Professionals: Facts & Figures 2021 Facts Sheet." June 10, 2021. https://www.dpeaflcio.org/factsheets/library-professionals-facts-and-figures.

Eva, Nicole, Mê-Linh Lê, and John Sheriff. "Less Money, Less Children, and Less Prestige: Differences Between Male and Female Academic Librarians." *The Journal of Academic Librarianship* 47, no. 5 (2021): https://doi.org/10.1016/j.acalib.2021.102392.

Faulkner, Ashley E. "Reflections on the Impostor Phenomenon as a Newly Qualified Academic Librarian." *New Review of Academic Librarianship* 21, no. 3 (2015): 265–68. https://doi:10.1080/13614533.2015.1070185.

Flores, Tracey T. "Breaking Stereotypes and Boundaries: Latina Adolescent Girls and Their Parents Writing Their Worlds." *Voices from the Middle* 25, no. 3 (2018): 22–25. https://www.academia.edu/36223905.

Foundation for California Community Colleges. "California Community Colleges Facts and Figures." Accessed August 12, 2021. https://foundationccc.org/About-Us/About-the-Colleges/Facts-and-Figures.

Gallin-Parisi, Alexandra. "An Academic Librarian–Mother in Six Stories." *In the Library with the Lead Pipe*. (May 2018). http://www.inthelibrarywiththeleadpipe.org/2018/academic-librarian-mother.

Gallin-Parisi, Alexandra. "It's a Marathon, Not a Sprint, and Other Lessons for Supporting Librarianship and Motherhood." *Library Leadership & Management* 31, no. 4 (2017): 1–14. https://doi.org/ 10.5860/llm.v31i4.7213.

Gonzalez-Smith, Isabel, Juleah Swanson, and Azusa Tanaka. "Unpacking Identity: Racial, Ethnic, and Professional Identity and Academic Librarians of Color." In *The Librarian Stereotype: Deconstructing Perceptions and Presentations of Information Work*, edited by Nicole Pagowsky and Miriam Rigby, 149–73. Chicago: Association of College and Research Libraries, 2014.

Hanna, Ashley-Marie Vollmer, and Debora Marie Ortega. "Salir Adelante (Perseverance): Lessons from the Mexican Immigrant Experience." *Journal of Social Work* 16, no. 1 (2016): 47–65. https://doi.org/10.1177/1468017314560301.

Jones, Angel M. "Letters to Their Attackers: Using Counterstorytelling to Share How Black Women Respond to Racial Microaggressions at a Historically White Institution." *International Journal of Qualitative Studies in Education* (2021): 1–13. https://doi.org/10.1080/09518398.2021.1942292.

Kendrick, Kaetrena Davis, and Ione T. Damasco. "Low Morale in Ethnic and Racial Minority Academic Librarians: An Experiential Study." *Library Trends* 68, no. 2, (2019): 174–212, https://muse.jhu.edu/article/746745.

Lacey, Sajni, and Melanie Parlette-Stewart. "Jumping Into the Deep: Imposter Syndrome, Defining Success and the New Librarian." *Partnership: The Canadian Journal of Library and Information Practice and Research* 12, no. 1 (2017): 1–15. https://doi.org/10.21083/partnership.v12i1.3979.

Machado, Amanda. "How the U.S. Taught Me That My Spanish Was Shameful." *NBC News*, Last modified March 26, 2019. https://www.nbcnews.com/think/opinion/how-u-s-taught-me-spanish-was-shameful-ncna986746.

Medina, Catherine, and Gaye Luna. "Narratives from Latina Professors in Higher Education." *Anthropology & Education Quarterly* 31, no. 1 (2000): 47–66. https://doi.org/10.1525/aeq.2000.31.1.47.

mindfulinlis (@mindfulinlis). 2023. Instagram. https://instagram.com/mindfulinlis?igshid=YmMyMTA2M2Y=.

Moore, Mignon R. "Women of Color in the Academy: Navigating Multiple Intersections and Multiple Hierarchies." *Social Problems* 64, no. 2 (2017): 200–205. https://doi.org/10.1093/socpro/spx009.

Nataraj, Lalitha, Holly Hampton, Talitha R. Matlin, and Yvonne Nalani Meulemans. "'Nice White Meetings': Unpacking Absurd Library Bureaucracy through a Critical Race Theory Lens." *Canadian Journal of Academic Librarianship*, 6 (December 2020): 1–15. https://doi.org/10.33137/cjal-rcbu.v6.34340.

Nohemi Lopez, Maria (@academicmujeres). 2023. Instagram. https://instagram.com/academicmujeres?igshid=YmMyMTA2M2Y=.

Odenweller, Kelly G and Christine E. Rittenour. "Stereotypes of Stay-at-Home and Working Mothers." *Southern Communication Journal* 82, no. 2 (2017): 57–72. https://doi.org/10.1080/1041794X.2017.1287214.

PayScale. "4 Working-Mom Stereotypes That Need to Go." Last modified July 5, 2016. https://www.payscale.com/career-news/2016/07/working-mom-stereotypes.

Peele, Thomas, and Daniel J. Willis. "California's Failure to Diversify Community College Faculty Tied to Arcane State Law." *EdSource*. Last modified March 1, 2021. https://edsource.org/2021/californias-failure-to-diversify-community-college-faculty-tied-to-arcane-state-law/648977.

Pitt, Jenelle S., Mya Vaughn, Aisha Shamburger-Rousseau, and LaKiesha L. Harris. "Black Women in Academia: The Invisible Life." In *Racial Battle Fatigue: Insights from the Front Lines of Social Justice Advocacy*, edited by Jennifer L. Martin, 209–23. Santa Barbara, CA: Praeger, 2015.

Poderistas® Latinas in Poder (@poderistas). 2023. Instagram. https://instagram.com/poderistas?igshid=YmMyMTA2M2Y=.

Reale, Michelle. *Becoming a Reflective Librarian and Teacher: Strategies for Mindful Academic Practice*. Chicago: ALA Editions, 2017.

Ro, Christine. "The Pervasive Problem of 'Linguistic Racism.'" *Worklife*, Last modified June 3, 2021. https://www.bbc.com/worklife/article/20210528-the-pervasive-problem-of-linguistic-racism.

Smith, Iain A., and Amanda Griffiths. "Microaggressions, Everyday Discrimination, Workplace Incivilities, and Other Subtle Slights at Work: A Meta-Synthesis." *Human Resource Development Review* (2022): 1–25. https://doi.org/10.1177/15344843221098756.

WeAllGrow Latina® (@weallgrowlatina). 2023. Instagram. https://instagram.com/weallgrowlatina?igshid=YmMyMTA2M2Y=.

We Here® (@wehere.space). 2023. Instagram. https://instagram.com/wehere.space?igshid=YmMyMTA2M2Y=.

Williams, Joan C. "The Glass Ceiling and the Maternal Wall in Academia." *New Directions for Higher Education* no. 130 (2005): 91–105. http://dx.doi.org/10.1002/he.181.

# Creating a Sense of Belonging for BIPOC Students in a Community College Library

*Andrew Kuo*

## Introduction

A large percentage of students in community colleges are Black, Indigenous, and People of Color (BIPOC). I currently work in a Northern California community college (CC) library in an urban, culturally diverse area that has faced challenges in different ways due to racism and discrimination. Contra Costa College (CCC) is a Hispanic Serving Institution (HSI) college with a racially diverse student body: 43.3% Hispanic, 17.1% African American, 13.8% Asian, 12.1% White, 6% Filipino, 5.5% Two or more Races (2017–18).[1] I have worked there for over fifteen years. Serving BIPOC students at CCC is significant as I can relate to, sympathize with, and empathize with many of our working-class students. I am an immigrant from Taiwan who immigrated to Pennsylvania when I was eight. I speak both Mandarin and English fluently. My parents worked in restaurants as waiters and once as a manager. They usually worked 10-12 hour days. As a manager, my father worked 16 hours on the weekends, and during the holidays, he would be lucky to have a full day off a week. After 15 years of this grueling schedule, on and off (sometimes they took time off due to injury), they saved enough money to open their restaurant. We all worked at the restaurant; my parents hired a chef, a prep cook, and two-weekend hostesses.

---

1   College Contra Costa, "2019 Student Success Scorecard," 2019 Student Success Scorecard Contra Costa College, 2019, https://scorecard.cccco.edu/scorecardrates.aspx?CollegeID=311.

Unfortunately, the restaurant failed. They returned to working as wait staff, and I went to college.

In examining topics of student equity in an HSI college, the emphasis should be on creating connections with students. These connections are part of creating a sense of belonging. A sense of belonging for students means the students feel welcomed to the college for who they are as individuals, respected, included, and understood. Moreover, BIPOC students have a sense of belonging when they see BIPOC faculty and staff on campus. The more men of color feel related to college settings, the higher their success rate.[2] The academic library is not just a part of college but a significant component of informal learning spaces on campus.[3] On CC campuses, the library's position as a study space, a group study space, and a casual study space is crucial, as CCs do not have as many informal study spaces as other institutions of higher learning.

As librarians, we must be aware of the possibilities of informal study space in supporting students' success by creating connections and belonging. I have chosen to write this chapter in a narrative style for two reasons. This style makes it more accessible for librarian readers. Part of the mission of this chapter is to bring more access to BIPOC students, so it makes sense to create an accessible chapter for librarians who can then better connect with students. As an author, the narrative style lets me to stay closer to the material. This is more natural for me and keeps me wholly engaged.

## Literature Review

Before delving into BIPOC students' library-related topics, it is helpful to relate how society affects BIPOC students, shaping dynamics and attitudes. These macro factors relate to BIPOC students' experiences in the library. The in-groups and the out-groups that exist in America set up many issues facing BIPOC students. Two of these issues are microaggression and stereotype threat. In the essay "Offensive

---

2 Frank Harris III, J. Luke Wood, and Vanessa Falcon, "Supporting Men of Color in Community Colleges: An Examination of Promising Practices and California Student Equity Plans," University of Southern California, last modified 2017. https://cue.usc.edu/files/2017/05/Report_Supporting_Men_of_Color_in_Community_Colleges.pdf, 15.

3 Kelly M. Broughton, "Students' Sense of Belonging in Study Spaces," (PhD Diss., Ohio University, 2019), 18.

Mechanisms" by Chester Pierce from the book *The Black Seventies*, he describes and details microaggressions. Microaggressions contrast to macroaggressions, which are "gross and obvious," such as lynchings.[4] Microaggressions are subtle, continuous, and an "offensive mechanism"[5] for White people to deploy against Black people to continue white supremacy. Pierce counted police tenor ghettoization as microaggressions, among other acts, to make Black people see themselves as "useless, unlovable, unable."[6] Microaggressions also lead to health problems and earlier deaths.[7] The importance of creating belonging becomes even more critical because of microaggressions. BIPOC students are more than just the sum of their academic achievements. They are people with histories and people whom society has already put in a specific category even before they join our campuses. We, as librarians, must be aware of this and fight microaggressions because this is a way to support BIPOC students with equity.

Related to microaggressions are stereotype threats. A stereotype threat is a self-evaluative threat where others' negative stereotypes affect one's actions so that one does not want to conform to being viewed as this stereotype by others or oneself.[8] One can see that this threat can be a drain on anyone taking a test, especially if it is a difficult test, because of the drain in processing the stereotype threat. In Steele's study, one group [is told] the usual instructions for tests, stating that it tests for intellectual ability, while another group [is told] that it tests for problem-solving ability.[9] The second group did better on the same test. He goes on to perform other studies to narrow down and confirm the fact that stereotype threat harms Black participants because it diverts attention, creates interfering self-consciousness, and increases frustration.[10] The key here is that reduction

---

4   Chester Pierce, "Offensive Mechanisms," In *The Black Seventies*, ed. Floyd Barrington Barbour (Boston, MA: Porter Sargent Publisher, 1970), 266.

5   Pierce, "Offensive Mechanisms," 266.

6   Pierce, 265–82, 268.

7   Pierce, 268.

8   Claude M. Steele and Joshua Aronson, "Stereotype Threat and the Intellectual Test Performance of African Americans," *Journal of Personality and Social Psychology* 69, no. 5 (1995): 797, https://doi.org/10.1037/0022-3514.69.5.797.

9   Steele and Aronson, "Stereotype Threat," 797.

10  Steele and Aronson, 799.

of stereotype threat is possible, perhaps even eliminated in certain circumstances, for Black students and other students facing stereotype threat (such as women in mathematics and socioeconomically challenged students) if the tests are presented without the usual introduction, but one that considers the stereotype threats of society at large.[11] Taking a larger view, beyond testing, it is not hard to postulate that BIPOC students are under stereotype threat as they make their way through their courses and their academic careers.

Stereotype threat could include stigma. Generally, when we think of stigmas, we think of those visible, such as blind people, and their societal treatment. Erving Goffman explores this, expanding the lay definition and going in-depth. The first distinction he makes is virtual social identity versus actual social identity, where the former is the identity observers assume based on their first impressions. The latter are the traits the person can be proven to possess.[12] Our assumptions about the stigmatized do not usually fit the person standing before us. This goes beyond seeing a person with a disability. Goffman covers many social categories that were stigmas in 1963, at the time of publication.[13] Those stigmas still exist today, to different degrees in America. The three stigma types listed are physical, psychological (homosexual, alcoholic, or abuser), and race, religion, and nationality.[14] He demonstrates his points, including how the stigma may or may not be visible and how some people hide it to escape broader societal judgment.[15] If the stigmatized were in a more accepting environment where they felt belonging, they would not be under as much stress. With reduced pressure, BIPOC students would find it more accessible to concentrate on their academic goals. Even though this chapter concerns creating belonging for BIPOC students, we can recognize that the library can also be a place where other stigmatized groups are accepted, such as trans people, LGBTQ+, and others. This intersectionality is crucial to improving library belongingness as staff think about and apply an open and welcoming attitude for all students. Indeed, when

---

11   Steele and Aronson, 810.

12   Erving Goffman, *Stigma: Notes on the Management of Spoiled Identity* (London: Penguin, 1963), 2.

13   Goffman, 2.

14   Goffman, 4.

15   Goffman, 6.

we look at the American standard of the in-group, it is absurd, and we must look to reduce our biases.

Recently, writings related to the topic of supporting BIPOC students in the academic library have grown. "Students' Sense of Belonging in Study Spaces" is an example.[16] It discusses the library's famous and current student uses: studying, group work, and general socializing. BIPOC students differ from White students in factors that make them comfortable on a college campus. BIPOC students prioritize respect, the ability to be one's authentic self, and safety versus White students who prioritize fun and friendliness.[17] BIPOC student find themselves under many intersectional categories including class, gender, being an international student, and being an English as a Second Language (ESL) student were included in the category of BIPOC students. One can see the intersectionality in this framework: those groups pushed to the margins by the dominant White culture sense this pressure and react to defend themselves. How effective we are at creating belonging necessitates an awareness of how students view us. From there, we can decide how best to approach students—sometimes interacting with them to confirm librarian perceptions. From there, librarians and library staff know that supporting BIPOC students' authentic selves and concerns for safety will create a stronger sense of belonging.

Southwestern University and Southwestern Community College completed a study on students' sense of belonging in the library entitled, *Mapping Sense of Belonging in Library Spaces*. The study found that "library policies, campus climate, and interpersonal interactions are factors in developing SB (sense of belonging)."[18] The four facets of belonging they focused on were psychological (feeling that they belong in a community), spatial (emotional and personal connections to a place), cultural ("ethos, practices, and policies of the institution" which affect SB), and sociocultural ("engaging and aligning activities with and imagining futures connected to communities of practice").[19] A CC BIPOC student shared that she didn't have a way of transferring

---

16   Kelly M. Broughton, "Students' Sense of Belonging in Study Spaces." (PhD Diss., Ohio University, 2019).

17   Broughton, "Students' Sense of Belonging in Study Spaces," 55.

18   Mapping Sense of Belonging in Library Spaces, 2020 Library Assessment Conference, Online, December 16, 2020.

19   Chodock, "Mapping Sense of Belonging in Library Spaces," 4.

her data, and she was surprised when the librarian offered her a flash drive; this made an impression on her, showing her that people cared in the library.[20] These areas can be helpful to consider when librarians want to implement positive change to be more inclusive of BIPOC students in the CC library. At the CCC library, we guide students to resources, and if they happen to be a physical book, we walk the student over to the item. This way, we finish assisting the students through the process, and they learn how to locate a book online to get it in hand. When I often walk a student to a book, we talk about their class or their day. Occasionally, these interactions may begin an ongoing conversation with the student. I have had students come back and pick up from our previous discussion.

The ACRL Frameworks threshold concept and the transformation of the learner to "acquire expertise in that field of knowledge."[21] In a CC library, this sort of transformation does not happen in a vacuum. Sometimes, the librarian is the catalyst for the student. Other times, it is the student interacting with other peers. In all these cases, having a sense of belonging allows for transformation. Belonging means students are connected to the college, not only intellectually but also through relationships. This aids the college in retaining the students.

bell hooks asked to look beyond academic measurements to consider the whole student. hooks believed that the student is not just there as an academic but a real person with emotions, spirituality, and body.[22] It is the professor's job to teach the intellect and the whole student. This means engaging the whole student to set the student's mind free[23] to explore new ideas and ways of living. hooks cited Paulo Freire as a model for this sort of exploration, where he encouraged students to participate and have a dialogue with him and other students.[24] This is important for BIPOC students because it will increase their connection to the course through their connection to the

---

20 Chodock, 7.

21 ACRL, "Framework for Information Literacy for Higher Education," Association of College & Research Libraries (ACRL), February 2, 2015, https://www.ala.org/acrl/standards/ilframework, 12, accessed March 2, 2022.

22 bell hooks, *Teaching to Transgress: Education as the Practice of Freedom* (New York, NY: Routledge, 1994), 14.

23 hooks, *Teaching to Transgress*, 13.

24 hooks, 14.

professor. For hooks, books are not separate from life; they apply to life. In exploring new ideas, old biases—such as stereotypes and outright racism—ought to be corrected. Related to this, she described how she was inspired by the monk Thich Nhat Hanh, who had the approach to teaching as a healer — teaching not only to the mind but the whole person in life.[25] hooks explains that professors must encourage student participation and take the whole student into account (this supports self-actualization).[26] hooks describes how many professors today are enabling the splitting of body and mind as they compartmentalize their lives.[27] The classroom is not a top-down paradigm but where all participants learn and change. In creating belonging, not only are librarians answering reference questions and creating a safe environment, but they are also learning from BIPOC student perspectives, including their life stories, academic journeys, knowledge, and aspirations. This not only creates connections with students but makes us better librarians. Listening to students allows the librarian to relate to the student in this way; the librarian can see opportunities to connect with students related to academic or other interests. This sets up lines of communication with students. The more relatable and connected the librarian is to students, the better the librarian has become, for these threads can create bonds that retain BIPOC students.

Another aspect to examine is that of cultural humility. Cultural humility is "self-evaluation of one's own background and expectations, committing to redress power imbalances, and building relationships."[28] Some in the CC library may find it not college-specific enough, but focusing on the human rather than the student aspect makes more sense. The student comes to us seeking to further their skills and knowledge, but every student also comes with non-academic histories that affect their performance in college. From this POV, it is easier to see how librarians can broaden the view of students to support them better. The process of acquiring cultural humility is not merely going through a list, but it is an ongoing process, the idea being that tutors continue to examine their background, beliefs, and behaviors to reach

---

25 hooks, 14.

26 hooks, 17.

27 hooks, 17.

28 Nicole Andrews and Josie Watanabe, "Cultural Humility as a Transformative Framework for Librarians, Tutors, and Youth Volunteers: Applying a Lens of Cultural Responsiveness in Training Library Staff and Volunteers," *Young Adult Library Services* 16, no. 2 (2018): 20.

their patrons better.[29] Not only tutors but librarians can also adopt this attitude of self-reflection. It helps students and librarians gain more knowledge and understanding of BIPOC students.

The more reflective a librarian is, the more they will likely see the different POVs that BIPOC students bring to the table. Librarians can better support BIPOC students by reflecting on their backgrounds and connecting with those groups by acknowledging the support they wish they had had as students. The hope is to make BIPOC students less ostracized and bring more understanding. This leads to stronger relationships, more fulfilling interactions between tutors and students, and a more welcoming library.[30] Many CC libraries could benefit from similar workshops tailored to their sites. Their workshops should focus on student demographics so they can see how to practically apply what they learn to their work. This allows librarians to refresh their thinking and explore new areas of BIPOC student support. Workshops that will enable librarians and library staff (including any library deans, directors, and leads) to connect open lines of communication can improve morale as they all pull the library in the same direction. The author discussed intersectionality and how other factors such as race, class, and gender, can also create overlapping discriminations and disadvantages.[31] Ongoing workshops can build upon BIPOC's understanding to branch out to these groups. This improves student support and shows librarians and staff that it is a lifelong process and natural to expand our knowledge and understanding as we grow in the profession. Cultural humility creates more belonging in libraries because it breaks down the barriers and differences between different groups and improves understanding and communication not just in a public library but also in a diverse community college library.

Twanna Hodge explains that the librarian should question their own values [32] because it is from this perspective that librarians can make fundamental changes that cultivate a "mutually respectful

---

29  Andrews and Watanabe, "Cultural Humility as a Transformative Framework," 20

30  Andrews and Watanabe, 20

31  Andrews and Watanabe, 21.

32  Twanna Hodge, "Integrating Cultural Humility into Public Services Librarianship," *International Information & Library Review* 51, no. 3 (March 2019): 269, https://doi.org/10.1080/10572317.2019.1629070.

relationship"[33] with public library patrons. This includes examining implicit bias: "automatic associations—connecting bits of information together for us."[34] These points relate to the stigmas in society, which are only virtual,[35] but sift through almost all people so that they need to be brought to consciousness and eliminated. Are we going to catch all of them? Unfortunately, no, but this is a lifelong journey. As librarians make changes, they connect more fully with patrons and support them better. To help identify implicit bias, Hodge notes the Implicit Association Test, which will bring these unconscious biases to the surface.[36] Once those biases are made conscious, she lists techniques to deal with them: 1.) replace biases with counter biases 2.) think of details that make people individuals 3.) "perspective taking": "imagine what it would be like to like to be in that group."[37] These techniques would apply to my library in that there are groups of students I did not have much contact with growing up, such as Latinx people. It is part of my job now to understand the Latinx community better and fill in the gaps in my knowledge to support them.

## Strategies for Supporting Belonging

A work that brings topics of immigration to the forefront in the CC library for BIPOC students in the CC library is the book *Borders & Belonging*. It discusses immigrant poverty and best practices for reaching those communities.[38] In the early twentieth century, American libraries were directed towards assimilating immigrant populations into White, Anglo-Saxon, Protestant middle-class values and mores; in practice, this was a one-way street where immigrants were supposed to listen and learn from White librarians and take on the librarians' values.[39] This viewpoint carried on into the present day for some libraries, creating a barrier for immigrants in their communities. It is

---

33  Hodge, "Integrating Cultural Humility," 269.

34  Hodge, 269.

35  Goffman, *Stigma: Notes on the Management of Spoiled Identity*, 2.

36  Hodge, "Integrating Cultural Humility," 270.

37  Hodge, 271.

38  Ana Ndumu, *Borders and Belonging: Critical Examinations of Library Approaches toward Immigrants* (Sacramento, CA: Library Juice Press, 2021), 159.

39  Ndumu, *Borders and Belonging*, 13.

much more accessible for immigrants if librarians try to meet them halfway by using Google on the fly to communicate simply through translated keywords. Of course, it is better to find staff that speak the immigrant's native language. Doing the extra work of being an on-demand translator ought to increase the salary of those who do this work. This is true for CC libraries, too. At CCC, I realize we have an asset in having library staff who speak Mandarin, Spanish, or Amharic. When libraries hire, applicants who speak other languages ought to be considered with an eye toward languages most often used by patrons. Frequently, the library may also fulfill the goal of diversity in hiring in this way.

## Library Environment

The environment is usually the first thing students notice when they enter the library. What are the first things they see when they enter? What will make a student feel more comfortable and included? Displays promoting diversity are a great way to show inclusivity; displays may include Black History Month, LGBTQ+ History Month, and Women's History Month. Rotating the displays monthly to promote different groups and show variety would be practical. There may be a display that speaks to a student, whether they let the library staff know or not. That moment can spark a student's curiosity, spirit, feeling, or intellect to explore a topic—maybe through the library's collections and resources. Encourage student workers, especially BIPOC students, to be involved in creating displays. They will be more attuned to student tastes. Leisure reading materials can include BIPOC authors who are popular with a diverse student population, including Angie Thomas, Colson Whitehead, Lisa See, Sandra Cisneros, and Matt de la Peña. Also, BIPOC student workers can help reach out to students online, be it Instagram, Facebook, TikTok, etc. These practices naturally allow BIPOC student expression, and the library will reach more students.

Library furniture and equipment are another consideration. Plenty of choices exist, but the cost may be prohibitive. Search for funding where possible: partner with different programs and departments on campus; work with the Business Office or the equivalent; brainstorm with your FOL (Friends of the Library); Instructional Equipment funds; lottery funds; and look for community funding. Librarians could create surveys to get ideas or rankings from students for possible changes. During the pandemic, electronic devices and internet access have been necessary. One could bridge the digital divide (the gap between those with access to computers and the internet and those without) by acquiring these devices, such as laptops and hotspots, for student checkouts. Today, the digital divide is apparent at CCs for students of color.[40] Income inequality has grown during the pandemic. Libraries should be able to apply for pandemic funding to acquire digital equipment and access for students.

On college campuses with all or most buildings named after European Americans of all White presidents, some BIPOC students have commented that it creates an intimidating environment.[41] To combat this perception, libraries could put up plaques that recognize the achievements of BIPOC scholars, educators, and leaders. They could draw from the history of the local community in which they reside. Instead of imagery or statues of European colonizers, they could have a plaque of the Indigenous people from that land to give credit where credit is due. Display plaque(s) in prominence so everyone can see them and let BIPOC students know they have value and a place within the library.

## Library Space Usage

The CC librarian can create an inviting and safe climate for BIPOC students. There are opportunities for librarians to relate to students and connect them to the CC. A roving librarian can improve the atmosphere of a library.[42] If technology is available to walk around with, that will help with any students who have questions. Circulating also allows for more interaction with students. Opportunities to learn student names are a way to create connections. For many students of color, experiencing care has not occurred from education staff. Some BIPOC students feel invisible, others feel under scrutiny. Some students think teachers or faculty only know their names when they are in trouble. After learning names, librarians can ask about students' academic

---

40  ACCT: The Association of Community College Trustees, "Digital Divide: How Technology Access Impacts Community Colleges across the United States During a Pandemic," ACCT: The Association of Community College Trustees is the Voice of Community College Leaders ACCT: The Association of Community College Trustees, May 2021, https://www.acct.org/files/ACCT_Digital_Divide_at_Community_Colleges_During_COVID_2021.pdf.

41  Ndumu, *Borders and Belonging*, 59.

42  Daniel A. Sabol, "Best Practices in Roving Reference Services: Six Steps for Success," *College & Research Libraries News* 80, no. 1 (March 2019): 46, https://doi.org/10.5860/crln.80.1.46.

progress, their interests, and their plans. Librarians have an opportunity to learn about students and share their own experiences or expertise. Some may have the same major as the librarian in college.

Librarians must maintain an atmosphere conducive to learning. It may not seem "nice" to halt bullying or other adverse situations, but it is part of our duty to uphold a safe environment for all students to study in. This is especially important for BIPOC students as they may often feel stigmatized. It falls on the librarian to create an equitable atmosphere for students to feel safe studying and learning. When situations arise, take a breath and learn about the difficulty from all perspectives before saying or acting in the moment if possible. We all have implicit biases and assumptions; to reduce implicit bias, listen to all parties before deciding. Afterward, librarians will type an official summary of events. Still, librarians can also sit down, probably near the end of the workday, and write out the event in a journal (as suggested by Hodge) to reflect on the occasion.[43]

## Microaggressions

Besides having to deal with the hardships of the pandemic, many BIBOC students deal with microaggressions. These adversely affect BIPOC students' sense of comfort, respect, and, possibly, safety on a college campus, likely leading to depression.[44] There are three types of microaggressions: micro assault (such as mumbling a racial slur); microinsult (such as a backhanded compliment: "He's so articulate." to describe President Obama); microinvalidations (such as Whites expressing colorblindness—this invalidates BIPOC experiences).[45] As an immigrant and Chinese American, I experienced these microaggressions growing up in Pennsylvania. Sometimes it was outright racism as White boys yelled "Chink!" to my face. I experienced micro-invalidations for years after I arrived in the United States through comments from random cashiers such as "Your English is so good!" I knew I was still a foreigner even though I spoke English without an accent

---

43  Hodge, "Integrating Cultural Humility," 272.

44  Laura Reid Marks, et. al., "Racial Microaggressions and Depression in Black College Students: The Role of Ethnic Identity," *Journal of College Student Psychotherapy*, (September 2021): 1–17, https://doi.org/10.1080/87568225.2021.1976607.

45  Akello Specia and Ahmed A. Osman, "Education as a Practice of Freedom: Reflections on bell hooks," *Journal of Education and Practice* 6, no. 17 (2015): 4.

(well, I had a DELCO [Delaware County, PA] Accent, but so did everyone else!). I am not going to assume other BIPOC students had the same experience as myself. Still, I will vouch for my own experiences, and I believe BIPOC students whenever they say they have experienced microaggressions.

As educators, we must support BIPOC students. We believe them before anything else. We must have policies in place for discriminatory incidents. How do we respond to situations we face in our workspaces as librarians? We cannot allow witnessed microaggressions in the library. When it happens, we must be ready to talk to students. We communicate to the aggressors how their words hurt other students. It is not funny. It is a big deal. As a BIPOC librarian, I share my own experiences with those who do not believe it hurts. We support BIPOC students. We share our experiences. We listen. If it is agreeable for all parties, we then bring them together to discuss the situation to understand better and end further microaggressions. In instances of microaggression that are not seen but reported by students, follow policy and mediate both parties with the possibility, in all cases, of referring it to management.

Yet, victims of microaggressions and stereotype threats need more than just empathy and support. To be an ally for any BIPOC or disenfranchised student requires learning about these groups and effective allyship. One must be amenable to taking steps to reduce microaggressions. As someone who grew up in Taiwan in the 1970s until I was eight years old, I can state that White people are viewed as animalistic (because of their different hair colors, like dogs or cats that also have different fur colors), hairy, smelly, and big-nosed. These are assumptions we had about White people. White people were automatically stigmatized as such until proven otherwise. I would let the White students know about these assumptions. I then ask them how it makes them feel and to imagine they are surrounded by 95% or more Asian Taiwanese every day;—knowing almost all of them hold such assumptions about their culture. I can then state how I witnessed how this translated into microaggressions: Taiwanese people touching White people's hair, sometimes without asking; kids pulling on White people's arm hairs; and Taiwanese sitting farther away from White people in public settings. Assuming is part of the problem. With understanding, we can begin to parse out the details and reasons why BIPOC students feel. We can then try to peel back the microaggression to the underlying, biased, stereotypical assumptions that prompted them. One can see how working from the same POV can increase communication. The librarian must remember the purpose and know both students' POVs. Sometimes, it is hard to move to understand, but it is at least possible to move to the White student acknowledging the hurt caused. The point is to build understanding and stop microaggressions.

Relatedly, microaggressions and xenophobia during the Trump Era have increased, not to mention outright racism, including hate crimes. As a BIPOC librarian, I cannot ignore the current climate of the United States regarding BIPOC. We all know how the George Floyd murder fueled riots and counter-protests of 2020. As COVID-19 occurred, President Trump's ignorant and inflammatory responses included calling it "Kung Flu."[46] Even a library dean picked up the term.[47] These comments, and others like them, led to more hate crimes against Asian Americans. The divisive vitriol of the Trump Era has many BIPOC fearful, depressed, and angry.

I have talked with BIPOC students in my library who sigh and throw up their hands as they go over the talking points from Trump, including anti-Asian comments related to Covid (but many times spilling over to Black Lives Matter and Trump's anti-Mexican immigration stance). As librarians, we must remember this when working with BIPOC students. The trauma for BIPOC means that librarians must be more aware than ever and more supportive of BIPOC students. Librarians can be more conscious and patient in listening, asking for additional reference interview questions, welcoming students, remembering to follow up, and seizing opportunities to engage with BIPOC students. If the question of bias/racism surfaces through assignments or conversations with students, ask the polite question(s) that probe if the student wants to discuss it. If they do, listen. Be supportive by acknowledging any of their concerns as a BIPOC student. Let them know they are not alone and that there are groups on campus and online that they can join for connection and support. If they want to be politically active, direct them to the relevant faculty, online resources, and community organizations. To support BIPOC students, learning about other cultures, appreciating them, and examining one's own beliefs and

---

46  BBC News, "President Trump Calls CORONAVIRUS 'Kung Flu'," BBC News, last modified June 24, 2020, https://www.bbc.com/news/av/world-us-canada-53173436.

47  Ray Pun (@raypun101), "Seriously? A Library Dean Wrote an ATG Post Calling Covid-19 the 'Wuhan Virus' & Quoting His Friend as Calling It 'Kung Flu,'" So much more." Twitter, May 12, 2020, https://twitter.com/raypun101/status/1260058143628775425?lang=en.

representations of others helps break down bias.[48] Working from this idea of viewpoint, we can then review our views of others, especially those outside our group. Documenting our own biases allows us to change at our own pace without the threat of others' judgments. Concurrently, microaggressions happen to BIPOC library staff. The profession must acknowledge that BIPOC library staff carry more emotional labor than their White colleagues. BIPOC library staff may need support through acknowledgment, discussion, "alone time," and finding a support group.

## Conclusion

A racist rant of "Go back to Asia!" was directed at me during this time. The problems of racism and bias are a genuine concern today. Since this incident happened in the service area of CCC, I can rationally assume that CCC students may be exposed to similar verbal, if not worse, assaults. It is something I keep in mind when serving BIPOC students. CCC students may all face different struggles, but being a BIPOC student adds another possible layer to their challenges. I am mindful of this, such as when I must relay or implement library policy so BIPOC students do not feel singled out, ignored, or mistreated. This mindfulness is not limited to library policies but extends to any areas of BIPOC student interactions that may be relevant. I believe racism was always here, as I experienced it as a child, just that the Trump Era made it more acceptable for racists to spout their hate speech and vitriol. As CC academic librarians, we must recognize these harms and support BIPOC students beyond platitudes.

---

48  Higgins, "Mitigating Implicit Bias."

## Bibliography

ACCT: The Association of Community College Trustees. "Digital Divide: How Technology Access Impacts Community Colleges across the United States During a Pandemic." ACCT: The Association of Community College Trustees is the Voice of Community College Leaders. ACCT: The Association of Community College Trustees, May 2021. https://www.acct.org/files/ACCT_Digital_Divide_at_Community_Colleges_During_COVID_2021.pdf.

Andrews, Nicole, and Josie Watanabe. "Cultural Humility as a Transformative Framework for Librarians, Tutors, and Youth Volunteers." *Young Adult Library Services* 16, no. 2 (2018): 19–22.

Association of College & Research Libraries. "Framework for Information Literacy for Higher Education." Association of College & Research Libraries (ACRL), February 2, 2015. https://www.ala.org/acrl/standards/ilframework.

Broughton, Kelly M. "Students' Sense of Belonging in Study Spaces." PhD Diss., Ohio University, 2019.

Contra Costa College. "Contra Costa College 2019 STUDENT SUCCESS SCORECARD." California Community Colleges 2019 student success scorecard. Contra Costa College, 2019. https://scorecard.cccco.edu/scorecardrates.aspx?CollegeID=311.

Chodock, Ted. "Mapping Sense of Belonging in Library Spaces." Library Assessment Conference — Building Effective, Sustainable, Practical Assessment, 2021. https://www.libraryassessment.org/wp-content/uploads/2021/09/197-Chodock-Mapping-Sense-of-Belonging.pdf.

Goffman, Erving. *Stigma: Notes on the Management of Spoiled Identity*. London: Penguin, 1963.

Harris, Frank, J. Luke Wood, and Vanessa Falcon. "Supporting Men of Color in Community Colleges: An Examination of Promising Practices and California Student Equity Plans." University of Southern California. Last modified 2017. https://cue.usc.edu/files/2017/05/Report_Supporting_Men_of_Color_in_Community_Colleges.pdf.

Higgins, Molly, and Rachel Keiko Stark. "Mitigating Implicit Bias." American Library Association. Last modified January 4, 2021. https://americanlibrariesmagazine.org/2021/01/04/mitigating-implicit-bias/.

Hodge, Twanna. "Integrating Cultural Humility into Public Services Librarianship." *International Information & Library Review* 51, no. 3 (2019): 268–74. https://doi.org/10.1080/10572317.2019.1629070.

hooks, bell. *Teaching to Transgress: Education as the Practice of Freedom*. New York: Routledge, 1994.

Marks, Laura Reid, Madeline Stenersen, Kimberly Adams, Daniel Lattimore, and Brittany C. Lee. "Racial Microaggressions and Depression in Black College Students: The Role of Ethnic Identity." *Journal of College Student Psychotherapy*, September 2021, 1–17. https://doi.org/10.1080/87568225.2021.1976607.

Ndumu, Ana. *Borders and Belonging: Critical Examinations of Library Approaches toward Immigrants*. Sacramento: Library Juice Press, 2021.

Phelps, Jordyn. "Trump Defends 2017 'Very Fine People' Comments, Calls Robert E. Lee 'A Great General'." ABC News. Last modified April 26, 2019. https://abcnews.go.com/Politics/trump-defends-2017-fine-people-comments-calls-robert/story?id=62653478.

Pierce, Chester. "Offensive Mechanisms." Essay. In *The Black Seventies*, edited by Floyd Barrington Barbour, 265–82. Boston: Porter Sargent Publisher, 1970.

Pun, Ray. "Seriously? A Library Dean Wrote an ATG Post Calling Covid-19 the 'Wuhan Virus' & Quoting His Friend as Calling It 'Kung Flu" So much more." Twitter. May 12, 2020. https://twitter.com/raypun101/status/1260058143628775425?lang=en.

Sabol, Daniel A. "Best Practices in Roving Reference Services: Six Steps for Success." *College & Research Libraries News* 80, no. 1 (2019): 46–47. https://doi.org/10.5860/crln.80.1.46.

Specia, Akello, and Ahmed A. Osman. "Education as a Practice of Freedom: Reflections on Bell hooks." *Journal of Education and Practice* 6, no. 17 (2015): 195–99. https://files.eric.ed.gov/fulltext/EJ1079754.pdf.

Steele, Claude M., and Joshua Aronson. "Stereotype Threat and the Intellectual Test Performance of African Americans." *Journal of Personality and Social Psychology* 69, no. 5 (1995): 797–811. https://doi.org/10.1037/0022-3514.69.5.797.

# Student Success and Equity in the Library
## Looking at our Community Campus Library Collections

*Edeama Onwuchekwa Jonah*

### Introduction

Since 1936, the American Library Association (ALA) has been actively engaged in combating all attitudes, behaviors, services, or programs that amount to the exclusion or restriction of a targeted group of people based on a designation of race, skin color, ethnic origin, or descent.[1] The ALA posits that collection development should reflect the philosophy inherent in Article I of the Library Bill of Rights, "Books and other library resources should be provided for the interest, information, and enlightenment of all people of the community the library serves. Materials should not be excluded because of the origin, background, or views of those contributing to their creation."[2] Academic libraries play a vital role in supporting strategic goals for diversity in American higher education through collection development; the selection of educational resources to support the academic

---

1 "B.3 Diversity (Old Number 60)," American Library Association, accessed August 28, 2022. http://www.ala.org/aboutala/governance/ policy manual/updatedpolicymanual/section2 /3diversity. Document ID: 5914dd45-6914-0c64-5192 88a6784af423.

2 "Diverse Collections: An Interpretation of the Library Bill of Rights," American Library Association, (2006), accessed December 7, 2022. http://www.ala.org/advocacy/intfreedom/librarybill/interpretations/diversecollections.

programming of students, and faculty/staff development.³ Community colleges are among the most diverse institutions in U.S. higher education.⁴ Nearly nine million students attend community colleges year-round in the United States, with a disproportionate percentage coming from underrepresented populations and more than two-thirds underprepared for higher education.⁵

According to the California Community Colleges Chancellor's Office (CCCCO), "disproportionate impact is a condition where some students' access to key resources and supports and ultimately their academic success may be hampered by inequitable practices, policies, and approaches to student support."⁶ The mission of community colleges is to educate the community, and academic libraries play an essential role in making that education accessible. Community college libraries can make more education accessible by having a diverse collection of diverse resources that reflect their student population. A diverse collection should contain content by and about a wide array of people and cultures to authentically reflect various ideas, information, stories, and experiences.

The California Community Colleges' (CCC) *Student Equity and Achievement* initiative set forth expectations for increasing specific measures of student success for California Community College students by closing achievement gaps for underrepresented students. According to the Student Equity and Achievement (SEAP) Program Updates, the Student Equity and Achievement (SEAP) Program was established in July 2018 with the goal of providing colleges more flexibility in spending related to equity and student services. This program supports educational opportunities and promotes student success, regardless of race, gender, age, disability, or economic circumstance.

---

3  John Napp and Arjun Sabharwal, "Academic Libraries and the Strategic Vision for Diversity in Higher Education" (paper presentation, 2019 ASEE Annual Conference & Exposition, Tampa, Florida, June 15, 2019): 12, https://peer.asee.org/academic-libraries-and-the-strategic-vision-for-diversity-in-higher-education.

4  Eboni Zamani-Gallaher and Dibya Choudhuri, "A Primer on LGBTQ Students at Community Colleges: Considerations for Research and Practice. New Directions for Community Colleges," *New Directions for Community Colleges* 155 (2011): 35–49.

5  "Community College FAQs," Community College Research Center, accessed October 16, 2022, https://ccrc.tc.columbia.edu/Community-College-FAQs.html.

6  Brice Harris, "Ensuring Equitable Access and Success: A Guide to Assessing and Mitigating Disproportionate Impact in Student Success and Support Programs." California Community College Chancellor's Office (2013), http://extranet.cccco.edu/Portals/1/SSSP/Matriculation/REPORT_DisportionateImpactCombined_09.17.13_FINAL.pdf.

Best practices in promoting diversity and inclusion in academic libraries are, however, a safe strategy for minimizing the gap across data sources and demonstrating the effectiveness of diversity initiatives in the academic library.[7] According to the Center for Urban Education, "equity-mindedness" refers to the perspective or mode of thinking exhibited by practitioners who call attention to patterns of inequity in student outcomes. It has also been considered as the process of framing the success of underserved and underrepresented students as an institutional and state responsibility.[8] In reference to looking at a community college campus library with an equity lens, the following questions are pertinent to be considered:

- How can library collections and resources be made to be racially and culturally sensitive, relevant, and reflective of the diversity of students on campus? A constant concern for libraries is providing a collection of appropriate resources to its patron population and holding ourselves accountable for fostering diversity and equity through our collection development plans.

- How does our library collection support our diverse student population, especially our Black, Indigenous, and People of Color (BIPOC) students? This will include dismantling some systemic and pervasive barriers within academic libraries to effectively provide services to the campus community.

- How can we increase library information literacy and student engagement, particularly among disproportionately impacted student groups? Working with students to provide insights into including diverse perspectives in scholarly collections for teaching, research, and learning.

Community colleges in the United States were born out of the necessity for educational opportunities and vocational training in smaller towns and a growing belief that education should be accessible to everyone.[9] With 1.8 million students at 116 colleges, the California Community Colleges is the largest system of higher education in the

---

7   Napp and Sabharwal, "Academic Libraries and the Strategic Vision," 12.

8   Megan Chase, Felix Eric, and Estela Bensimon. *Student Equity Plan Review: A Focus on Racial Equity* (Los Angeles, CA: Rossier School of Education, University of Southern California, 2020).

9   "B3 Diversity (Old Number 60)."

country.[10] Community colleges began in the early twentieth century to create a more highly skilled workforce through local education.[11] From inception, community college founders and advocates have supported access to higher education for those who had until then been denied or deemed unworthy based on race, sex, ethnicity, or socioeconomic status.[12] The history of the California Community Colleges (CCC) has been shaped by social justice and equity movements led by actions ranging from statewide legislation to individual colleges and "key stakeholders."[13] Community colleges in California and other states nationwide are considered some of the most diverse higher education institutions in the United States. Students vary in age, ethnicity, religion, educational background, and economic status.

The 21st-century college student population is the most diverse in our nation's history, characterized by the intersection of race, gender, sexual orientation, religion, family composition, age, and economic status. The educational pathways for students in community colleges differ from other traditional higher education institutions in their academic pursuits and purposes. California Community Colleges play a critical role in the country's educational system. Community colleges offer students of any background, regardless of socioeconomic status, a chance to experience higher education and learn in an accepting and open environment. California Community Colleges provide career education and workforce training, guaranteed transfer to four-year universities, degree and certificate pathways, and basic skills education in English and math.[14] The community college provides opportunities to those who need their college experience to be flexible and affordable. Students are encouraged to enroll, to state a major course of

---

10  Michelle Velazquez Bean, and Teresa Aldredge, Karen Chow, Lynn Fowler, Arthur Guaracha, Tanya McGinnis, LaTonya Parker, and Graciela Saez-Kleriga, "Academic Senate for California Community Colleges," The Role of the Library Faculty in the California Community College, 2019, accessed. August 29, 2022, https://www.asccc.org/papers/role-library-faculty-california-community-college.

11  Richard L. Drury, "Community Colleges in America: A Historical Perspective," Inquiry 8, no. 1 (2003): 1–6, accessed December 11, 2022. https://files.eric.ed.gov/fulltext/EJ876835.pdf.

12  Chelsea Contrada, "Information Literacy and Instruction: Reference and Information Literacy in the Community College Library," Reference & User Services Quarterly, 59, no. 1 (2019): 12–16, accessed December 11, 2022, https://journals.ala.org/index.php/rusq/article/view/7220/9868.

13  Michelle Vazquez Bean and et. al, "Academic Senate for California Community Colleges."

14  "Key Facts," California Community Colleges, accessed December 6, 2022. https://www.cccco.edu/About-Us/Key-Facts.

study, and to persevere toward graduation.[15] Due to the diverse nature of community college students, the information needs will vary widely because of nontraditional ages, ethnicity, language, and cultural differences, as well as disparities in learning and physical ability.[16]

Community college libraries are unique institutions that aim to combine service and learning through a lens of equity and social justice. They provide access to the resources and services students need to succeed academically, whether it be technical assistance, research help, computer access, or just a safe and quiet place to study.[17] Beyond providing services for the campus community, community college libraries can interact with the public uniquely and create programming that serves the surrounding communities. Community college libraries advocate and work for students; they not only offer resources and services that emphasize the importance of education but also keep social justice at the heart of their mission by advocating for access and equity. By supporting cultural competence in the library, librarians and staff assist in making the library a safe and comfortable space. Community college libraries genuinely care about the students and less about creating or supporting institutional research, as other academic libraries are required to achieve relevancy. This chapter seeks to stir a discussion for improving diversity and equity regarding a library's collection development policy, reviewing library resources through an equity and diversity lens, and indirectly improving student success, especially for marginalized student groups in community colleges.

## The Role of Academic Libraries in Supporting Equity and Diversity

Academic libraries are considered the intellectual hubs of their campus and have a role in shaping diversity and the conversation on diversity and inclusion through culturally competent collection management

---

15 Daniel Overfield and Roy Coleen, "Academic and Public Library Collaboration: Increasing Value by Sharing Space, Collections, and Services," *American Library Association Institutional Repository* (2013): 1–8.

16 Phyllis Pistorino, "Intercultural Competence for Community College Librarians," *School of Information Student Research Journal* 10, no. 1 (2020): 7.

17 Contrada, "Information Literacy and Instruction," 12–16.

and hiring and promotion practices.[18] The role of libraries in supporting institutional goals for equity, diversity, and inclusion can be direct and indirect, depending on the library's mission and goals. The support is direct where academic libraries are integral to the strategic goals for information literacy.[19] Academic libraries can articulate direct support through collection development, reference, and instruction. Reframing the role of libraries in terms of diversity, equity, and inclusion (DEI) within the contexts of critical pedagogy, instructional design, and information literacy teaching and learning is an offer to librarians seeking to rethink not only their approach to instruction but also the goals and actions of libraries more generally.

Critical information literacy was described as an approach that encourages connections with students and faculty and brings meaning to librarians' work and students' learning.[20] Critical librarianship offers a framework for thinking about our work that asks how library structures came to be and what ideologies underpin them.[21] Library liaison programs, in which librarians are "assigned to a specific client base, personalized, a relationship-centered system of service delivery," have been shown to be a valuable component of higher education in the U.S.[22] In addition to being classroom and subject discipline liaisons, CC librarians have indicated that their libraries liaise with several other campus units, including counseling, distance education first-year experience programs, veterans centers, and writing/tutoring centers. Beyond these roles, librarians shared their liaison experiences to connections with satellite campuses, child development centers, and prison programs.[23] Academic librarians who are considered library liaisons engaged in these different service provisions, references, and instruction show a lot of commitment to diversity and

---

[18] Napp and Sabharwal, "Academic Libraries and the Strategic Vision," 12.

[19] Napp and Sabharwal, 12.

[20] Eamon Tewell, "The Practice and Promise of Critical Information Literacy: Academic Librarians' Involvement in Critical Library Instruction," *College & Research Libraries*, 79, no. 1 (2018): 10–34, https://doi.org/10.5860/crl.79.1.10.

[21] Emily Drabinski, "What Is Critical about Critical Librarianship?" *Art Libraries Journal* 44, no. 2 (2019): 49–57, doi:10.1017/alj.2019.3.

[22] Mary Wahl, "Library Liaison Services in US Community Colleges: Findings from a National Survey." *Journal of Library Outreach and Engagement* 1, no. 2 (2021): 58–77, accessed December 6, 2022, https://iopn.library.illinois.edu/journals/jloe/article/view/807/706.

[23] Wahl, "Library Liaison Services in US Community Colleges," 58–77.

inclusion by making recommendations and selecting culturally diverse resources. Equity, diversity, and inclusivity are core values of librarianship and are among the principles that guide the development of our collections.

## Libraries and Collection Development

According to the Academic Senate for California Community Colleges Position Paper,[24] collection development is the process through which materials are chosen for the collection and removed from the collection when they no longer meet curriculum standards; librarians should work with discipline area faculty to achieve this goal. The ALA's glossary of terms[25] asserts that everyone deserves equitable rights and opportunities. ALA further recognizes that institutionalized inequities based on race are embedded into our society and are reinforced through social institutions and perpetuated by policies, practices, behaviors, traditions, and structures. For example, many schools and communities continue to target or exclude hundreds of thousands of students each year on account of race, sex, gender, national origin, religion, and disability, among other factors.[26] Libraries are a microcosm of the larger society and play an essential and unique role in the communities they serve; they must seek to provide an environment free of racism through policies and practices and create a safe space where all are treated with respect and dignity. Ciszek and Young affirmed that "libraries wishing to assess a collection for diversity should have a clear definition of diversity in place before assessment."[27]

A significant challenge facing today's libraries is developing and updating traditional and digital collections and services to meet the needs of multiple generations of users with differing approaches to information seeking.[28] The perspective on diversity has changed considerably over the past few decades, the same as discourse on diversity

---

24   Michelle Vazquez Bean and et. al,"Academic Senate for California Community Colleges,"

25   Michelle Vazquez Bean and et. al,

26   American Library Association, "ODLOS Glossary of Terms," September 7, 2017, accessed December 2, 2022, http://www.ala.org/aboutala/odlos-glossary-terms.

27   Matthew Ciszek and Courtney Young, "Diversity Collection Assessment in Large Academic Libraries," *Collection Building* 29, no. 4 (2010): 154–61, doi: 10.1108/01604951011088899.

28   Ciszek and Young, "Diversity Collection Assessment in Large Academic Libraries," 154–61.

has shifted from visual dimensions (gender and race) towards subtler ways of identifying people based on their ethnicity, race, ability, language, gender, sexual orientation, religion, and national origin. In 2012, the Association of College and Research Libraries (ACRL) Board of Directors approved diversity standards developed by ACRL's Racial and Ethnic Diversity Committee. In its standards, the committee stated that libraries must develop collections "inclusive of the needs of all persons in the community the library serves."[29]

According to ALA,[30] best practices in collection development assert that materials should not be excluded from a collection solely because the content or its creator is considered offensive or controversial. Refusing to select resources due to the potential controversy is considered censorship, as is withdrawing resources. Choosing books regarded as "controversial" can be incredibly stressful for librarians, with many making selection decisions to self-censor based on fear of losing their jobs.[31] Challenges to these diverse books have not just come from library patrons; they have also resulted from self-censorship by librarians. According to a 2019 report from the ALA, the Office for Intellectual Freedom (OIF) "has noticed a representative pushback by those who believe that a more diverse and just society poses a threat to their beliefs and their way of life."[32] Despite these challenges, libraries are responsible for defending against challenges that limit a collection's diversity of content.

Creating collection development policies to serve culturally diverse user groups must be considered. Having a thorough collection development policy can guide librarians' efforts in dealing with book challenges and provide materials that best meet the needs of patrons. Without a collection development policy, a library has no clear understanding and guidelines of decisions to take and no benchmark against which to measure its decisions or progress. Libraries without collection development policies are like businesses without business

---

29  Lynn Silipigni Connaway, *The Library in the Life of the User: Engaging with People Where They Live and Learn*, (Dublin: OCLC Research, 2015), 226.

30  "Diverse Collections: An Interpretation of the Library Bill of Rights," American Library Association, (2006), accessed December 7, 2022, http://www.ala.org/advocacy/intfreedom/librarybill/interpretations/diversecollections.

31  "Diverse Collections."

32  Rebecca Hill, "The Problem of Self-Censorship," in *Intellectual Freedom Issues in Schools*, ed. April M. Dawkins (Santa Barbara: Libraries Unlimited, ABC-CLIO, 2021), 88.

plans. It's important to note that even a library with written policy statements suffers if they are not consulted, reviewed, revised, and updated regularly.

Librarians should review collection development policies and procedures regularly to ensure that they meet the information needs for access to library and information resources. This review could include services and technologies by all community college patrons, "especially those who may experience language or literacy-related barriers; economic distress; cultural or social isolation; physical or attitudinal barriers; racism; discrimination on the basis of appearance, ethnicity, immigrant status, religious background, sexual orientation, gender identity, gender expression."[33]

## Promoting Student Success and Equity in the Library

To promote students' success and equity in the library, librarians should be charged with sourcing, vetting, and acquiring content to meet their users' evolving needs. Cook-Harvey, Darling-Hammond, Lam, Mercer, and Roc define equity as "the policies and practices that provide every student access to an education focused on meaningful learning—one that teaches the deeper learning skills contemporary society requires in ways that empower students to learn independently throughout their lives."[34] Cook-Harvey et al., further explained that such an equitable education requires "competent and caring educators...who are supported by adequate resources.... each student can develop his or her full academic and societal potential."[35] Libraries at community colleges uniquely provide a spectrum of information literacy instruction, references, and materials circulation to meet their diverse students' needs.

Librarians at community colleges face unique challenges in serving diverse populations and must be exceptionally culturally competent to

---

33 Kathy S. Rosa, The State of America's Libraries: A Report from the American Library Association, (Chicago: American Libraries, 2016), accessed January 13, 2020, http://www.ala.org/news/state-americas-libraries-report-2019.

34 "Diverse Collections."

35 Channa M. Cook-Harvey, Linda Darling-Hammond, Livia Lam, Charmaine Mercer, and Martens Roc, *Equity and ESSA: Leveraging Educational Opportunity Through Every Student Succeeds Act*. (Palo Alto, CA: Learning Policy Institute, 2016): 36.

provide equal access, engage students, and affect learning.[36] Librarians must begin reevaluating their library collections to ensure that the diverse voices widely represented are easily discoverable and accessible. It is essential for the collection development librarian and other librarians in their respective colleges to review their collection development policy and make their library a welcoming space for their diverse population. Displaying books by BIPOC authors and focusing on topics of race and culture to highlight the presence of BIPOC voices across their library collections is also vital to promoting Equity in the Library. Beyond book displays, the Equity Librarian, in collaboration with the other librarians, can create library guides with access to diverse resources and promote awareness of the availability of library resources. From a broader perspective, the California Community College libraries use an integrated feature through the library platform (ILS or LSP) Alma/Primo to display digital and video book collections to make them searchable.

## Collection Assessment

Librarians often use the terms assessment and evaluation interchangeably. The differences can sometimes be determined based on the intent of the analysis. Very often, the aim of the assessment is to determine how well the collection supports the goals, needs, and mission of the library or parent organization.[37] Collection assessment is the evaluation of library collections (print, e-resources, and non-print materials), which can be carried out periodically with the help of feedback and suggestions received from the regular users of the library. It is one of the important activities of an academic library as it must cater to the needs of its users.[38] ACRL's 2016 top trends in academic libraries acknowledge that "There has been a remarkable shift to the incorporation and integration of more continuous, ongoing,

---

36 ACRL Racial and Ethnic Diversity Committee, "Diversity Standards: Cultural Competency for Academic Librarians: April 2012," *College & Research Libraries News* 73, 9 (2012): 552.

37 Cary Cuiccio and Marie Husby-Slater, "Needs Assessment Guidebook: Supporting the Development of District and School Needs Assessments," State Support Network (2018), accessed December 7, 2022, https://files.eric.ed.gov/fulltext/ED606124.pdf.

38 Singh Har and Preeti Mahajan, "Library Collection Assessment: A Case Study of two Universities in the Region of Punjab, India," *Chinese Librarianship: An International Electronic Journal* 39 (2015): 52–69.

flexible, and sustainable review of collections rather than ad-hoc project-based models."[39]

Evaluation aims to examine or describe collections in their terms or about other collections and checking mechanisms, such as lists. Evaluation and assessment provide librarians with a better understanding of the collection and the user community.[40] The librarian gains information that helps determine if a collection is meeting its objectives, how well it serves its users, and in which ways or areas it is deficient. With collection assessment, creating or adopting systems for assessment management is essential. Assessment management systems help higher education educators, including librarians, manage their outcomes, record and maintain data on each outcome, facilitate connections to similar outcomes throughout an institution, and generate reports. Ideally, assessment management systems are used by an entire institution, but libraries can take the lead and pioneer their use at individual institutions.

Many community college libraries have begun reevaluating their collections to ensure representation and that those collections are easily discoverable and accessible. For example, the California Community College Library Services Platform (LSP) has set up a DEI task force to identify and collect potentially offensive terms discovered in bibliographic records while considering individual institutional needs and concerns.

Beyond the collection assessment process in colleges and libraries, workshops can be designed to create an equity-minded view regarding the library collection. Some questions that could be used for the assessment process could include the following:

- Does the campus library collection policy have a diversity and equity component?

- How can we ensure that library collections and resources are racially and culturally sensitive and relevant and reflect the diversity of students on campus?

---

39 ACRL Research Planning and Review Committee, "2016 top Trends in Academic Libraries: A Review of the Trends and Issues Affecting Academic Libraries in Higher Education," *College & Research Libraries News*, 77 no. 6, (2016): 274–81.

40 Peggy Johnson, *Fundamentals of Collection Development and Management* (Chicago: ALA Editions, an imprint of the American Library Association, 2018), 127–133.

- How can we increase library information literacy and student engagement, particularly among underrepresented students?

Workshop sessions with student success and equity with the library collection focus can be organized to educate faculty, staff, and students on issues regarding the library's collection; it could also discuss the titles found in the College Library and create awareness and emphasis on improving information literacy skills for the students.

## Recommendations

Library collections have historically reflected white, Western, Christian, cis-heteronormative, able-bodied men and excluded or sidelined authors, artists, and publishers who do not fit into these dominant and privileged groups. Librarians can address these injustices by actively acquiring and promoting content created by historically oppressed, underrepresented, and underserved communities that support and honor the diversity in the university and the larger global society. It is essential that library collections present topics from multiple viewpoints. Likewise, the library's exhibits and displays should include diverse perspectives while adhering to college standards. In consultation with stakeholders, library faculty and administrators should adopt, regularly review, and update collection development policies that guide the selection, acquisition, and deaccession of library materials. When purchasing electronic resources, we evaluate accessibility for users with disabilities and require licenses that disproportionately protect users' privacy. Some of the recommendations gathered from other research that will help promote equity, diversity, and inclusion:

### *Collection*

- Clarify and clearly articulate the library's definitions of diversity, equity, and inclusion, which could develop into a DEI Mission Statement & Equity Diversity Inclusion Library Plan.
- Review the library's collection development policy and strengthen diversity commitment, including strategic and systematic procedures for assessing and maintaining diverse collections.
- Encourage librarians to ensure open and equitable access to digital and electronic resources.

- Learn more about adding inclusive, non-Library of Congress subject headings to catalog records.
- Library faculty should be involved in college governance, retaining the same rights and responsibilities as all other faculty.

## Funding

- Create a dedicated collection development fund to build the library collections of BIPOC scholars and works focused on DEI and anti-oppression work.
- Investigate grant opportunities and campus partnerships for increasing diverse holdings.
- Maintain a "wish list" of titles and collections related to diversity.
- Include library faculty in the college budget allocation process and work with discipline faculty to ensure that expenditures align with department and college-wide needs.
- Prioritize funding for collecting works from historically marginalized writers of small press publications, graphic novels, and literature-in-translation (to name only a few examples).
- Negotiate where the libraries' collection development funding comes from and direct those funds according to our values.

## Outreach

- Collaborate with students, faculty, and the campus community to solicit suggestions on diverse resources.
- Partner with academic and co-curricular programs to inform our collection decisions and welcome feedback from community members.
- Seek clarification (consider author identities, perspectives, geographic location, and historical timeframe).
- Collect in various media formats, recognizing the many ways to take information.
- Highlight diverse collections in book displays and book lists on your website, social media, and in-person recommendations to students, staff, and faculty.

- Divest from content providers who partner with organizations that harm BIPOC communities, mainly through the sale of surveillance data to law enforcement.

## Conclusion

A typical mission of any community college is to provide a venue for lifelong learning, to make higher education more accessible, and to offer a comprehensive educational program. Colleges can achieve this mission and beyond by intentionally making efforts to look at their collections with an equity-minded lens. Librarians can create a welcoming and inclusive library space by developing a collection that represents the holistic diversity of the students on campus and the wider educational community, whether by providing books or other resources for leisure or research, teaching, and learning. The strengths of librarian selectors include professional knowledge, awareness of students' reading and study habits, a solid commitment to undergraduates who have not yet selected a major, an understanding of the library collection, and overall knowledge of the curriculum (in many cases), and concern for technical and licensing issues that the faculty may not appreciate. Library resources that reflect the students' experiences and languages tell the students that their identities and their experiences matter.

### Bibliography

ACRL Racial and Ethnic Diversity Committee. "Diversity Standards: Cultural competency for academic librarians: Approved by the ACRL Board of Directors, April 2012." *College & Research Libraries News*, 73, no. 9 (2012): 551–61. Accessed December 12, 2022. https://crln.acrl.org/index.php/crlnews/article/view/8835/9457.

ACRL Research Planning and Review Committee. "2016 Top Trends in Academic Libraries: A Review of the Trends and Issues Affecting Academic Libraries in Higher Education." *College & Research Libraries News*, 77 no. 6, (2016): 274–81. Accessed December 12, 2022. https://crln.acrl.org/index.php/crlnews/article/view/9505/10798

American Library Association. "Diverse Collections: An Interpretation of the Library Bill of Rights." (2006). Accessed December 7, 2022. https://www.ala.org/advocacy/intfreedom/librarybill/interpretations/diversecollections.

American Library Association. "B.3 Diversity (Old Number 60)." Accessed November 30, 2022. http://www.ala.org/aboutala/governance/ policy manual/updated policy manual/section2/3diversity.

American Library Association. "Library Bill of Rights." Accessed December 7, 2022. https://www.ala.org/advocacy/intfreedom/librarybill.

American Library Association. "ODLOS Glossary of Terms," September 7, 2017. Accessed December 8, 2022. http://www.ala.org/aboutala/odlos-glossary-terms.

Chabot, Lisabeth, Wayne Bivens-Tatum, Heather L. Coates, M. Kathleen Kern, Michelle Leonard, Chris Palazzolo, Lorelei Tanji, and Minglu Wang. "2016 top trends in academic libraries. A Review of the trends and issues affecting academic libraries in higher education." *College & Research Libraries News* 77, no. 6 (June 2016): https://crln.acrl.org/index.php/crlnews/article/view/9505/10798.

Chase, Megan M., Eric R. Felix, and Estela Mara Bensimon. *Student Equity Plan Review: A Focus on Racial Equity.* Los Angeles, CA: Rossier School of Education, University of Southern California, 2020. Accessed December 7, 2022. https://static1.squarespace.com/static/5eb5c03682a92c5f96da4f-c8/t/600f48b93e23721b6ca72efa/1611614397014/CCC+Equity+Plan+Review_A+Focus+on+Racial+Equity.pdf%5B47%5D.pdf.

Ciszek, Matthew P., and Courtney L. Young. "Diversity Collection Assessment in Large Academic Libraries. "*Collection Building* 29, no. 4 (2010): 154–61.

Community College Research Center. "Community College FAQs," https://ccrc.tc.columbia.edu/Community-College-FAQs.html. Accessed December 7, 2022.

Connaway, Lynn Silipigni. *The Library in the Life of the User: Engaging with People Where They Live and Learn.* Dublin: OCLC Research, 2015.

Contrada, Chelsea. "Information Literacy and Instruction: Reference and Information Literacy in the Community College Library." *Reference & User Services Quarterly* 59, no. 1 (2019): 12–16.

Cook-Harvey, Channa M., Linda Darling-Hammond, Livia Lam, Charmaine Mercer, and Roc Martens. *Equity and ESSA: Leveraging Educational Opportunity Through Every Student Succeeds Act.* Palo Alto, CA: Learning Policy Institute (2016).

Cuiccio, Cary, and Marie Husby-Slater. "Needs Assessment Guidebook: Supporting the Development of District and School Needs Assessments." State Support Network (2018). Accessed December 3, 2022. https://files.eric.ed.gov/fulltext/ED606124.pdf.

Drabinski, Emily. "What Is Critical about Critical Librarianship?" *Art Libraries Journal* 44, no. 2 (2019): 49–57. Accessed December 3, 2022. https://doi.org/10.1017/alj.2019.3.

Drury, Richard L. "Community Colleges in America: A Historical Perspective." *Inquiry* 8, no. 1 (2003): 1–6. Accessed December 3, 2022. https://files.eric.ed.gov/fulltext/EJ876835.pdf.

Harris, Brice W. "Ensuring Equitable Access and Success: A Guide to Assessing and Mitigating Disproportionate Impact in Student Success and Support Programs." Accessed December 12, 2022. http://www.3cmediasolutions.org/sites/default/files/EnsuringEquitableAccessAndSuccessREPORT_DisportionateImpact_091713.PDF.

Hill, Rebecca. "The Problem of Self-Censorship." In *Intellectual Freedom Issues in School Libraries*, edited by April M. Dawkins, 88–92. Santa Barbara: Libraries Unlimited, ABC-CLIO, 2021.

"Key Facts California Community Colleges Chancellor's Office 2022." Accessed November 1, 2022. https://www.cccco.edu/About-Us/Key-Facts.

Johnson, Peggy. *Fundamentals of Collection Development and Management*. Chicago: ALA Editions, 2018.

Napp, John, and Arjun Sabharwal. "Academic Libraries and the Strategic Vision for Diversity in Higher Education." Paper presented at 2019 ASEE Annual Conference & Exposition, Tampa, Florida, June 15, 2019. Accessed October 4, 2022. https://peer.asee.org/academic-libraries-and-the-strategic-vision-for-diversity-in-higher-education.pdf.

Overfield, Daniel and Coleen Roy, "Academic and Public Library Collaboration: Increasing Value by Sharing Space, Collections, and Services," Paper presented at the meeting for the Association of College & Research Libraries, Indianapolis, Indiana, April 10–13, 2013. Accessed December 4, 2022. http://www.ala.org/acrl/sites/ala.org.acrl/files/content/conferences/confsandpreconfs/2013/papers/OverfieldRoy_Academic.pdf.

Pistorino, Phyllis. "Intercultural Competence for Community College Librarians." *School of Information Student Research Journal* 10, no. 1 (2020): 7.

Rosa, Kathy. *The State of America's Libraries: A Report from the American Library Association*. Chicago: American Libraries, 2016. Accessed January 13, 2020. http://www.ala.org/news/state-americas-libraries-report-2019.

Singh, Har, and Preeti Mahajan. "Library Collection Assessment: A Case Study of two Universities in the Region of Punjab, India." *Chinese Librarianship: An International Electronic Journal* 39 (2015): 52–69.

Tewell, Eamon. "The Practice and Promise of Critical Information Literacy: Academic Librarians' Involvement in Critical Library Instruction." *College & Research Libraries* 79, no. 1 (December 2022). https://crl.acrl.org/index.php/crl/article/view/16616.

Velazquez Bean, Michelle, Teresa Aldredge, Karen Chow, Lynn Fowler, Arthur Guaracha, Tanya McGinnis, LaTonya Parker, and Graciela Saez-Kleriga. "Academic Senate for California Community Colleges." The Role of the Library Faculty in the California Community College, 2019. Accessed March 21, 2021. https://www.asccc.org/papers/role-library-faculty-california-community-college.

Wahl, Mary. "Library Liaison Services in US Community Colleges: Findings from a National Survey." *Journal of Library Outreach and Engagement*, 1, no. 2 (2021): 58–77. https://cclibrarians.org/outlook/april-2019/library-liaison-services-california-community-college.

Zamani-Gallaher, Eboni M., and Dibya Devika Choudhuri. "A Primer on LGBTQ Students at Community Colleges: Considerations for Research and Practice." *New Directions for Community Colleges* 155 (2011): 35–49.

# Testament of Perseverance
## A Journey Through Tenure

Shamika Jamalia Morris Simpson

## Introduction

Are you a magnifying glass or a telescope? A magnifying glass enlarges a particular view or element, thus focusing only on that view or element. A telescope brings far objects close to get a better and clearer view of distant objects. Metaphorically speaking, I used both instruments as a lens to view my work experiences and potential. I used to magnify negative and traumatic work experiences. I would replay them repeatedly like late-night sitcoms. I was so focused on the negative that I could not see beyond my current circumstances, which led to a sense of dread every time I had to report to work. Kaetrena Davis Kendrick introduced the phrase "low morale" in librarianship, which is "the degree to which an employee harbors negative feelings about his or her workplace or dissatisfaction with aspects of the work or workplace."[1] In this essay, I will reflect on my experience as a probationary tenure track faculty librarian at a community college. I will also reflect on how self-care helped me pull myself out of a "low morale" rut. I learned to shift my magnifying glass to view positive work experiences and use my telescopic lens to focus on career goals, manifest innovative ideas, and foster continuous improvement via professional development.

---

1   Kaetrena Davis Kendrick, "The Low Morale Experience of Academic Librarians: A Phenomenological Study," *Journal of Library Administration* 57, no. 8 (2007): 847. doi:10.1080/01930826.2017.1368325.

I wish to add my experience to the research and exploration of racialized and anti-Black attitudes, which explores their impact on Black librarians. "Reflection is deliberate and intentional. It is a process that we consciously undertake, in the professional sense, to take stock of our practice."[2] "Speaking up and taking control of our narrative is vital to our healing from the trauma [colleagues and institutions] have caused."[3] My experience, while unique to me, provides an example of the experience of an academic librarian. I desire for my experience to be a catalyst for change by 1) igniting tenured faculty, particularly those with positive experiences, to examine academic policy, practice, and behavior that lead to the negative experiences for some faculty, 2) providing people of color who wish to become academic librarians with perspective, and 3) compelling administrators in academia to deeply examine the tenure process and the experiences of tenure-track faculty of color during their probationary period and take action.

My academic librarian career has not been easy. The injustices I have faced and currently face are rooted in anti-Blackness. The University of San Francisco's Multicultural Resource Center defines anti-Blackness "as being a two-part formation that both strips Blackness of value (dehumanizes) and systematically marginalizes Black people. This form of anti-Blackness is overt racism."[4] My experience is not an isolated one; other Black faculty, staff, and managers have experienced the same anti-Black treatment at the same institution. From my experience, it is difficult to speak out against injustices as they are never addressed or resolved. You can be labeled as difficult, angry, and unprofessional when speaking out. The term "unprofessional" in Aysa Gray's article "The Bias of 'Professionalism' Standards" was defined by Tema Okun and Keith Jones, grassroots organizers and scholars, as "white supremacy culture or the systemic, institutionalized centering of whiteness."[5] It is noteworthy to mention some of the anti-Black

---

2   Michelle Reale, *Becoming a Reflective Librarian and Teacher: Strategies for Mindful Academic Practice* (Chicago: American Library Association, 2016), 2.

3   WOC+Lib, "Statement against White Appropriation of Black, Indigenous, and People of Color's Labor," WOC+LIB (blog), September 3, 2021, accessed August 2, 2022, https://www.wocandlib.org/features/2021/9/3/statement-against-white-appropriation-of-black-indigenous-and-people-of-colors-labor.

4   Multicultural Resource Center, "Racial Equity & Anti-Black Racism," accessed February 25, 2022, https://mrc.ucsf.edu/racial-equity-anti-black-racism.

5   Aysa Gray, "The Bias of 'Professionalism' Standards," *Stanford Social Innovation Review*, 2019. https://doi.org/10.48558/TDWC-4756.

racism I faced was from by non-Black faculty of color. Systems of anti-Blackness, such as white adjacency and colorism, perpetuate racist systems. Simmons defines white adjacency as "a person from a marginalized background within society in terms of race, and at the same time, receiving benefits similar to those identified as white."[6]

## From Grad School to New Librarian

My position as a collection development and outreach librarian is a unique one. My responsibilities are collection development, acquisitions, and outreach. This position resulted from the retirement of the collection development librarian and the vacated outreach librarian position. Our library department's collection development focused on acquisitions and deselection. The administration did not present an explicit collection of development priorities outlined. There was a collection development policy. However, it needed to be reviewed and updated. Additionally, there was a need to realign the collection to students' curricular, informational, and recreational wants and needs. In my opinion, this was just as important as student curricular needs. For example, the addition of graphic novels, Young Adult (YA) fiction, and pop culture titles to attract students who would not necessarily visit the library. As the previous librarian performed it, the outreach part of the position hadn't taken a solid form, with outreach efforts being infrequent. In addition to implementing the collection development plan, I also had to implement a student engagement plan. Our department needed to have established guidelines regarding outreach. Although the administration's expectations of improving student engagement were high, more was required to achieve this, including a budget. The entire department would need to be built from the ground up. I created new outreach systems that focused less on community engagement via programs and more on marketing library materials in the physical library and online via social media and resource guides. I also adopted new service models, such as having wall-to-wall new books facing out towards the library lobby area, including QR code finding aids within the physical collection to lead library users to online resources, and providing snacks.

---

6 Dailyn Simmons, "The Unspoken Truth," *Daily Sundial* (Northridge, CA), February 28, 2020. https://sundial.csun.edu/156565/opinions/the-unspoken-truth/.

I knew there would be a learning curve when I accepted the position. I would perform a job typically performed by three librarian positions: collection development, acquisitions, and outreach. I understood that innovative ideas, policies, or procedures may take longer to implement. Before my hire, I prepared for my new role. I enrolled in the Association for Library Collections and Technical Services (ALCTS) classes, Intro to Collection Development and Intro to Acquisitions. I participated in webinars and workshops to reinforce and supplement my library graduate school education. I also enrolled in the Social Media Marketing certificate program at California State University, Dominguez Hills. I wanted a well-rounded understanding of expectations for my role. I met with the electronic resources librarian about the library book budgets and accounts. She had a vast knowledge of the budgets, and her staff temporarily handled the purchases of print materials. In our meeting, she informed me that I would take on the additional task of acquiring electronic books. The administration did not include the acquisition of electronic books in the job description, announcement, or interview. At that moment, I was overwhelmed with emotions of dread and anxiety. I was desperately trying to learn my new role. "How could I take on another job responsibility?" I explained that although this might be possible, it was not feasible. The librarian was persistent, but we reached an unspoken agreement once I explained that I was willing to consider the possibility.

The following week, in a librarian meeting, the dean announced that I would be taking over the responsibility of electronic books. Based on this dean's statement that I would manage anything with the word "book," it was apparent that the dean had limited knowledge of libraries and librarians. It was also evident that the dean and electronic resources librarian met privately to discuss the management of electronic books. When I reflect on this story, I think about the dean in my story who had a single story about eBooks. She made assumptions based on false information. In a TED Talk, Chimamanda Ngozi Adichie speaks about "The Danger of a Single Story."[7] To demonstrate her single-story phenomenon, she shares a few life experiences. In one story, her mother hired a new live-in domestic helper or a "house boy."[8] His name was Fide. The only thing she knew about Fide was that he was

---

7  Chimamanda Ngozi Adichie, "The Danger of a Single Story," TED YouTube video, 18:33. October 13, 2009, https://youtu.be/D9Ihs241zeg.

8  Adichie, "The Danger of a Single Story," 18:33.

poor. Her mother sent old clothes and food to Fide's home. Adichie's family took a trip to Fide's village, and Fide's mother showed them a basket that Fide's brother made. Adichie explained that she didn't understand how his brother was able to make the beautiful basket. All she was told about Fide and his family was that they were poor, and "it had become impossible for [her] to see them as anything else but poor. Their poverty was [her] single story of them."[9] I would have loved to explain to the dean by providing an alternate perspective; however, I wasn't allowed to do so. As a probationary tenure-track faculty, I feared for my job. I questioned the timing of the assignment. Was the assignment strategically assigned during my probationary period? What would have resulted if I had attempted to tell the library dean, "No"?

## First Probationary Tenure Review

There were four people on my probationary tenure committee. I met with them individually to discuss the evaluation reports they had written based on their observations of my work. Two were glowing, one was good, and my last was shockingly terrible. I received the "needs improvement" mark based on hearsay from another colleague. A mark of "needs improvement" was an automatic non-renewal of the contract. I was livid. The contract language was clear that the evaluation report must reflect observations performed during the 50-minute observation. It was apparent that not only did the person who gave me a lousy evaluation not observe me with his own eyes, but he was complicit in ruining the career of a new librarian to fuel the spite of another. I quickly learned that I would not receive an observation nor be honestly evaluated based on my merits or accomplishments. Instead, one or more colleagues in my department evaluated my popularity and likeability. As Tressie McMillan Cottom states, "For some of us, being competent has always been an illusion."[10] As a probationary faculty member, I was at the mercy of tenured colleagues. These colleagues hold the power. Your future depends on their recommendations. Serita Echavez See describes tenure as "Tenure means total unaccountability. With tenure, you get to do anything you want. And that begets not freedom but forms of irresponsibility, apathy, and racism

---

9   Adichie 18:33.

10  Tressie McMillan Cottom, *Thick* (New York: The New Press, 2019), 81.

that consolidate rather than trouble the relationship between power and knowledge."[11] As a result of my first probationary tenure review, I withdrew. I became disconnected and distrustful of others.

Not every member of my tenure committee was dishonest or operated outside of the faculty contract. I struggled with being authentic while trying to fulfill the roles and responsibilities of an academic librarian. If I shared an idea, revised a department policy/procedure, proposed a new task method, and more, I was dismissed, ignored, and labeled. Bethea states, "You may become a wealthy and highly educated Black woman, but still, when you're seen, you're seen as everything that a white supremacist society associates with being a Black woman: poor, uneducated, promiscuous, unattractive, sassy, loud. You walk into every room at a deficit. Unacceptable. Unaccepted."[12] Damasco and Hodges state, "job responsibilities of library faculty can encompass a broad range of activities rather than a single task like teaching. For example, librarians who teach regular bibliographic instruction sessions usually have other responsibilities as well, such as regular reference desk hours."[13] The evaluation criteria were biased for non-instructional faculty (such as librarians and counselors) as all the requirements revolved around classroom teaching. Living up to "faculty standards"[14] is a hidden component of the evaluation process. As a new faculty librarian, I struggled to balance collection development, acquisitions, outreach activities, reference desk hours, college service committee obligations, one-shot instruction sessions, class teaching, and department meetings. There isn't any separate tenure evaluation criterion for instructional and non-instructional faculty. Damasco and Hodges argue that "given [the] differences one might expect some variance between the tenure policies that govern library faculty and teaching faculty at the same institution."[15]

---

11   Serita Echanez See, "Talking Tenure," in *Written/Unwritten: Diversity and the Hidden Truths of Tenure*, (Chapel Hill: University of North Carolina Press, 2016), 155.

12   Aiko D. Bethea, "Vulnerability, Shame Resilience, and the Black Experience" in *You Are Your Best Thing*, eds. Tarana Burke and Brene Brown (New York, NY: Random House, 2021), 180.

13   Ione T. Damasco and Dracine Hodges, "Tenure and Promotion Experiences of Academic Librarians of Color," *College & Research Libraries* 73, no. 3 (2012): 286, https://doi.org/10.5860/crl-244.

14   Damaso and Hodges, "Tenure and Promotion Experiences of Academic Librarian of Color," 287.

15   Damaso and Hodges, 286.

One semester, I worked on a few projects that required a significant amount of research. I submitted a (release time) request asking my former library manager to be off from the reference desk schedule. Full-time librarians at my institution are responsible for a specific area of assignment in addition to reference desk hours. I did not think that my request was unreasonable or that I was asking for special privileges. Full-time librarians were scheduled for three- to four-hour reference desk shifts during this period. My supervisor accused me of asking for favors. My supervisor said my colleagues would want the same opportunity if they granted my request. Conversely, a white male colleague was granted this allowance for three consecutive semesters before I asked; only he received leave approval. This behavior was commonplace for the former library manager, who is Indian, to favor and support white male colleagues. He regularly praised their ideas and work campus-wide, minimizing and negating my work.

My last probationary tenure evaluation meeting did not go well. The expectation during this meeting was for me to sign a false and unsupervised evaluation. I asked my evaluator to leave my office several times to allow me a moment to pull myself together. I refused to break down in tears in his presence. He refused to leave. He could not understand why I was upset. I had to get away from this toxic situation, so I left, sat in my car, and cried. I had to call a friend to calm me down. I would have gone home, but I had a reference desk shift assigned to me. I would never burden anyone else by not showing up, so I remained in my car until it was time for my reference desk shift. I returned with a smile and started my transition to help students. Kawanna Bright uses the term "deep acting"[16] to describe a form of "emotional labor."[17] Bright explains, "With deep acting, the employee expresses the expected emotion rather than the felt emotion."[18] Furthermore, "how the employee actually feels, how they express those feelings, and the ramifications of their decisions are what make up the essence of emotional labor."[19] On the inside, I was trembling because I was about to be unemployed, but I could not in good conscience allow

---

16  Kawanna Bright, "A Woman of Color's Work is Never Done: Intersectionality in Reference and Information Work," in *Pushing the Margins*, ed. Rose L. Chou and Annie Pho (Sacramento: Library Juice Press, 2018), 169.

17  Bright, "A Woman of Color's Work is Never Done," 168.

18  Bright, 169.

19  Bright, 169.

this to stop me from providing quality service to students. I didn't realize I was "deep acting"[20] then. "Deep acting" helped me to navigate my "low morale,"[21] even if it was short-term. See's statements regarding the tenure process rang true; "It seems impossible to come through the process intact or unscarred whether one is retained or fired."[22]

## Self-care & LIS

My first year as a full-time, tenure-track librarian differed from what I expected. I had a level of optimism. I was joining a team prioritizing student achievement and promoting, marketing, and branding the library as a premier resource center. Instead, I found a maelstrom of politics, backchannel communication, inequitable work distribution, favoritism, microaggressions, racism, and the practice of taking credit for others' academic integrity and the misattribution of recognition for academic integrity. It may seem like I suffered from a case of "vocational awe,"[23] the belief that librarians and the library profession are essentially good and beyond critique. Instead, I suffered from assuming that my colleagues could set their differences aside for the greater good of the students. I started at this institution as a staff member and previously worked at four other libraries; I understood no profession is beyond critique or reproach.

There was an eighteen-month reprieve when the Coronavirus (COVID-19) pandemic hit. The stay-at-home order was a blessing in disguise. I could work from home, thus removing me from a toxic work environment. For the Black community, we were also dealing with the heinous and senseless murder of George Floyd.[24] Black people are not new to being treated as less than human or victims of police brutality,

---

20   Bright, 169.

21   Kendrick, "The Low Morale Experience of Academic Librarians" 847.

22   See, "Talking Tenure," 152.

23   Fobazi Ettarh, "Vocational Awe And Librarianship: The Lies We Tell Ourselves," *In the Library with a Lead Pipe* 58, no. 4 (2018): 141, accessed August 1, 2022, https://www.inthelibrarywiththeleadpipe.org/2018/vocational-awe/.

24   Evan Hill, et. al. "How George Floyd Was Killed in Police Custody," *New York Times* (New York, NY), Jun. 20, 2020, A24L, https://www.nytimes.com/2020/05/31/us/george-floyd-investigation.html.

police misconduct, or "Stand Your Ground" laws.[25] From Trayvon Martin, Eric Garner, and Michael Brown, just to name a few.[26] From the Middle Passage experience to slavery to Jim Crow to the lynching of Black people, that never ceased.[27] The only difference now was that the pandemic forced people who intentionally ignored systemic racism, anti-Blackness, and white supremacy to sit down and watch police brutality in real-time.[28] The stay-at-home order was a blessing for me. Even though the world was in chaos, I could use this time to reignite my passion for librarianship, social justice, professional development, and building networks with library folks outside of my institution.

The stay-at-home order also provided me with the time and opportunity to take professional development classes and attend workshops and webinars for free or discounted rates. I earned two certificates focused on diversity, inclusion, and the facets connected to these ideals. I stepped outside my comfort zone, joined new professional library associations, participated in leadership and mentor programs, and was elected to be in association leadership roles. I connected with library folks outside my institution and realized I needed more information, opportunities, and growth. I no longer felt isolated and alone. Library groups and social media accounts for Black and librarians of color, such as *We Here, Black Librarians*, and *Onlylibraryfans* (formerly *BIPOC in LIS*),[29] and more, showed me that Black librarians everywhere had similar experiences. I had a newfound support system.

I learned to focus on my self-care. I learned how to practice breathwork. I started crafting, baking, and gardening again. I decluttered and redecorated my home. I also learned to meditate. Working nonstop took its toll on my mental, emotional, and physical health. I had high blood pressure, frequent migraines, and thinning hair. My work life

---

25 National Conference of State Legislatures, "Self Defense and 'Stand Your Ground'", February 9, 2022, accessed August 2, 2022, https://www.ncsl.org/research/civil-and-criminal-justice/self-defense-and-stand-your-ground.aspx.

26 Darran Simon, "Trayvon Martin's Death Sparked a Movement That Lives on Five Years Later," *CNN online*, February 27, 2017, https://www.cnn.com/2017/02/26/us/trayvon-martin-death-anniversary/index.html.

27 LowCountry Digital History Initiative, "The Middle Passage," *LowCountry Digital History Initiative*, accessed August 2, 2022, http://ldhi.library.cofc.edu/.

28 Evan Hill, et. al., "How George Floyd Was Killed in Police Custody".

29 Wehere.space (@wehere), Instagram, https://www.instagram.com/wehere.space/; Black Librarians (@blacklibrarians), Instagram, https://www.instagram.com/blacklibrarians/; Onlylibraryfans (@onlylibraryfans), Instagram, https://www.instagram.com/onlylibraryfans/.

took me away from my family. My kids suffered as I dealt with work-related trauma. I did not have time for family fun and often worked on work tasks or projects during their school activities. They no longer had a mother. A saving grace was discovering the *GirlTrek* podcast series.[30] To reconnect with my family, I had to reconnect with myself. *GirlTrek* is a campaign "to heal intergenerational trauma, fight systemic racism, and transform Black lives."[31] Black women are encouraged to commit to "walking towards your healing and liberation."[32] I accepted the challenge, and when the live GirlTrek podcast would air, I would take a work break, walk around my neighborhood, and listen. Walking and taking breaks away from my homework space helped me clear my mind, sleep better, and get my high blood pressure under control.

## Recommendations

I turned my anger, isolation, depression, and frustration into activism. First, I created a Black Lives Matter resource guide. This guide was my avenue to make a statement against the injustices that Black people face. It was my rally call against institutional performative diversity. Libraries, institutions, companies, supporters, and allies began writing diversity and Black Lives Matter support statements. During this time, stores, websites, and more all had BLM statements; however, from my experience, accepting the diversity or Black Lives Matter statements at face value was hard. When I read the statements, I often wondered who was in the room when the administration wrote these statements. How are employees of color-treated? Does the statement reflect the genuine nature of the company/institution? Does the statement reflect a commitment to a new equitable direction for the company/institution? For example, my institution uses the term "culture of care." It is an informal term that refers to the importance of employees and their well-rounded health and being. I believe this term to be performative because it checks the diversity box to make the institution seem like it is moving in a new direction that considers its employees. I was unable to reconcile this term with what I experienced.

---

30 T. Morgan Dixon, et. al., "Foremothers: Octavia Butler," August 4, 2017, in *Black History Bootcamp*, produced by GirlTrek, podcast, MP3 audio, 34:49, https://blackhistorybootcamp.com/foremothers-day-21-octavia-butler/.

31 "Walking for Healing and Liberation," *GirlTrek*, accessed July 27, 2022, https://www.girltrek.org/about-us/.

32 "Walking for Healing and Liberation," *GirlTrek*.

Too often, these declarations are in direct opposition to the treatment of Black people. Empty, surface-level diversity statements are an attempt to gaslight marginalized folks. Creating the Black Lives Matter (BLM) guide helped me to find my voice again. I was at the point in my career where I would sit quietly and let folks do whatever they wanted. My opinion and contributions should have been more appreciated and validated. I thought the only way I could survive was to isolate myself as much as possible. The Black Lives Matter guide not only helped me find my voice but later became the catalyst that activated our campus identity groups to create resource guides to break down barriers and celebrate their cultures.

Figure 1    Black Lives Matter LibGuide from Shamika J. Simpson

Ultimately, in dealing with complex and traumatic situations, you must find a few or many tools that will help you cope. Before you fill your toolbox, evaluate your situation and determine if you wish to stay at your institution. Leaving a toxic situation is an option. My decision to stay was based on the current openings for collection development or acquisitions librarian positions, pay equivalence, the disruption of my children's routines and lives, and the possibility of restarting the tenure process. If you decide to stay, as I have, you must fill your toolbox with a few or many tools that will help you handle adverse situations. For example, a morning yoga class to center yourself before work, a high-energy exercise class to let off steam, a sister circle, journaling, walking during breaks, and more could assist in alleviating stress. The most essential tool is having a friend, family member, or colleague call when you are in full crisis mode. It helps to have someone "talk you off" the proverbial ledge. There isn't one formula that works for everyone. Finding the tools that will assist you in difficult situations takes time.

## Conclusion

My journey to become a tenured faculty has been challenging. My institution will be opening physically soon, and all employees will return. As I rejoin my co-workers in the library, I must be intentional and disciplined about focusing on my self-care. This means balancing my workload, recognizing triggers, and speaking up when needed. I must hold my institution accountable when inequitable workloads persist. I will continue using a telescopic lens to step outside my comfort zone and manifest my visions for my career and work. Looking to the future, I plan on creating a green space in the library with real and faux plants. An indoor green space would provide a safe place on campus for students to get away, sit quietly, meditate, pray, and center themselves when they cannot do so outside. The green space could become a community place for guided yoga and meditation sessions. I plan to connect some subject areas with the collection's academic and vocational departments and programs. While searching for books in the leisure reading section, students can take a pamphlet that markets a creative writing program. I am excited to try new ideas. I wish the folks who made my tenure process a traumatic experience would have allowed me to be me. My desire to help students and provide students with resources that can help them academically and enhance their personal lives are intertwined. I would have loved to implement some of my ideas earlier on. Simple words of support or encouragement or simply listening beyond your understanding can go a long way in nurturing new library faculty.

## Acknowledgments

I thank my many friends and family who have supported me. I dedicate this chapter to my husband, Byron, who is my rock, compass, and support. My children, Jaden, Jeremiah, and Zainah, lost quality time with me due to the demands of a new career. My parents, Anthony and Everlena, who are both revolutionaries and activists in their own right; Dele Ladejobi, my brilliant friend, colleague, and mentor; my new BCALA friends and mentors, K.C. Boyd, Richard Ashby Jr., and Karen Lemmons.; and to all the BIPOC librarians who continue to endure, just as I have/am. Finally, I would like to thank my friends who encouraged me to persist even when I wanted to quit. This is a testament that you can persevere despite everything.

## *Bibliography*

Adichie, Chimamanda Ngozi. "The Danger of a Single Story," 2009, TED YouTube video, 18:33. https://youtu.be/D9Ihs241zeg.

Bethea, Aiko D. "Vulnerability, Shame Resilience, and the Black Experience." In *You Are Your Best Thing,* edited by Tarana Burke and Brene Brown, 179–90. New York: Random House, 2021.

BIPOC_in_LIS (@bipoc_in_lis), Instagram, https://www.instagram.com/bipoc_in_lis/.

Black Librarians (@blacklibrarians), Instagram, https://www.instagram.com/blacklibrarians/.

Bright, Kawanna. "A Woman of Color's Work is Never Done: Intersectionality in Reference and Information Work." In *Pushing the Margins*, edited by Rose L. Chou and Annie Pho, 163–95. Sacramento: Library Juice Press, 2018.

Cottom, Tressie McMillan. *Thick*. New York: The New Press, 2019.

Damasco, Ione T., and Dracine Hodges. "Tenure and Promotion Experiences of Academic Librarians of Color." *College & Research Libraries* 73, no. 3 (2012): 279–301. https://doi.org/10.5860/crl-244.

Dixon. T. Morgan, and Vanessa Garrison. "Foremothers: Octavia Butler." August 4, 2017, in *Black History Bootcamp*, produced by GirlTrek, podcast, MP3 audio, 34:49, https://blackhistorybootcamp.com/foremothers-day-21-octavia-butler/.

Ettarh, Fobazi. "Vocational Awe And Librarianship: The Lies We Tell Ourselves." *In the Library with a Lead Pipe* 58, no. 4 (2018). https://www.inthelibrarywiththeleadpipe.org/2018/vocational-awe/.

Gray, Aysa. "The Bias of 'Professionalism' Standards." *Stanford Social Innovation Review*, 2019. https://doi.org/10.48558/TDWC-4756.

Hill, Evan, Ainara Tiefenthäler, Christiaan Triebert, Drew Jordan, Haley Willis, and Robin Stein. "How George Floyd Was Killed in Police Custody." *New York Times*. Jan. 24, 2022. https://www.nytimes.com/2020/05/31/us/george-floyd-investigation.html.

Kendrick, Kaetrena Davis. "The Low Morale Experience of Academic Librarians: A Phenomenological Study." *Journal of Library Administration* 57, no. 8 (2007): 846–78, accessed August 2, 2022. doi:10.1080/01930826.2017.1368325.

LowCountry Digital History Initiative. "The Middle Passage." Accessed August 2, 2022, http://ldhi.library.cofc.edu/.

National Conference of State Legislatures. "Self Defense and 'Stand Your Ground'." February 9, 2022, Accessed date August 2, 2022, https://www.ncsl.org/research/civil-and-criminal-justice/self-defense-and-stand-your-ground.aspx.

Oxford Languages, s.v. "colorism (n.)." (Northridge, CA). Accessed February 22, 2022, https://www.merriam-webster.com/dictionary/colorism.

Reale, Michelle. *Becoming a Reflective Librarian and Teacher: Strategies for Mindful Academic Practice*. Chicago: American Library Association, 2016.

See, Serita Echanez. "Talking Tenure." In *Written/Unwritten: Diversity and the Hidden Truths of Tenure*. edited by Patricia A. Matthew, 148–61. Chapel Hill: University of North Carolina Press, 2016.

Simon, Darran. "Trayvon Martin's Death Sparked a Movement That Lives on Five Years Later." Last modified Feb 27, 2017. https://www.cnn.com/2017/02/26/us/trayvon-martin-death-anniversary/index.html.

Simmons, Dailyn. "The Unspoken Truth." *Daily Sundial (Northridge, CA)*, February 28, 2020. https://sundial.csun.edu/156565/opinions/the-unspoken-truth/.

UCSF Multicultural Resource Center. "Racial Equity & Anti-Black Racism." Accessed March 5, 2022. https://mrc.ucsf.edu/racial-equity-anti-black-racism.

WeHere.space (@wehere), Instagram, https://www.instagram.com/we-here.space/.

WOC+Lib. "Statement against White Appropriation of Black, Indigenous, and People of Color's Labor." *WOC+LIB* (blog). Last modified September 3, 2021. https://www.wocandlib.org/features/2021/9/3/statement-against-white-appropriation-of-black-indigenous-and-people-of-colors-labor.

**Honoring Our Labor**
Reflections on Our Work

# Learning from the Brown Body
## Xicana Feminism in the Community College Library

*Eva M.L. Rios-Alvarado*

*The [brown] body is a pedagogical device, a location of recentering and recontextualizing the self and the stories that emanate from that self.*
Cindy Cruz[1]

*Be a dangerous woman, be a jaguar.*
Elizabeth Irene Martinez[2]

## Introduction

This chapter was written during the context of work prior to the 2020 global pandemic and within *pandemic pedagogy*,[3] that is teaching in the times of a pandemic. I emphasize the COVID-19 pandemic as it was still in progress as I wrote this chapter. The year 2020 was one of the most challenging years as a librarian educator, community member, and as a woman of color; in a nation that continually demonstrates to

---

1  Cindy Cruz, "Toward An Epistemology of a Brown Body," in *Chicana/Latina Education in Everyday Life: Feminista Perspectives and Epistemologies*, ed. Dolores Delgado Bernal, Alejandra Elenes, Francisca E. Godinez, and Sofia Villenas (Albany: State University Press, 2006).

2  Elizabeth Martinez, *A Jaguar in the Library: The Story of the First Chicana Librarian* (Moorpark: Flor y Canto Press, 2020).

3  Kiara Lee-Heart, "Pandemic Pedagogy: A Call to Educators to Bring Their Classrooms to Reality," *Learning for Justice*, accessed March 21, 2021, https://www.learningforjustice.org/magazine/pandemic-pedagogy-a-call-to-educators-to-bring-their-classrooms-to-reality.

negate my teaching, existence, creativity, liberation, and autonomy. It is within the time of pandemic pedagogy when the college I work at, which serves about 50,000 students, and growing, worked a full year and a half remotely. Many educators and students are now returning to our institutions feeling unsafe, unacknowledged, sick, and not ready for the coming variants which seem to have no end.[4] Some campuses are even going back to remote teaching or even implementing remote work hours into the work week, with uncertainty. In a moment of a double edged-sword, students are encountering growing challenges from understanding how college works, from the pain of the pandemic, and the political climate. Many students (including community college workers) are barely functioning in college while we are asked to perform as if nothing ever happened, and yet students and employees are experiencing higher levels of mental health crises, anxiety, domestic violence, poverty, housing insecurity, joblessness, low morale, and burn-out, to name a few.[5] Colleges are addressing some of these challenges as they can, mainly through equity as a fix-it response. Yet, colleges cannot fix the totality of these structural realities with their current means. Equity is not liberation.

In this chapter, I share how community college librarians and colleges are part of a larger social-political educational context where a singular decision-making focus solely on metrics will not fully provide and account for needed change in our lives and education. Attention to our collective experiences in higher education and our educational stories bring in valuable information which is often not given equal time in decision making. I use this chapter to show how our experiences can teach us to change and strengthen our educational spaces. People of color in their higher educational pathways will continue to feel barriers while colleges are hyper-focused on solving "the gap." When the gap is the failure and inability of institutions, of democracy, to solve racism, settler-colonialism, social injustice barriers, class inequalities, gender discrimination, homophobia, amongst others.[6] More focus

---

4   Kaetrena Davis Kendrick, Amanda M. Leftwich, and Twanna Hodge, "Providing Care and Community in Times of Crisis: The BIPOC in LIS Mental Health Summits," *College & Research Libraries News* [Online] 82, n. 8 (2021): 358, https://doi.org/10.5860/crln.82.8.358.

5   Jon Marcus, "As Admissions Season Descends, Warning Signs Appear for Low-Income Applicants," *The Washington Post*, accessed February 19, 2021.

6   Gilda L. Ochoa, *Academic Profiling: Latinos, Asian Americans, and the Achievement Gap* (Minnesota: University of Minnesota Press, 2013), 21.

and energy, outside/inside of our colleges, should be placed on liberational practices and methods to address and rectify the social realities students and communities are feeling and what we are tasked to solve in higher education. Ignoring our collective realities and our relational experiences, as we move into the future of education, in the community college and library setting will result in further denial and prolong the healing and justice needed now.

I work in the state of California, which has a distinct set of students, communities, and geographic indicators. The state has a massive community college system. Community college students in California are part of a larger educational, social, economic, and political infrastructure as are the librarians who work in these colleges. Equally of value is not to overlook who is teaching, leading, and working, and more importantly learning in these spaces. In the California Community Colleges (CCC) there are 116 colleges with approximately 1.8 million students statewide. In the year 2017–2018, out of 1.8 million students, (44.54%) identified as Hispanic, (0.43%) Native American, (5.9%) African American, (11.56%) Asian, (2.69%) Filipino, (0.41%) Pacific Islander, (3.82%) Multi-Ethnicity, (25.88%) White, and (4.77%) Unknown.[7] These numbers show us the currency of who is attending California colleges in the CCC system, but what of their experiences? Taking these numbers closer to home, at my Southern California community college, where we are the largest single-district community college in the state, the demographic trends are like the State in that the campus is over half Latinx (also referred to in data fields as Hispanic) in student population.

The lack of racial/ethnic representation in our faculty is vividly expressed by way of student-to-faculty data, where we know students of color are in the classrooms of mostly white faculty. According to the campus facts, about (0.16%) of the students at the college are American Indian and Alaskan Native, (18.64%) Asian, (3.46%) are African American, (10.86%) White Non-Hispanic, (6%) Unknown, (3.62%) Pacific Islander/Filipino, (2.54%) Multi-Ethnic, and about (54.73%) of the student body identifies as Latinx. On the other hand, the demographics of tenured faculty indicate who is teaching at these institutions. According to the data collection system of the California Community

---

7 "Key Facts: General Facts," California Community Colleges, accessed date October 2021. https://www.cccco.edu/About-Us/Key-Facts.

Colleges Chancellor's Office, Data Mart, in the year 2020, statewide, there were only 117 (0.64%) academic tenured faculty/tenured track (TF/TT) who identified as Native American, Alaskan Native 91 (0.50%) TF/TT, 1,876 (10.32%) TF/TT Asian, 1,093 (6.01%) African American TF/TT, 3,265 (17.96%) Hispanic TF/TT, 272 (1.50%) Multi-Ethnicity TF/TT, 1,114 (6.13%) Unknown, and 10,352 (56.94%) White Non-Hispanic TF/TT.[8]

In a state with over 39 million people, 1.8 million community college students reside at 116 different colleges where people of color are not being hired sufficiently at college settings where we are needed. The demographics of the college tenured faculty do not adequately represent the student body demographics statewide and at the campus I work.[9] We must pause here to note this as an effect of settler colonialism, where white supremacy most definitely shows in the hiring and retention of staff, faculty, and administrators. These factors weigh heavily into our lives and learning. Some ways include but are not limited to, how people learn, who people learn from, and the political and cultural agendas of our leaders which impact our workspaces and ability to be who we are at work. Furthermore, our campuses reside on Native American lands with very low Native presence in our student body, faculty, and staff. This indicates a historical and current neglect into how the Native mind, voice, and thought come into our campuses with little regard to the historic reality that we live and work on Native lands. In 2020, on my campus there were two Native American, Alaskan Native (0.49%) tenured faculty and (0.16 %) of students identified as Native American and Alaskan Native, according to an internal, not public facing, campus database.

## Where to Start? I Start from Libertad

Feminist and class consciousness are at the root of my pedagogy and the basis of how I maneuver in libraries and in my teaching. With my years, I learned I have always been a feminist, but I had not fully rationalized it until I was in my early 20s when I came to a more complex

---

8   "Faculty & Demographics: Data Mart," California Community Colleges Chancellor's Office Management Information Systems Data Mart, accessed date October 16, 2021. https://datamart.cccco.edu/Faculty-Staff/Staff_Demo.aspx.

9   U.S. Department of Education, *Advancing Diversity, and Inclusion in Higher Education: Key Data Highlights Focusing on Race and Ethnicity Promising Practices* (Washington D.C.: U.S. Department of Education, 2016), accessed October 16, 2021, https://www2.ed.gov/rschstat/research/pubs/advancing-diversity-inclusion.pdf.

consciousness of my Xicana feminist identity that I continue to evolve with and critique. This happened while taking a Chicana Feminism class taught by Dr. Dionne Espinoza at California State University, Los Angeles in the early 2000s. Even though my mother had raised me with feminist principles without naming it as such, in Dr. Espinoza's class, I developed the academic vocabulary, and was given the opportunity to meet other feminist scholars by learning about and being part of feminist organizations such as Mujeres Activas en Letras y Cambio Social (MALCS).[10] MALCS and the process of being in an all *mujeres* (womens) and gender non-binary space provided me a sense of worth, that was not felt at any point previously in my education, and helped prepare me for the borders Brown women face in higher education and what I would come to encounter and re-encounter in my librarian faculty roles.

I am a Xicana[11] community college librarian from what is known now as the Southwest United States, specifically Tovaangar[12] or the Los Angeles area, near Ochuunga, also known as the Northeast Los Angeles area. Most people wouldn't know, the "L" in my name is one of my middle names: *Libertad* (freedom). Purposefully, I was given this name by my father as a symbol of the revolution he wanted to see in the world for all people. His gesture and lineage have always been a symbol of the resistance that colonized, oppressed peoples still have in their hearts and spirits. Libertad is not just a word for me, it is my name, it is also part of everything I want for others, myself, and our sacred spaces of learning and life.

My families are from the peoples of northern Mexico, the states of Zacatecas, Coahuila, and Chihuahua. Each of my *abuelitos* (grandparents) has a different immigration history to Southern California. I come from a humble working-class background. My families have worked hard in this country (and in Mexico) under many different circumstances and geo-political narratives. We are and have been farm workers, miners, social workers, educators, nannies, domestic laborers, military veterans, and now a librarian, amongst other professions. We have served and continue to give.

---

10  "MALCS Mission," Mujeres Activas en Letras y Cambio Social (MALCS), accessed July 10, 2021, https://malcs.org/about/.

11  Ana Castillo, *Massacre of the Dreamers: Essays on Xicanisma*, (Albuquerque: University of New Mexico Press, 2014), 219.

12  Sean Greene and Thomas Curwen, "Finding Tovaangar: Mapping the Tongva Villages of LA's Past," *Los Angeles Times online*, accessed May 9, 2019.

Even with the richness of who I am culturally, the reality for Brown *mujeres* (women), like me, regardless of faculty status or not, is that our places of employment, even in libraries, come with institutional challenges, where we encounter many obstacles impacting our lives and work. Furthermore, in the community college library and the discipline of Library and Information Science (LIS) we work within an oppressive apparatus as practitioners and learners within higher education.[13] Although there is a trending rise of policies in favor of diversity, equity, inclusion, and anti-racism in higher education, LIS actively and passively feeds into colonial, racist, and hetero-patriarchal legacies calling for remedies and reciprocity for many communities.[14] As a result of the historical-to-present reality of active settler colonialism that extends to education and therefore the library; the imperialist mindset is alive and active in the library.[15] We tangibly encounter toxicity and violence in college education by way of white-dominant oppressive practices[16] (even perpetuated and supported, surprisingly, by people of color), controlling how education happens, who is hired, who stays, college/library policies, leadership models, funding/spending, and how we spend our time at work. Oppression in education informs what happens at the community college in all facets of its operation and therefore has a hand in controlling student knowledge production and the experiences of future generations. I often ask myself while at work feeling the weight of these structures, what would a college operated and guided by women of color feminist ways or other types of liberational methods look and feel like for students, employees, and our communities? This chapter explores some insights into how we can start to get there.

---

13  Nicola Andrews, "It's Not Imposter Syndrome: Resisting Self-doubt as Normal for Library Workers," *In the Library with the Lead Pipe*, (2020), https://www.inthelibrarywiththeleadpipe.org/2020/its-not-imposter-syndrome/, accessed January 23, 2022; Alexandria Brown, James Cheng, Isabel Espinal, Brittany Paloma Fiedler, Joyce Gabiola, Sofia Leung, Nisha Mody, Alanna Aiko Moore, Teresa Y. Neely, and Peace Ossom-Williamson, "Statement Against White Appropriation of Black, Indigenous, and People of Color's Labor," WOC+LIB, September 3, 2021, https://www.wocandlib.org/features/2021/9/3/statement-against-white-appropriation-of-black-indigenous-and-people-of-colors-labor.

14  E.J. Josey, ed., *Black Librarian in America* (Metuchen: Scarecrow Press, 1970), vii-xvi; "CICSC/AIS Land Acknowledgement Toolkit," California Indian Culture and Sovereignty Center, accessed February 12, 2021. https://www.csusm.edu/cicsc/.

15  Joel Spring, *Deculturalization and the Struggle for Equality: A Brief History of the Education of Dominated Cultures in the United States* (New York: Routledge, 2022), 1.

16  Raymond Pun and Jessica Bustos, "Understanding Barriers and Experiences of Library Advocacy Work by Library Workers of Color: An Exploratory Study," *The Political Librarian* 5 no. 1, (2021): 14.

First, we must start with our reality. As Brown women in spaces of education we are expected to ask for permission to exist and when we do not ask for permission, we are overly questioned, ignored, deemed dangerous, or treated as if we are not qualified. Despite hundreds of years of resistance, Indigenous and Brown women continue to share our aspirations to thrive in a world, including our workspaces, that constantly peel away at our wholeness.[17] From the discipline and living theory of Latina/x/Chicana/x Studies we learn this is a historically ongoing phenomenon and centrally described here in the United States of America (U.S.).[18] Brown women inform us of a higher education and workplace where our *palabra* (words) is invalidated, our work underfunded, often met with hostility, resistance, and disapproval.[19] As a result of this inhumanity, we have faced within all institutional settings, Brown women developed what Espinoza, Cotera, and Blackwell call *movidas* (acts of resistance on their own terms) to work around the oppressions Brown women have encountered inside and outside of the educational system in the U.S.. *Movidas* is one method Brown women have used in relation to how we continue to operate and thrive within an oppressive tradition in all areas of U.S. society, namely in this chapter within higher education, which manifests into our community college jobs. This book reflects and analyzes who librarians of color are in community college now and offers insights. One thing remains critically important as we move our profession forward and work within the oppressive and often racist spaces: we must continue to bring our cultural identities (and experiences) to our jobs as we do our LIS pedagogical work. However, as has been my experience, Brown women working and learning in community college libraries are subject to methods that are contrary to our cultural realities. This brings me to how and why libraries and librarians can learn from our experiences, and how Brown bodies are central to leading the ways Chicana/x feminisms are part of a path to liberatory practices in community college education. In my work as a community college student equity and outreach librarian, students have consistently told me

---

17  Elizabeth Martinez, *A Jaguar in the Library: The Story of the First Chicana Librarian* (Moorpark: Flor y Canto Press, 2020), 9.; Nancy L. Godoy-Powell, Elizabeth G. Dunham, "21st Century Community Outreach and Collection Development: ASU Chicano/a Research Collection," *Journal of Western Archives* 8, no. 1 (2017): 1.

18  Maylei Blackwell, "Chicana Insurgencies: Stories of Transformation, Youth Rebellion, and Campus Organizing," in ¡*Chicana Power!*, ed. Maylei Blackwell (Austin: University of Texas Press, 2011), 43–64.

19  Martinez, *A Jaguar in the Library*, 9–17.

they want to connect with educators in ways that relate to their political, cultural, and ethnic frameworks. Therefore, we must not hide our identities. Instead, we must proudly adorn ourselves with the beauty and wisdom of our *culturas* (cultures) and implement our knowledge, even if we are challenged and met with disapproval, via the power of our ancestral *movidas* lineage.

I invite the reader to reflect on their own identities and experiences in relation to their present and future work. Taking time to understand who we are in connection with what we do informs our purpose and direction.[20] I will share my reflections by exploring how my experiences inform my librarianship, and how my outreach and pedagogical work is part of a *Xicana feminist librarianship*. I will discuss how settler colonialism and by extension white supremacy continues to harm people of color in higher education with a few examples from my experiences teaching and working at community colleges, in the United States, specifically in Southern California. I will also share some ways that we can restructure our work and leadership in the community colleges by looking to the guiding and ever-growing methods of Latina/x/Chicana/x Feminist practices, with a focus on Chicana/x lens. There are limitations to expressing everything in one chapter. Keep in mind, what I share in this chapter is related to my ways of knowing and I acknowledge there are many more venues for liberation within education and libraries. I apply what I have learned thus far, as lessons in my life, and I invite the reader to ruminate from my life's perspective; a Xicana Librarian. With that in mind, I challenge the profession to deeply reflect; what would our work be like if we authentically implemented and centered women of color feminist practices and methods into our work in the community colleges and the community college library?

## My Brown Body: Pedagogies of the Home in Xicana College Librarianship

As I have come to learn from Chicana/x Studies, our Brown bodies are powerful sites of memory and knowledge and at the same time allow Brown women, queer, and gender non-binary peoples to use their experiences and narratives to develop creative solutions and strategies for our lives. Cindy Cruz's work on the Brown, queer body, via

---

20 Char Booth, *Reflective Teaching, Effective Learning: Instructional Literacy for Library Educators* (Chicago: American Library Association, 2011), 17.

her educational research work, tells us that our Brown bodies become, "an agent, witness, and provocateur."[21] Cruz encourages that the Brown body be viewed as a "pedagogical device."[22] Cruz's ideas promote agency to connect who we are, our backgrounds, and our stories to empowerment within education, that come from what we have, are, and will experience.

Another insight of the Brown body is by educator Dra. Dolores Delgado-Bernal, who builds on the foundational work of Gloria Anzaldúa, where she shares, "the brown body channels our abilities and powers via the generational memory of our brown bodies while in our educational spaces."[23] As a *Xicana*, I have relied on the works of feminist leaders and the legacies of my mother, my grandmothers, my *nina* (godmother), to inform my positionality in relation to my geography, history, sexuality, and political awareness, spirituality, and teaching.

My Brown body as a pedagogical device in LIS as a community college librarian invites a conversation and analysis with lessons through my experiences. In my experience as a Brown woman in LIS, I have many stories. One resonating reality I continually encounter is how Brown women are not valued. This is because Brown women are not valued in education and in society. As we learn from *pedagogies of the home*, a concept created by Chicanas, this concept allows Brown *mujeres* (women) to resist oppressions by drawing on the production of knowledge from our homes into our sites of learning.[24] When I realized I was using the lessons from my home in my librarian work, it made sense to me and connected why I care so deeply for our community. In my librarian training and education there were no classes that could teach me about working with people genuinely, like my mom showed me in my community. Considering our knowledge outside of the educational system, we are equipped, grounded, and have more intentionality as we frame our learning and teaching in context. I have

---

21 Cindy Cruz, "Toward An Epistemology of a Brown Body," in *Chicana/Latina Education in Everyday Life: Feminista Perspectives and Epistemologies*, ed. Dolores Delgado Bernal, Alejandra Elenes, Francisca E. Godinez, and Sofia Villenas (Albany: State University Press, 2006), 62.

22 Cruz, "Toward An Epistemology," 76.

23 Dolores Delgado Bernal, "Learning and Living Pedagogies of the Home: The Mestiza Consciousness of Chicana Students," in *Chicana/Latina Education in Everyday Life: Feminista Perspectives and Epistemologies*, ed. Dolores Delgado Bernal, Alejandra Elenes, Francisca E. Godinez, and Sofia Villenas (Albany: State University Press, 2006), 115.

24 Delgado Bernal, "Learning and Living Pedagogies," 115.

extended some of the lessons from my own home to my work as a librarian and educator. Although the work of *pedagogies of the home*, as I understand, focuses on Chicana students, I believe these practices extend to the workspace. Dra. Delgado Bernal points out, "Chicana feminist pedagogies focus on the ways Chicanas teach, learn, and live the foundations for balancing and resisting systems of oppression, ... [where] this knowledge is passed from one generation to the next—often by mothers."[25]

I have found connections between what I learned from my mother, outside of school, to my job as a librarian in the workplace. Acknowledging and contextualizing these powerful moments inspires me to think of all the lessons others experience yet are denied honoring within our current metrics-focused educational setting that devalues women of color feminist thought and ways. My *mamí* (mother) is the first person who schooled me in the art of genuine communication. A great lesson which I observed and learned from her in my youth and to this day. I watched her as a child be in spaces with other people from such a genuine and loving place. She showed me how to be in the community and how to care for other people in the community by listening and exchanging. Going to the *panadería* (bakery), how she held space, even when people belittled her or devalued her spirit, and in all the places she would take me, she has always had the gift of building community and using her gifts of genuine communication with others. As a Brown woman, elders and community, my mom, *tías* (aunts), *abuelitas* (grandmothers), and her *comadres* (homegirls), essentially women, have been critical teachers who have graced my life, while I reflect and try to understand more about who I am in the LIS profession and in my academic work.

The people who loved and showed me how to care for others as a child have inspired my Xicana feminist librarianship. The lessons I was shown in my early years, purposefully or not purposefully, were by the women in my family and are part of how I practice library outreach to the community and in my teaching. We each have our own lessons and experiences. I encourage all community college librarians to reflect on who has taught you, where you have learned, how you have learned, and how you are teaching and treating others. These are the lessons framed so powerfully by Dra. Delgado Bernal. Our homes are

---

25  Delgado Bernal, 114.

not always perfect and sometimes sites of pain and violence, similarly, so are our workspaces. Yet, they offer Brown *mujeres (women)* generational strategies and life information in ways that the institution is incapable of providing.[26] Love, sacrifice, survival, joy is something textbooks cannot teach, but our homes and other sites of learning (outside of the classroom) are some of our first teachers.

My *mamí* has been wealthy in the love that surrounded her in the form of women. Growing up, our family was always far away and destroyed by the American lie, but she somehow made her own family. She co-built a circle of women around her and me. Essentially, I grew up in her women's *círculos* (Chicana empowerment circles). Being brought up by some badass social workers and service workers cradled my development, since my mom had left her community in San Bernardino, California as a young adult to escape sexual abuse, poverty, and the lack of opportunity. She had to make choices on her own, and I ended up with her in the Ochuunga area (Northeast Los Angeles area)[27] and different parts of the city. Women have always been my safety net, energy source, and guidance network. Women have always taught me, loved me, believed in me, sometimes not believing in me, hurting me, but women are who I have learned from in my home and have informed my ways of being with others. They taught me lessons of love, trust, respect, community, patience, laughter, and hard work, to name a few. As outreach librarians we work with people and therefore trust is a critical starting point. From the work we do, we cross paths with many people of color who have had poor experiences or treatment in some libraries and educational settings in their lifetime. There are still misunderstandings about who librarians are and why we exist. Sometimes, or maybe a lot of the time, as outreach librarians we work hard to ensure people feel the community college library is for them. Skills I have learned from women, in my home, are skills lent to working with students, faculty, and staff who are unsure of coming to the library. I'm not sure what all students' previous library experiences have been, but if I am honest, it sometimes is not a positive one as I have learned from listening to students and campus employees.

---

26  Delgado Bernal, 115.

27  Sean Greene and Thomas Curwen, "Finding Tovaangar: Mapping the Tongva Villages of LA's Past," *Los Angeles Times online.* May 9, 2019.

## Reflections on Outreach & Xicana Feminist Librarianship Lens

Every college has its own employee contracts and expectations. Outreach librarians are professors and can earn tenure (at most community colleges). As outlined in the community college's goals and mission, our primary directive is to teach. We also must contractually provide service hours to the campus, do collection development work, reference desk hours, and we are expected to do work related to our different job titles and descriptions. Given the large spectrum of activities and duties[28] it's really a job where we are not given time to rest or reflect and are expected to constantly produce and report on our production. Numbers, not people, are valued.

As I reflect on my educational experience in relation to my role as an educator, women experience demoralization all too much in higher education even after we are told education is the dominant pathway to equity.[29] People who identify as Indígena, Chicana/x, Latina/x, Afro-Latina/x, Asian-Latina/x, and Native American experience similar contradictions and therefore places in the academy and community such as MALCS are vital to our wellbeing. Working in a community college library is different from other types of libraries. "No one is turned away," is a common motto I hear to describe the community college. There are of course similarities, yet the focus of our work, as faculty, is to support and teach college students of all ages and educational backgrounds. The setting retains university-type politics and *academic banging* (a term created by me and friends in college to understand why some scholars felt superior to us when we shared that we graduated from a state university).

College librarian outreach work is spent with the people in the college community. The classroom is any place we go. When we do outreach, we can manifest, reinvent, and inspire others to be part of information spaces (online or in person) to promote lifelong learning and information access.[30] Through library outreach, student-to-librarian relation-

---

28  Michelle Velazquez Bean, and Teresa Aldredge, Karen Chow, Lynn Fowler, Arthur Guaracha, Tanya McGinnis, LaTonya Parker, and Graciela Saez-Kleriga, "Academic Senate for California Community Colleges," The Role of the Library Faculty in the California Community College, 2019, accessed March 21, 2021, https://www.asccc.org/papers/role-library-faculty-california-community-college.

29  Angela P. Harris and Carmen G. González. *Introduction to Presumed Incompetent: Intersections of Race and Class for Women in Academia*, ed. Gabriella Gutierrez, Yolanda Flores Niemann, Carmen G. González, and Angela P. Harris (Logan: University State University Press, 2012), 1.

30  "About Us: Facts and Figures," Mt. San Antonio College, accessed January 23, 2022. https://www.mtsac.edu/about/overview/facts-and-figures.html.

al experiences extend to places such as library events, outreach programs, social media, and beyond. From working and leading various types of projects at my college, students tell me they feel connected when librarians show care and intent in our outreach. Although the work we do in outreach librarianship spreads welcoming library messages across campus, not everyone is supportive of librarian outreach work.[31] Some struggle to understand and quantify how outreach work contributes to both the library and the college in a meaningful way. As outreach librarians, creativity and forward thinking can require resources, including money, which the college and library administrators are resistant to provide because we are not seen as important or deemed worthy of such funds. Our work is not always perceived by administrators and peers in a positive and cost-effective light. Ironically, leadership and colleagues feel empowered to dictate how our work should happen and feel inclined to have a hand and say in our work without considering outreach librarian leadership. For these and other reasons, we are not always given the same level of support, understanding, and respect that our peers experience.

One experience that really threw me off balance a few years back was when a library administrator, in an unrelated meeting, felt inclined to talk down to me and proceeded to negatively speak to me sternly saying, "I have no idea what you do and how you use your time!" Yet, that same year we had a record number of library programs attended by students, and collaboratively created with non-librarian discipline faculty and staff across campus. I led a team to help spread the message of the library, through our outreach work, to about 1,000 students within a few academic terms. Our library Instagram account gained over 900 followers when it started at 35 followers: a remarkable change from a few years before when the account was handed to me. These were only some areas of my work, and all librarians teach, do reference desk hours, do collection development, liaise, and provide service hours to the college. More research and writing about outreach librarian work and philosophy is needed to better illustrate how community college outreach librarians' contributions support the institution so we can get the resources needed and deserved to support students without reluctance, obstacles, or unnecessary added labor.

---

31  Peter Barr and Anthea Tucker Beyond, "Saints Spies and Salespeople: New Analogies for Library Liaison Programs," *In The Library With The Lead Pipe*, (Sep 19, 2018). https://www.inthelibrary-withtheleadpipe.org/2018/beyond-saints-spies-and-salespeople/.

Our work as outreach librarians happens in a student, staff, faculty consciousness raising reality. Essentially, the college outreach librarian inspires a curiosity that cannot always happen within the library classroom walls or an online learning management classroom. Our work is layered. Let it be known, librarian outreach work is not just an outreach table with pamphlets, it's a human-to-human interaction which requires awareness, cultural competence,[32] and tact. Outreach work involves much more than people skills. Our work is directly tied to our educational political philosophy and our critical social consciousness.[33] While we follow the same library mission and overarching college goals as our colleagues, as outreach librarians we do our jobs in ways which are profoundly worth more than is given credit. We orchestrate collaborative opportunities to ensure our work happens in tandem with students, staff, faculty, and state education initiatives (such as student equity and achievement program, AB 705[34] also known as multiple measures, and others). We build relationships with campus stakeholders, to the benefit and visibility of the library, and facilitate a relationship for others to build on their own with the library services, resources, collections, while helping students understand how to access navigational capital.[35] Conversely, to four-year universities, in the community college setting most students are first-generation, just learning about college, and scholarly practices. And, therefore, for those we reach in our work, using the library might not happen until a student has transferred or might not manifest itself in the physical realm immediately.

I urge our colleges to learn and respectfully incorporate liberational philosophies and practices, such as Latina/x/Chicana/x Feminist (and other critical frameworks and practices) into the college day-to-day business, as a starting place and radical alternative to the business of education. To include them at the forefront of the college operations, and to do so in authenticity and love. Why not hire leaders from the community and not just career people who have no investment in

---

32 "Diversity Standards: Cultural Competency for Academic Libraries," American Library Association, accessed February 2022, http://www.ala.org/acrl/standards/diversity.

33 Paulo Freire, *Teachers as Cultural Workers: Letters to Those Who Dare Teach* (Boulder: Westview Press, 2005), 97.

34 "What is AB705?," Assessment and Placement, California Community Colleges, 2018, accessed February 2022, https://assessment.cccco.edu/ab-705.

35 Michelle M. Espino, "Exploring the Role of Community Cultural Wealth in Graduate School Access and Persistence for Mexican American PhDs," *American Journal of Education, Racial Diversity in Graduate Education*, 120, no. 4 (August 2014): 554, https://doi.org/10.1086/676911.

educational justice and liberation. Latina/x/Chicana/x Feminist ways can change the culture of our campuses, and we must continue to bring radical thought with critique and practice beyond the classroom into decision making into governance. Derived from Indigenous ways and practices, Chicana/x Feminism (and other feminist practices, including Black feminist) ideas have guided and held me within higher education, when there was no one who understood or cared to think from these value systems or other value systems that challenged how people are treated in LIS (learners and practitioners). Specifically, in my life, Latina/x/Chicana/x and Black feminist theory has shown me to question and resist spaces and acts of oppression, which continue to govern the education system. The ideas from Dolores Delgado-Bernal's *pedagogies of the home*, Dionne Espinoza, Maria Cotera, and Maylei Blackwell's *movidas praxis*, and Cindy Cruz's theorizing on the importance of the *Brown body*, to name a few feminist theories/practices, are great starting places to understand many of the students in our colleges and to address the oppressiveness felt by workers and students alike within libraries and education.

I have practiced Latina/x/Chicana/x feminist, liberational ideas into my librarianship over the years. It is possible to include liberational frameworks that can be incorporated into community college governance practices, leadership models, and educational practices to magnify the lives of students in ways that resonate with who we are and our communities. Equally, it is vital for librarians to have an educational philosophy extending beyond library standards. There is a great choice and responsibility to not replicate systems of oppression, even when others do not understand why it matters. In college professional development, communication models, leadership models, classrooms, and more; Chicana/x/Latina/x Studies offers a critical analysis of racism, gender, sexuality, and class struggle, to name a few. These are all themes' students face in their lives that equity work is meant to address. Yet, equity fails to offer an analysis of colonialism needed in our educational spaces, especially as some states are trying, and in some cases succeeding, to ban ideas counter to the European American experience.[36]

---

36 Rashawn Ray and Alexandra Gibbons, "Why are States Banning Critical Race Theory?" Brooking's Institution Blog, FIXGOV (blog), last modified November 2021, https://www.brookings.edu/blog/fixgov/2021/07/02/why-are-states-banning-critical-race-theory/.

## Reflections on Connecting Settler Colonialism to College Education

Some Native American students on campus have told me we have books in the library that say their tribe is no longer here. Through my outreach work, the Native American and Inter-Tribal Student Alliance, a Native student organization, is creating a student booklist of books they want in our library collection, so we can include and center their learning needs and cultures with dignity. Settler colonialism has a major hand in actively dismantling the lives of Native peoples specifically, and people of color, where our campuses are located. The campus I work at holds a responsibility to the Tongva peoples (the original peoples of the Los Angeles Basin and greater LA-area) and Natives peoples whose land we live on, work, and grow with. I, too, have my own history with the land I work on, and grew up on. It is a responsibility of mine to work in framing and rewriting my positionality here. When we look at employee and student demographic data, the numbers and stories indicate a lack of investment in the hiring of Native faculty at my college and statewide. When we listen to Native people share their experiences and read these data points, we are really talking about how settler colonialism has impacted Native American lives in California Community Colleges (CCC). Brown people are also part of the colonial context and some of us are Native American peoples and/or Indigenous peoples, unable to connect with this history or have been denied access due to genocide, displacement, assimilation, and other policies placed upon us, including terminologies, words like Hispanic and Latinx. Some of us also have a settler past and must find ways to be present with our past.

We also know representation, specifically that of ethnic and racial diversity, is something students want on our campuses. Historically across the nation, students have organized and protested to create centers and push for courses on college campuses that uplift and educate about ethnic diversity on college campuses. On the campus I work on, El Centro, the Latinx/Chicanx student support program, was birthed out of the calls and demands for Ethnic Studies by students and the community. Native students and allies, more recently, have been advocating for a Native American student center and classes taught by Native American faculty and staff. The first person who held a position of leadership at the Native center was immediately fired and the center exists as one small office with one part-time, hourly employee. These indicators are markers of how Native people have been treated, with the short history of the center, and highlight how funding is shamefully dispersed to support the Native community at the campus, historically.

As an engaged librarian, I have seen student activists, for instance those students who advocated for these centers, take extra time out of their schooling hours to battle for authentic representation in the employee demographics and in the services and courses provided to students. These students often face getting lower grades, with all the work they put into their political work on campus, because they feel a sense of responsibility to their communities to fight for Ethnic Studies and other services to support students to come. Colleges are settings where the minds of people of color are learning and growing, and all the while being taught and governed by people who do not understand their lives and ways of being.

## Conclusion

Currently, education continues to be a numbers game with new state laws in which students are ushered through a point-valued, outcomes-based, educational system tied to state funding. Similarly, librarians are experiencing pressure to provide exact measures as to how we support getting students through college via success statistics. This bears weight on our funding and political power on campus. While we work in these highly data-driven environments, work as an outreach librarian focuses more on connecting with students authentically and consciously. In our work at the college, we must develop trust, genuine communication methods, and take note of what students are asking for and experience to ensure students feel comfortable developing who they are and their goals. Talk with students. Listen to students. Learn from them and teach with them. This means letting go of hierarchy and oppressive means of educating and leading. Really, the only way anything has changed on my campus is when students have demanded it, which is why working alongside students is critical. We can equally make similar changes in our work by bringing who we are, our *pedagogies of the home*, to the workplace.

During the pandemic, the Chicanx/Latinx student program, El Centro, asked me to co-collaborate on a presentation titled "What does it mean to be a Latina Fem?" Students, staff, and faculty from across campus attended online and showed support and made it very clear they want more events like these and more faculty representation closer to the student demographics/needs. Currently, I am writing a grant to encourage students to get active in a feminist professional organization called MALCS. MALCS is the feminist organization shared with me in my early years at CSU, Los Angeles. For the first time in my library career, I feel I am doing the work of the Xicana feminist librarian educator I want to be instead of doing the work others want to assign to me. Structures and people are in place to block and slap liberational educators on the wrist, as I have witnessed, but I will always push back for my community with a *movidas* (acts of resistance on their own terms) lens. When we align who we are to what we do, and what the community wants for a just society, we are giving the best possible service to our profession. Learning from our Brown bodies, our legacies and experiences lay the foundations for what is next in our profession.

As academic librarians, with a cultural awareness and critical consciousness, we can uplift more than the student body. We can uplift each other as employees and make deep changes if we are united and have trust. Our work adds *sazón* (spice), *dendê* (palm oil), and brings with it the cultural awareness students want and crave in their learning. The work we build in our community colleges, usually on our own, adds to the operations and the prestige of the community college and supports student goals. Not everyone can understand our ways of being as college employees because many of us are in spaces of cultural isolation, as people of color in our libraries and colleges, as the demographics show in this chapter.

Too often we need to feel acknowledged by these organizations, people(s), and institutions who truly only care about status, accreditation, checking off all the boxes in reports to the state and making enrollment. However, our most valuable constituents are students and community. Equity can only go so far, we need liberation! Students and our communities are the people we need to look to for validation and recommendations in our education work. I would much rather have the support and acknowledgement of my community than an award. Not all librarians or information workers will resonate with the messages in this chapter. However, information workers need to acknowledge that our identities and experiences have wisdoms that want to be part of the library work. Our communities need your reflections, resistance, and critical analysis. We all can use our experiences to improve and expand our discipline, workspaces, and education overall. I urge community colleges and college libraries to invite a conversation and incorporation of how WOC feminist practices, in our work, can make our community college spaces of learning truly liberational. It's time to change the way we do work in the community college. I start with my Brown body; I start with Libertad.

## Reflective Questions for Your Practice

- Who has influenced your growth, from childhood to the present?
- What themes, ideas, concepts, frameworks, epistemologies inform who you are?
- What matters to you most as an educator?
- What are the faculty, staff, student, and administrator demographics on your campus?
- What matters are students organizing for politically on your campus and how can you support these demands?
- How can you start to incorporate what you care about into your workspace (including your culture(s), critical consciousness, and educational political philosophy)?
- What is the history of your campus, and what is the relationship with the original people(s) where your campus is located?
- How can you enable students to have better access to campus funding for their goals? For example, what processes do you need to know, and who do you need to know?
- How are decisions made in your department? Who holds the most power and why?

### Bibliography

Andrews, Nicola. "It's Not Imposter Syndrome: Resisting Self-doubt as Normal for Library Workers." *In the Library with the Lead Pipe.* (2020). https://www.inthelibrarywiththeleadpipe.org/2020/its-not-imposter-syndrome/.

American Library Association. "Diversity Standards: Cultural Competency for Academic Libraries." Accessed February 2022. http://www.ala.org/acrl/standards/diversity.

Barr, Peter., and Tucker, Anthea. "Beyond Saints Spies and Salespeople: New Analogies for Library Liaison Programs." *In The Library With The Lead Pipe*, (September 19, 2018). https://www.inthelibrarywiththeleadpipe.org/2018/beyond-saints-spies-and-salespeople/.

Blackwell, Maylei. "Chicana Insurgencies: Stories of Transformation, Youth Rebellion, and Campus Organizing." In *¡Chicana Power!*, edited by Maylei Blackwell, 43–64. Austin: University of Texas Press, 2011.

Brown, Alexandria, James Cheng, Isabel Espinal, Brittany Paloma Fiedler, Joyce Gabiola, Sofia Leung, Nisha Mody, Alanna Aiko Moore, Teresa Y. Neely, and Peace Ossom-Williamson. "Statement Against White Appropriation of Black, Indigenous, and People of Color's Labor." *WOC+LIB*, September 3, 2021. https://www.wocandlib.org/features/2021/9/3/statement-against-white-appropriation-of-black-indigenous-and-people-of-colors-labor.

California Community Colleges Chancellor's Office Management Information Systems Data Mart. "Faculty & Demographics: Data Mart." January 24, 2001. https://datamart.cccco.edu/Faculty-Staff/Staff_Demo.aspx.

California Community Colleges. "Key Facts: General Facts." Accessed. January 24, 2021. https://www.cccco.edu/About-Us/Key-Facts.

California Community Colleges. "What is AB705?," Assessment and Placement, 2018. Accessed February 2022, https://assessment.cccco.edu/ab-705.

California Indian Culture and Sovereignty Center. "CICSC/AIS Land Acknowledgement Toolkit." Accessed February 2021. https://www.csusm.edu/cicsc/.

Castillo, Ana. *Massacre of the Dreamers: Essays on Xicanisma*. Albuquerque: University of New Mexico Press, 2014.

Castillo-Montoya, Milagros, and Torres-Guzmán, Maria E. "Thriving In Our Identity and In the Academy: Latina Epistemology as a Core Resource." *Harvard Educational Review*, 82, no. 4 (2012): 540–56.

Char Booth, *Reflective Teaching, Effective Learning: Instructional Literacy for Library Educators*. Chicago: American Library Association, 2011.

Cruz, Cindy. Toward An Epistemology of a Brown Body." In *Chicana/Latina Education in Everyday Life: Feminista Perspectives and Epistemologies*, edited by Dolores Delgado Bernal, Alejandra Elenes, Francisca E. Godinez, and Sofia Villenas, 59–76. Albany: State University Press, 2006.

Delgado Bernal, Dolores. "Learning and Living Pedagogies of the Home: The Mestiza Consciousness of Chicana Students." In *Chicana/Latina Education in Everyday Life: Feminista Perspectives and Epistemologies*, edited by Dolores Delgado Bernal, C. Alejandra Elenes, Francisca E. Godinez, and Sofia Villenas. Albany: State University Press, 2006.

Espino, Michelle M. "Exploring the Role of Community Cultural Wealth in Graduate School Access and Persistence for Mexican American PhDs." *American Journal of Education, Racial Diversity in Graduate Education* 120, no. 4 (2014): 545–74. https://doi.org/10.1086/676911.

Espinoza, Dionne, Cotera, María Eugenia, and Maylei Blackwell. *Chicana Movidas: New Narratives of Activism and Feminism in the Movement Era*. Austin: University of Texas Pres, 2018.

Freire, Paulo. *Teachers as Cultural Workers: Letters to Those Who Dare Teach*. Boulder: Westview Press, 2005.

Godoy-Powell, Nancy L., and Dunham G., Elizabeth. "21st Century Community Outreach and Collection Development: ASU Chicano/a Research Collection." *Journal of Western Archives*, 8 no. 1 (2017): 1–6. https://doi.org/10.26077/0c74-272d.

Greene, Sean, and Curwen, Thomas. "Finding Tovaangar: Mapping the Tongva Villages of LA's Past." *Los Angeles Times online*. Accessed May 9, 2019. https://www.latimes.com/projects/la-me-tongva-map/.

Harris, Angela P., and Carmen G. González. "Introduction." In *Presumed Incompetent: Intersections of Race and Class for Women in Academia*, edited by Gabriella Gutierrez Yolanda Flores Niemann, Carmen G. González, and Angela P. Harris. Logan: University State University Press, 2012.

Josey, E.J. ed., *Black Librarian in America*. Metuchen: Scarecrow Press, 1970.

Kendrick, Kaetrena Davis, Amanda M. Leftwich, and Twanna Hodge. "Providing care and community in times of crisis: The BIPOC in LIS Mental Health Summits." *College & Research Libraries News* [Online] 82, n. 8, (September 2021): 358–60. https://crln.acrl.org/index.php/crlnews/article/view/25125/32978.

Lee-Heart, Kiara, & Learning for Justice. "Pandemic Pedagogy: A Call to Educators to Bring Their Classrooms to Reality." Accessed March 21, 2021, https://www.learningforjustice.org/magazine/pandemic-pedagogy-a-call-to-educators-to-bring-their-classrooms-to-reality.

Marcus, Jon. "As admissions season descends, warning signs appear for low-income applicants." *The Washington Post*, February 19, 2021, https://www.washingtonpost.com/local/education/college-admissions-wealth-gap-covid/2021/02/18/8c606766-712d-11eb-b8a9-b9467510f0fe_story.html.

Martinez, Elizabeth I. *A Jaguar in the Library: The Story of the First Chicana Librarian*. Moorpark: Flor y Canto Press, 2020.

Mt. San Antonio College, "About Us: Facts and Figures," Accessed January 23, 2001. https://www.mtsac.edu/about/overview/facts-and-figures.html.

Mujeres Activas en Letras y Cambio Social (MALCS). "MALCS Mission." Accessed July 10, 2021. https://malcs.org/about.

Ochoa, Gilda L. *Academic Profiling: Latinos, Asian Americans, and the Achievement Gap*. Minnesota: University of Minnesota Press, 2013.

Pun, Raymond, and Jessica Bustos. "Understanding Barriers and Experiences of Library Advocacy Work by Library Workers of Color: An Exploratory Study." *The Political Librarian* 5, no. 1 (2021): 14. https://journals.library.wustl.edu/pollib/article/id/8558/.

Ray, Rashawn, and Alexandra Gibbons. "Why are States Banning Critical Race Theory?" *Brooking's Institution Blog, FIXGOV* (blog). Last modified November 2021. https://www.brookings.edu/blog/fixgov/2021/07/02/why-are-states-banning-critical-race-theory/.

Spring, Joel. *Deculturalization and the Struggle for Equality: A Brief History of the Education of Dominated Cultures in the United States.* New York: Routledge, 2022.

U.S. Department of Education. *Advancing Diversity and Inclusion in Higher Education: Key Data Highlights Focusing on Race and Ethnicity Promising Practices.* Washington D.C.: U.S. Department of Education, 2016. https://www2.ed.gov/rschstat/research/pubs/advancing-diversity-inclusion.pdf.

Velazquez Bean, Michelle, Teresa Aldredge, Karen Chow, Lynn Fowler, Arthur Guaracha, Tanya McGinnis, LaTonya Parker, and Graciela Saez-Kleriga. "Academic Senate for California Community Colleges." The Role of the Library Faculty in the California Community College, 2019. Accessed March 21, 2021. https://www.asccc.org/papers/role-library-faculty-california-community-college.

# Now We Are Strangers to Each Other
## Reflections on My Onboarding Process

*Dele Chinwe Ladejobi*

## Introduction

I have celebrated many years as a full-time tenured faculty member and librarian at my institution. I marked significant career milestones in my Library and Information Science (LIS) professional practice. This accomplishment would not have been possible were it not for the students and my colleagues who have mentored and encouraged me over the years and believed in my capabilities. As the current Library Department Head (DH), I have committed myself to a hands-on approach to managing the department's day-to-day operations. This environment quietly roiled with many conflicts, both personal and operational. The enterprise lacked a sense of wholeness and coherence. I could only wonder at the type of image we projected to our college community. Strangely enough, these dysfunctions became a genuine catalyst that compelled me to reach back for ideas and inspiration in the liberal and open-minded lessons originating in the days of my onboarding.

Accordingly, many of our departmental practices have taken a new direction to achieve a more equitable workplace for the library faculty, staff, and student workers. The administration aimed to break long-existing tensions and communication breakdowns, a necessary sea of change. The administration overhauled policies to become egalitarian, proactive, and involved in the library's operations. This included engaging in open meetings and supporting our coworkers to take the initiative in confidently using original ideas to improve service areas. Investing in positive workplace autonomy led to enhanced engagement that evolved into an enthusiastic, more profound student-centered commitment to creating a dependable and nurturing academic environment for our students.

The Cambridge English Dictionary defines onboarding as "the process in which new employees gain the knowledge and skills they need to become effective members of an organization."[1] A study of small businesses by Jansons revealed that a structured and thorough long-term onboarding process for new hires is a critical component of setting new employees up for success from their first day of employment.[2] Since the early 1990s, library professional associations have recognized that a positive onboarding process is a significant factor in recruiting and retaining minority employees. However, three main issues were responsible for the inadequate recruitment and retention of minority academic librarians: lack of institutional commitment to change and accountability, personal and institutional racism, and barriers to advancement and retention.[3]

Onboarding requires continuous mentoring, transparency, collaborative efforts, and effective communication across all levels of an institution or organization and involves immersing new employees in the culture of the workplace. This process "begins when a new employee is offered a position and ends when the employee is considered fully functional. It covers an employee's first year, incorporates various offices and functions, addresses the whole range of employee needs (equipment, accounts, training, networking), and is strategic in focus. Employees actively participate in the onboarding process."[4] A positive onboarding experience is essential because it promotes employee commitment and inclusivity. It helps create healthy work relations and transparent communication processes, thereby eliminating barriers obstructing shared decision-making, ultimately creating a hostile work environment.

---

1   "Onboarding," ONBOARDING | Definition in the Cambridge English Dictionary, accessed February 27, 2022, https://dictionary.cambridge.org/us/dictionary/english/onboarding.

2   Pete Jansons, "Study: Only 50% of Small Businesses Have a Structured Onboarding Process," CareerBuilder for Employers, July 18, 2017, https://resources.careerbuilder.com/small-business/more-companies-need-structured-onboarding.

3   Janice Y. Kung, K-Lee Fraser, and Dee Winn, "Diversity Initiatives to Recruit and Retain Academic Librarians: A Systematic Review," *College & Research Libraries*, 81, no. 1 (8 January 2020): 98, accessed February 28, 2022, https://doi.org/10.5860/crl.81.1.96.

4   Jolie O. Graybil, Maria Taesil Hudson Carpenter, Jerome Offord Jr., Mary Piorun, and Gary Shaffer, "Employee Onboarding: Identification of Best Practices in ACRL Libraries," *Library Management* 34, no. 3 (2013): 201. accessed February 28, 2022, https://dx.doi.org/10.1108/01435121311310897.

This chapter explains my onboarding process as a new librarian and how my experience positively shaped my professional foundation and career. Having worked at the same institution for many years, presenting my onboarding experience in a reflective narrative personalizes my story to engage the reader's understanding of how a healthy onboarding and mentoring process is critical in the retention of employees. Additionally, I will draw some noticeable comparisons between the onboarding experiences of my colleagues hired in recent years to show how a hostile work environment impacted our individual experiences by hampering our ability to build positive relationships and ultimately creating communication barriers that obstructed our decision-making process for over a decade.

## New Employee to Finding My Footing

Hall-Ellis found that "onboarding improves library retention and productivity…a well-designed and coordinated onboarding process assimilates new employees into the organization and equips them with the tools and resources needed for professional and personal success."[5] Harpelund stressed that if properly implemented, onboarding can ensure higher engagement, organizational readiness, better time-to-performance, better retention, and lower stress.[6] On the contrary, where no structured onboarding exists, there is low employee morale, less engagement, less employee confidence, and a lack of trust within the organization. Jelinek maintained that developing, implementing, and maintaining a strategic and successful employee onboarding program includes many moving pieces. This entails guiding the new employee through the correct completion of paperwork, learning about the organization's cultural norms and values, getting to know coworkers, how decisions are made, and making sure the new hire feels comfortable and empowered to work effectively by providing them with the right resources, information, and technology at the correct times.[7] The benefits of a positive onboarding process with-

---

5   Sylvia D. Hall-Ellis, "Onboarding to Improve Library Retention and Productivity," *The Bottom Line* 27, no. 4 (2014.): 138, accessed February 28, 2022, http://dx.doi.org/10.1108/BL-10-2014-0026.

6   Christian Harpelund, *Onboarding: Getting New Hires off to a Flying Start* (Bingley: Emerald Publishing Limited, 2019), 2–3.

7   Paul Jelinek, "The Impact of Good and Bad Employee Onboarding Experiences," Intelligence at Work (blog), September 17, 2020, accessed February 28, 2022, https://www.ceridian.com/blog/the-impact-of-good-and-bad-onboarding-experiences.

in an academic library include a better work environment, retention, enhanced efficiency, teamwork, reducing "miscommunication, and showing the new employees that they are valued and part of the team."[8]

The inspiring quality of leadership that existed during the formative years of my employment became instrumental in establishing the foundation of my career as a librarian. During this period, the core beliefs of my professional values were firmly laid and worked to unite the purpose of my decisions and actions to come. It was a framework of personal ethos committed to recognizing equity and diversity, consciously respecting cultural and racial sensitivity, and being intentionally inclusive. Later, as my professional responsibilities grew, these principles took another form and evolved into a teaching philosophy and pedagogy that would be purposefully structured so that each student in my courses would feel included, heard, and seen as a unique member. The success of this practice is in the feedback I receive from my students each semester. I had an unforgettable onboarding experience that truly bonded me to the college and was the best year for which an employee could ask.

My outgoing Library DH was a woman to emulate for all her accomplishments within the college and the community city-wide. She inspired me with her pioneering leadership efforts and excellent service. She was the college's first African American/Black librarian and Library DH. She was an incredible mentor and supported colleagues from diverse backgrounds, especially people of color, to serve in leadership positions at the college and other institutions. She was instrumental in hiring the second African American/Black librarian at the college, who later served as the Library DH. She was the first person of color to serve as the faculty Academic Senate President and the Faculty Union President, respectively. She paved the way for Black, Indigenous, and People of Color (BIPOC) Librarians and inspired a Latino librarian to serve as the second person of color elected to Academic Senate President. As her participation in city affairs expanded, she was elected to serve as the first African-American Board member on the Unified School District Board of Education. She served four terms as the Board President.

---

8   Jamia Williams, "The Importance of Onboarding within the Academic Library." *Advocacy, Legislation & Issues* (Online), June 18, 2021, accessed February 28, 2022, https://www.ala.org/advocacy/diversity/odlos-blog/academic-libraries-onboarding.

Indisputably, she was a trailblazer and left an indelible mark on me as an optimistic Black woman. She exemplified the professional qualities that would open themselves to become part of a person's onboarding experience. I was her third Black Librarian hired before she retired from the college. I am currently serving for the third time as the Library DH. My incoming Library DH mirrored her qualities. He, too, was a valuable supervisor, mentor, and role model to me. He was meticulous about attention to detail and had excellent leadership skills. Within the first days of our acquaintance, it became clear that he had given thought and preparation to ease me into my new role in the department. Our DH provided my entire office to ensure my immediate ability to start work successfully. When I arrived on my first day, everything was ready for me to commence work and join departmental operations. We had lunch together, during which he introduced me to our coworkers and colleagues from within and outside the library department at both campuses. Afterward, he would occasionally invite other librarians and me for breaks at the faculty lounge located inside the cafeteria. This was intentional on his part to strengthen ties within the department, and we would talk freely about anything or anyone. It was also the perfect networking place to meet other faculty members. We even had a few things in common. We both share the same birthday, graduated from the same library graduate school, and are passionate about cataloging. He served as the cataloging librarian until my hire. When the library technician who had worked with him for years as a copy cataloger refused to recognize "the new, young lady," i.e., me, our DH told her in my presence to do whatever I said in my role as her immediate supervisor. This changed the game immediately. She showered me with respect, and in time, we became coworkers who trusted and depended on each other. Our positive new relationship would not have been possible had it not been for the proactive guidance of our DH.

At about the same time, the dean of our school, a white female with a brisk, energetic managerial style, took the initiative to ensure the new faculty in her school would have an optimal and collegial introduction to our workplace. As a part of an extensive onboarding process, she made sure her secretary gave each of us a folder with information about "who's who" on campus with the names and functions of every building on both campuses. We received a schedule of the dates and times when she would walk with us around campuses to meet and greet other administrators, faculty, and staff. She introduced us (and had us introduce ourselves) at every department meeting, gathering, and on College Day, an annual welcome back event for administrators, faculty, and staff, and an opportunity where the administrators set the tone for the next Academic Year. The tone is convivial and upbeat as everyone receives updates on the college's recent accomplishments, present concerns, issues, and higher education goals for the future. Our dean encouraged us to participate in professional development activities actively and even found funds to support us financially. She genuinely cared about our professional well-being and urged us to chat with her about any concerns or issues.

All the librarians worked collegially inside the library, and we did not allow our differences to interfere with our work, including the department's policies and procedures. Within our group, the continuum of onboarding standards served to further the immersive process and solidified and confirmed my abilities. This motivated me to step fully into my role. I joined in writing reports required by the institution, including the department plan, program review, and the library's section of the college accreditation report. We wrote justifications for money to buy books for the library textbook reserves and general collections, hired staff and student workers, opened both campus libraries during the summer, and made budget augmentations to employ more part-time librarians to help cover the reference desks. We all wrote or contributed to these, and I felt fully engaged.

We practiced inclusivity to the core. We agreed that all communications originating from the library should be reviewed by and incorporate input from *all of us*. No one, not even the DH, disseminated any memo, email, or any other form of communication outside the department without the item being first reviewed by all the full-time and often part-time librarians. We were like the proverbial "well-oiled wheel." We valued face-to-face professional conversations and, during meetings, discussed how we could accomplish our goal of showcasing the library's services and resources. Together, we would share our ideas and strategize on which campus-wide committees to join to represent the department to its best advantage comprehensively. We divided up professional development activities, allowing everyone to attend multiple workshops, training, and conferences. We shared what we learned and offered to train each other. There was no competition among us. We had healthy working relationships, and everyone in the department profited.

Group solidarity, cooperation, and goodwill pertain to the pressures of the work environment and are central precepts of onboarding. It transpires through example. Onboarding demonstrates the experienced individual's commitment to conscientiously extend receptivity to the newcomer, confirming and validating their place and position within the commonalities of academia. The onboarding process aims to create an attachment between the new employee and the institution. As is within human nature, attachment begins through positive human relations. At that time, in my department, onboarding was the foremost guiding principle put in practice to embed positive, collegial associations between employees deeply. Our group unity was a product of lessons learned in onboarding.

## Seasoned Employee

The goal of the onboarding process includes familiarizing new employees with an organization's strategies and assisting new employees with understanding how their work will contribute to the organization's mission and vision.[9] My four-year probationary tenure review process was a learning, nurturing, and mentoring period. My tenure faculty committee members encouraged me to gain experience by serving on various committees to learn about shared governance and college culture. I served on several college-wide committees, including curriculum, instructional planning, and accreditation. I still serve as the library department's representative in the faculty union. Being a member of various committees helped me engage and interact with faculty from other departments and learn firsthand about the faculty work processes, including contracts, wages, evaluation, and improving working conditions.

I recall my experience serving as a member of the accreditation committee. Part of my duties was to meet and consult with administrators at all institutional levels. It was challenging work because I had no previous experience with some of the tasks ahead, and the lack of background made it a daunting prospect. There was an enormous amount of statistical data to manage. Even so, my colleagues continued to encourage and remind me of the excellent service I provided to our students. The chair of the accreditation committee was endlessly

---

9   Jolie O. Graybil, et. al, "Employee Onboarding," 202.

patient and supportive. The chair walked me through the steps, including helping me schedule appointments with colleagues I needed to interview to complete my tasks. He would often come to my office to deliver all the reports and statistical data I needed and assist me with interpreting the data. He loved numbers and took great pride in explaining these to me. I do not like numbers; nothing he said made sense to me. He figured out ways to simplify these for me. Ultimately, I completed a comprehensive report, and he told me he was very proud of my work. That was the last time I served as a member of the Accreditation Committee. I still contribute to writing the library portion of the Accreditation Report.

Although we had some challenges, these were the years when librarians from diverse backgrounds worked together regardless of our differences, respected each other's perspectives, and acknowledged each other's beliefs and backgrounds. We recognized that our cultural foundations and experiences helped to mold who we have become. We did not allow our different viewpoints to deter us from our purpose because we knew that, in the end, the students would suffer the consequences of our discord. Therefore, we stayed focused on promoting student success, as evidenced in our actions through every aspect of library operations and endeavors. Best of all, there was transparency. We were unafraid to dialogue, no matter how uncomfortable we were with the topic.

Years later, hiring a new dean opened a progressive era and made a positive impact by giving impetus to the career aspirations of BIPOC information workers. She paved the way for us to advance to the department chair position in our respective areas. Under the new dean's leadership, encouragement, and support, BIPOC Library Department Heads, including me, emerged because she believed we could do the job just as well as anyone else. She questioned why there had not been a BIPOC Library DH in many years. She discovered that all of us had school-aged children, who made it difficult to fully commit to the administrative duties of the DH and our work as full-time faculty. She cared about the welfare of employees and was flexible with individual schedules to ensure that our work did not take away from family time. She demonstrated authentic leadership in recognizing and addressing challenges in a way that would provide opportunities for professional growth. Her characteristic approach was to be supportive rather than critical, which helped to spark everyone's confidence in mastering the new system. Those were the good old days when people talked *to* each other and meant what they said when we used "my" to describe the higher-ups in terms of a close, connected affiliation: *my* dean and *my* DH because they *knew* and *valued* me.

## Latter Years

In recent years, we have experienced persistent discord and ongoing contradictions between principle and practice. This created instability and deep divisions plaguing our library department, eventually becoming the distressing new normal. Some librarians, especially Black librarians, feel that our voices are unheard and that our work is marginalized, discounted, and treated as incidental. Today's new hires often need the healthy onboarding, mentoring, and work experience that made me the resilient librarian I am today. Instead, they receive a traumatizing experience. There is a major breakdown in the fabric of our department and a marked decline in communication with each other, both interpersonal and group, as well as verbal and written. Our hostile, exclusionary work environment has impacted our professional experiences by hampering our ability to build positive relationships and ultimately created a myriad of barriers that obstructed our decision-making process for nearly a decade. The library department stagnated and went into a long period of decline. We are worse than strangers in our interactions with one another.

Compared to my onboarding experience, which I described earlier, our newly hired librarians' introduction to community college librarianship has been very discouraging, mentally draining, and disillusioning. Usually, new faculty benefitted from the deliberate and seamless integration into college life and assumed their rights and roles in step with their colleagues. They learned about the contract and college culture and networked with their cohort. Some departments, such as ours, deviated from the rule of lending departmental guidance and support at the most interpersonal level. This was due to changes in the college administration that filtered down into the library's leadership. The omission was handily justified using the rationale that tutelage received by new faculty at the college level is sufficient for them to function proficiently in performing assigned tasks and meeting faculty requirements, especially during the tenure review process.

Such is the case in our library department. The college hired two BIPOC librarians in the same year. They only received onboarding routinely coordinated for the new hire cohort by the Union, Academic Senate, or the college. I was informed about this matter as the union representative. One of the BIPOC librarians reported her frustration at finding on the first day, there was no office, computer, cabinets, or telephone available to her. In short, she never felt welcomed. She also reported that the Library DH has yet to meet with her regularly about her progress and understanding of job responsibilities, such as reports, job duties and other faculty duties. However, the DH always pointed out her mistakes or mishaps. At the time of my onboarding, the department heads viewed their position as a stakeholder in the success or failure of new faculty. They were eager to support them during this transition to academic life. A new faculty member could always depend on the DH to be at hand to make introductions, ease conversation, and help spark meaningful connections. In contrast, as she attended campus-wide events alone, people would ask superficial questions such as when she started working here and where she had worked. Remembering the exhilaration of my introduction as a new faculty, this was troubling and confusing.

In retrospect, this change is a paradigm shift. Until now, these duties would have transferred to the "new generation." But it was not, and the omission became a point of origin for some of our most serious problems. Onboarding advocated teamwork over autonomy and transparency over private agendas or alliances. It served as a memorable, singular period set aside for new employees. Through onboarding, supportive new professional relationships would emerge, and they would be welcomed and mentored through a faceted understanding of the responsibilities and obligations of achieving tenure. Some years later, a weakening in this belief system occurred. It was understated and so subtly hidden within the library department that I could not clearly articulate it. The deterioration of our internal organization had begun to creep in. Initially, I felt disconcerted by the shift, and in the interest of keeping the peace, I decided to weather through my uneasy perception of this strange interlude. However, the red flags started to rise as full-time librarians stopped having our bimonthly meetings to discuss matters of importance to the departmental goals. Before this opportunity to communicate with each other was severed, librarians would unanimously agree on a resolution and initiate accountable steps for improvement. Inertia spread through the department. There was no longer a leader whose purpose was to act as a vehicle in moving our decisions forward. Librarians would find out later that the DH "discussed these decisions further" with personally selected librarians and, after the concurrence of a chosen few, decided against acting on the decision we had already agreed upon as a group.

Unsurprisingly, going up the chain of command, there has developed a feeling of uncertainty regarding our relationship with higher administrators. It is problematic when the library deans do not have an LIS degree and lack any relevant experience in the field, consequently having limited critical knowledge of the intricacies of library operations. Our full-time faculty contract already recognizes the department heads as the ombudsperson, and they are supposed to represent the faculty (of which librarians are part) and all members of their departments to the deans positively and equally without favoritism. The Library DH is our primary conduit of formal and informal communication to the Dean. We relied on the strength of character of the DH to fight the temptation to exploit this ready access to the Dean as an opportunity to push their agendas, opinions, and partialities to specific individuals. Over time, it became clear that this is precisely what was happening; some of us were being misquoted and misrepresented.

We attempted several honest endeavors towards building and supporting team efforts to open an active dialogue to air our perspectives, sincerely address controversial issues, and find remedies. All efforts to initiate discussions and uphold collegial practices that build trust and make an organization function optimally were swept under the rug or dismissed outright. In our department, all these factors magnified the empowerment and perception of entitlement for the privileged few. They were detrimental to the healthy well-being of employees as they questioned one's work and value, but also inhibited professional growth because people were not valued or heard. These practices resulted in undue stress for some library workers; they contributed to discouragement, resistance, distrust, and dissatisfaction, especially for the BIPOC librarians and librarians from other races who risked being penalized because their viewpoints differed from those of the leadership.

To accomplish our goals today, we must encourage good leadership through transparency and accountability. We must start by reviewing our policies and practices, amending them to reflect the changing times, accepting our flaws and weaknesses, and building on our strengths. This will take courage and hard work. The librarians have our tasks cut out for us. As much as possible, my goal is to restore transparency, encourage a healthy work-life balance, and create an inclusive environment in our department where no one would feel that their voice is not heard.

## Conclusion

What I described in my onboarding journey is also a checklist for the practical steps of ethical awareness of onboarding goals to embrace for employee retention and success. The essential nurturing of the onboarding experience formed the core of my career as a librarian and was encouraged by people who kindled a sense of revelation about the potential of academic professionalism, values, and fellowship. Their receptivity highlighted the kindness of these individuals to me as a newcomer, their humor, and their friendly recognition that I brought my singular aptitudes and talents. I felt attached to the institution through the mentorship of colleagues at every organizational level because of my successful onboarding. These tenets are essential to the central theme of onboarding and quite eloquently capture the crucial elements for a successful onboarding process.

We recently hired a full-time tenure-track librarian. I look forward to introducing my new colleague to our department's practices of transparency and inclusion. For me, it comes as a long-awaited opportunity to restore the traditions of onboarding and secure memorable experiences that are indispensable in inspiring them to continue to discover their strengths throughout their career. People may question whether the onboarding experience I described in my formative years could ever exist again at my institution, specifically in our library. I believe my experiences show that an effective onboarding model does work. It is an inevitable component of productivity—the natural reaction against change and the consequent struggle to adapt. Not everyone looks forward to the experience; even the naysayers would not deny the high stakes to be won or lost.

Our future leadership skills must evolve to embrace the complexity of a diverse and inclusive workplace. It will be a worthwhile and enduring transformation. More than ever, I firmly believe that each of my library colleagues has experience and hidden potential. We must diversify our styles and try different strategies to reach them. For the first time in many years, full-time librarians actively engage in decision-making through weekly meetings and work together to standardize department policies and processes. We convene action-based, project-oriented meetings to address and plan specific tasks and then follow each stage through to completion. Although differences will naturally arise, we work together as a team. I am confident of my leadership abilities, ability to work well with diverse groups of people, and communication skills, which I believe have been successfully employed to motivate and bring out the best in everyone I have worked with. Our department policies and training manuals are being revised or newly written with input from other library employees across many work areas. Their thoughtful and careful examination of library processes reveals new perceptions and outlooks regarding our service responsibilities.

Institutions of higher learning will benefit from my experience by examining their onboarding processes and identifying the steps to reaching out and establishing trust when cultivating a new generation of talented educators. Looking and listening outward, I can see the same challenges troubling other institutions. They are often benignly unaware of the image they project and the lack of a human wholeness that reaches out to include everyone. I would urge them to find common concerns left over from their best philosophies and use these to discover a new way forward in establishing an academic community that provides a relatable, welcoming, and positive work environment for BIPOC librarians.

## *Bibliography*

Cable, Daniel M., Francesca Gino, and Bradley R. Staats. "Reinventing Employee Onboarding." *MIT Sloan Management Review* 54, no. 3 (Spring, 2013): 23–28.

Edwards, Ronald G. "Recruiting More Minorities to the Library Profession: Responding to the Need for Diversity." *Association of College & Research Libraries*, 1999. Accessed July 28, 2022. https://www.ala.org/acrl/sites/ala.org.acrl/files/content/conferences/pdf/edwards99.pdf.

Graybill, Jolie O., Maria Taesil Hudson Carpenter, Jerome Offord Jr, Mary Piorun, and Gary Shaffer. "Employee Onboarding: Identification of Best Practices in ACRLLibraries." *Library Management* 34, no. 3 (2013): 200–18. https://dx.doi.org/10.1108/01435121311310897.

Hall-Ellis, Sylvia, D. "Onboarding to Improve Library Retention and Productivity." *The Bottom Line* 27, no. 4 (2014): 138–41. http://dx.doi.org/10.1108/BL-10-2014-0026.

Harpelund, Christian. *Onboarding: Getting New Hires Off to a Flying Start*. Bingley: Emerald Publishing Limited, 2019. https://doi.org/10.1108/9781787695818.

Jansons, Pete. "Study: Only 50% of Small Businesses Have a Structured Onboarding Process." CareerBuilder for Employers. July 18, 2017. Accessed February 28, 2022. https://resources.careerbuilder.com/small-business/more-companies-need-structured-onboarding.

Jelinek, Paul. "The Impact of Good and Bad Employee Onboarding Experiences." *Intelligence at Work* (blog). September 17, 2020. Accessed February 28, 2022. https://www.ceridian.com/blog/the-impact-of-good-and-bad-onboarding-experiences.

Jimenez, M.F., Laverty, T.M., Bombaci, S.P. et al. "Underrepresented Faculty Play a Disproportionate Role in Advancing Diversity and Inclusion." *Nature Ecology & Evolution* 3, no. 7 (2019): 1030–1033. https://doi.org/10.1038/s41559-019-0911-5.

Kung, Janice Y., K-Lee Fraser, and Dee Winn. "Diversity Initiatives to Recruit and Retain Academic Librarians: A Systematic Review." *College & Research Libraries* vol. 81, no. 1 (8 January 2020): 96–108. https://doi.org/10.5860/crl.81.1.96.

"A Leadership Guide for Promoting Race Equity and Inclusion in the Workplace Web." November 2019. Accessed February 28, 2022. https://scchildren.org/wp-content/uploads/Leadership_Guide_for_Promoting_RFI_in_the_Workplace_web.pdf.

"Onboarding." *ONBOARDING | Definition in the Cambridge English Dictionary*. Accessed February 27, 2022. https://dictionary.cambridge.org/us/dictionary/english/onboarding.

"Report on Onboarding and Orientation for Librarians and Other Library Staff." (Online) April 2014. Accessed February 28, 2022. https://www.mcgill.ca/maut/files/maut/pic_onboarding_and_orientation_report_-_april_2014.pdf.

Snyder, Lori, and Erin Crane. "Developing and Implementing an Onboarding Program for an Academic Library: Strategies and Methods." *Library Leadership & Management* vol. 30, no. 3 (2016): 1–6. Accessed February 28, 2022. https://doi.org/10.5860/llm.v30i3.7164.

"Steps to a Successful Onboarding Process." 2009. *Workforce Management* 88, no. 7 (Jun 22, 2009): 1.

Wilkin, Binnie Tate. "Bobbie Smith: Former Coordinator of Libraries Long Beach City College and Recently Retired Member and President Long Beach Unified School District Board of Education." In *African American Librarians in the Far West: Pioneers and Trailblazers*, 221–28. Lanham, Maryland: Scarecrow Press, 2006.

Williams, Jamia. "The Importance of Onboarding within the Academic Library." *Advocacy, Legislation & Issues* (Online), June 18, 2021. https://www.ala.org/advocacy/diversity/odlos-blog/academic-libraries-onboarding.

# Racelighting
## Understanding BIPOC community college library workers' experience with questioning their own realities

*Terezita Reyes Overduin*

## Introduction

Racelighting is a process described by scholars Dr. J. Luke Wood and Dr. Frank Harris III as "the process whereby People of Color question their thoughts and actions due to systemically delivered racialized messages that make them second guess their own lived experiences [and realities] with racism."[1] It is related to the psychological phenomena of gaslighting,[2] first defined by Barton and Whitehead, wherein victims question their reality, memories, and sanity. Racelighting applies the concept of gaslighting to the long-term effects of racial microaggressions on Black, Indigenous, and People of Color (BIPOC) and provides a framework for understanding the lived experiences of BIPOC community college library workers in their daily work and interactions.

Wood and Harris's work has helped me understand and work through my experience as a community college librarian. My first two years as a BIPOC community college librarian were fraught with confusing

---

1. J. Luke Wood and Frank Harris III, "Racelighting: A Prevalent Version of Gaslighting Facing People of Color–Higher Education," *Diverse Issues in Higher Education* (February 12, 2021): https://diverseeducation.com/article/205210/.

2. Russell Barton and J. A. Whitehead, "The Gas-Light Phenomenon," *Lancet* (London, England) 1, no. 7608 (June 21, 1969): 1258–60, https://doi.org/10.1016/s0140-6736(69)92133-3.

interpersonal and organizational interactions. I needed help navigating the work environment, the organizational structure, and the closed-door approach to library work. I felt that I wasn't understanding something or doing something wrong and that my work wasn't valuable. However, after finding a community with other BIPOC library faculty and staff, I understood this was a pervasive problem. I found that the confusion and doubt I experienced were the product of institutional and interpersonal racism and even had a name: racelighting. Storytelling is rich and helps marginalized groups create community and understand the institutional structures we find ourselves. It was only through hearing the stories of others that I was able to understand and cope with my own experiences. This is especially helpful in the esoteric structures of higher education institutions, where each campus climate is different and nuanced. This chapter seeks to analyze the experiences of BIPOC library workers through the lens of racelighting, using my own story as an example.

## My Experience as a Community College Librarian

Acclimating to a position in a new organization is always a challenging process. New jobs mean new bosses, coworkers, offices, and dynamics. As I entered a new librarian position at one of the California Community Colleges (CCC), I tried to put my best foot forward and forge new connections with my colleagues. As a professional librarian coming from California State University with seven years of experience behind me, I was excited to begin discovering what working was like at a community college. I found that the administrative structure within this new institution was complicated to make sense of; in my previous academic librarian positions, the library department had a dean and a dedicated administrator responsible for the library's staff, faculty, and operations. Additionally, my previous deans were former librarians or someone with thorough knowledge of the processes of an academic library. However, while the community college library department had a dean, they were rarely present in the library. Their office was in another building, and I didn't see them or get a chance to meet with them until I'd been an employee of the college for two months. The dean was also the supervisor of several other departments and programs. They had very little time to spend in the physical library building, much less time to think about our department and the needs of its staff and faculty. Later, I discovered that Human Resources (HR) and the institution at large viewed the dean as my boss and the library's first-level supervisor, even though the dean had very little first-hand knowledge of how the library operated or what went on within its walls. As a new faculty member at the college, it was difficult to understand the administrative structure of a department with very little administrative presence and why the library had an administrator who did not thoroughly understand the day-to-day workings of the department they were assigned to oversee.

The person who showed me around and gave me my first tasks was the library coordinator. The library department (and every other department on campus) had a coordinator, a faculty member from that department chosen by the dean in consultation with other department faculty. In other departments, the person in this position would primarily oversee scheduling classes and field student complaints. Things in the library were more ambiguous. As a department without classes, the coordinator would instead supervise the scheduling of daily library operations and librarian schedules, including library instruction sessions, reference desk shifts, and field student complaints. The library is a unique place on campus, where coordination of programs, projects, and schedules is the heart of all activity. Thus, the library coordinator was a "de facto" position of management and power for our department.

My first indication that power and leadership structures in this institution were capricious came about four weeks into the job. I'd just finished a casual chat with another librarian about a program they had worked on. After leaving their office, the library coordinator called me into her office and asked me what I had spoken about with the other librarian. I told her, and she asked me to check with her before communicating with other faculty. Confused, I asked her to repeat herself. She did: "Please check with me before meeting with other librarians." I was in an utter state of shock! Was I just banned from speaking with my colleagues unless the coordinator was aware in advance? I didn't know what to do or what to say. I just said, "Okay," smiled, and left the room. Returning to my desk, I still couldn't make heads or tails of what happened. Had I misunderstood her? Was there something I was missing? After a few days, I assumed that there must be something that I wasn't understanding, and I decided to pretend the whole thing didn't happen.

I discovered that this wouldn't be a single, isolated incident. I continued to be distrusted and disrespected. Any input I managed to provide was not acknowledged or discussed; my questions and concerns went unanswered. Specific rules or policies only applied to me or were not required of other faculty. This confused me. I'd succeeded in other academic librarian positions previously. I'd done good work in those different positions. Why was this happening? Thinking I was still misunderstanding something, I continued to ask anyone I could, whether in the library department or elsewhere on campus, for clarification on how the management of the library was supposed to work and what precisely the role of the coordinator was. After getting different answers depending on who I asked, I felt lost. I was disoriented and frustrated and could not contribute meaningfully to this library and its institution.

## Racelighting as a Process

Racelighting is part of a detailed process comprising many components. Wood and Harris describe the process as beginning with antecedents such as White supremacy and systemic oppression.[3] These antecedents inform interpersonal biases, which lead to the expression of microaggressions, which result in the BIPOC experience of questioning their reality (e.g., racelighting). They explain, "although microaggressions are the means by which someone experiences racelighting, the process through which these messages serve to accumulate and distort the realities of People of Color is race lighting."[4] As BIPOC go through their daily work, the cumulative toll of microaggressions of all kinds causes them to question their experiences and blame themselves for the negative interpersonal interactions. BIPOC suffers when, in truth, these experiences are the result of the conscious or unconscious biases upheld by the normalized societal structures of white supremacy. Wood and Harris further expound, "...when experiencing racelighting, People of Color may be led to second guess their experiences, feelings, capabilities, knowledge, decision-making, recollections, and basic humanity."[5] Racelighting is part of the interpersonal

---

[3] Wood and Harris III, "Racelighting in the Normal Realities," 18.

[4] Wood and Harris III, 21.

[5] Wood and Harris III, "Racelighting: A Prevalent Version of Gaslighting Facing People of Color–Higher Education," accessed October 14, 2022, https://www.diverseeducation.com/opinion/article/15108651/racelighting-a-prevalent-version-of-gaslighting-facing-people-of-color.

structures of racism as experienced in BIPOC's daily lives and professional environments.

As BIPOC have daily experiences with bias and racism in the form of microaggressions, both in personal and professional contexts, we often come away wondering, "What just happened? Did they say that? I must not have heard correctly." As a result of the subliminal message in microaggressions that the person is somehow inferior, BIPOC wonders if they, themselves, are to blame. The concept of racelighting highlights these reactions and collects them into a definable phenomenon. Wood and Harris further argue that the process of racelighting leads to other race-related psychological phenomena, such as Racial Battle Fatigue, Stereotype Threat, and Imposter Syndrome.[6]

Racelighting is a process by which BIPOC are disoriented: they wonder what happened and why it happened and try to dismiss it by labeling it as a misunderstanding. In this confused state, they may be hesitant to ascribe these experiences to racialized messages or race-based rationale. Especially if there are other conflating circumstances, BIPOC may look for other possible explanations to decipher our experiences. Some questions might include: is it because of my gender, age, or sexual orientation, is it because of my position within the institution, or is it just because of my personal views, methodologies, or approaches to work? Nevertheless, we should not allow the intersection of our identities or any other circumstance to excuse microaggressions and their effects. BIPOC library workers should remember that the primary outcome of racelighting is to disorient the affected individual.[7] People who experience racelighting are unsure of their experiences, and that doubt seeps into the individual's consciousness, causing them to begin doubting many aspects of their thoughts, abilities, and identity. If a BIPOC library worker has an interaction that results in the outcomes of racelighting, it would be unreasonable to discount race as a possible factor.

---

6   William Smith, "Black Faculty Coping with Racial Battle Fatigue," in *A Long Way to Go: Conversations about Race by African American Faculty and Graduate Students* ed. Peter Lang (New York: Peter Lang, 2004), 171–90; Claude M. Steele, "A Threat in the Air: How Stereotypes Shape Intellectual Identity and Performance," *American Psychologist* 52, no. 6 (1997): 613–29, https://doi.org/10.1037/0003-066X.52.6.613; Pauline Rose Clance and Suzanne Ament Imes, "The Imposter Phenomenon in High Achieving Women: Dynamics and Therapeutic Intervention," *Psychotherapy: Theory, Research & Practice* 15, no. 3 (1978): 241–47, https://doi.org/10.1037/h0086006.

7   Wood and Harris III, "Racelighting in the Normal Realities," 10.

## Racelighting and Microaggressions in the LIS Profession

Racelighting is a natural extension of literature documenting microaggressions and racist structures in the LIS profession. Alabi's research has established microaggressions as a core component of the LIS profession and working environment.[8] Alabi's research also demonstrates that the racial microaggressions and disparity of treatment based on race that is a factor (e.g., observed) in other groups and working environments also persists in the library and information science (LIS) field. Additionally, Sweeney and Cooke's work analyzing informal conversations on social media surrounding microaggressions reveals a wealth of evidence that the structures of white supremacy and institutionalized racism are alive and well among some of the members of our profession.[9] They also recognize that microaggressions play a significant role in perpetuating power structures, noting that "microaggressions can simultaneously reaffirm the privilege and power of those delivering the microaggressive remark and disenfranchise the person at whom the remark is aimed."[10]

Further, as library staff and faculty, we also struggle with the perceptions and stereotypes that students, other faculty, and academia hold against the Library and Information Science (LIS) profession. The work of Arroyo-Ramirez et al. discusses the role of microaggressions in the experiences of BIPOC librarians as both coming from internal (colleagues and co-workers) and external (students, staff, faculty, and administration from outside the library) sources. They explain that microaggressions aimed at those in the library profession based on our occupation and the assumptions that people make about libraries and library workers.[11] Alwan, Doan, and Garcia's research demonstrates the wide range of microaggressions made against librarians based solely on their occupation and the "subordinate" status of

---

8   Jaena Alabi, "Racial Microaggressions in Academic Libraries: Results of a Survey of Minority and Non-Minority Librarians," *The Journal of Academic Librarianship* 41, no. 1 (January 1, 2015): 47–53, https://doi.org/10.1016/j.acalib.2014.10.008.

9   Miriam E. Sweeney and Nicole A. Cooke, "You're So Sensitive! How LIS Professionals Define and Discuss Microaggressions Online," *The Library Quarterly* 88, no. 4 (October 1, 2018): 375–90. https://doi.org/10.1086/699270.

10  Sweeney and Cooke, "You're So Sensitive!," 384.

11  Arroyo-Ramirez, et. al., "The Reach of a Long-Arm Stapler: Calling in Microaggressions in the LIS Field through Zine Work," *Library Trends* 67, no. 1 (2018): 107–08, https://doi.org/10.1353/lib.2018.0028.

librarians on college and university campuses as viewed by other faculty members of different disciplines.[12] This may be influenced by the fact that librarians' work is often not fully understood or appreciated by our fellow faculty, administration, or the institution broadly.[13] The assumptions and stereotypes about librarians and library work are another source of bias against our work and another facet of intersectionality that library workers must grapple with.

## Administrative Response

As I continued in this position, I tried different approaches to library work at my community college, such as focusing on my strengths or student needs. I joined this profession to help others, especially marginalized first-generation students like myself. I focused on projects tackling equity issues such as library anxiety, access, and user experience. I hoped that if I didn't interact as much with my colleagues, I would have fewer negative interactions and build my credibility. However, this did not help to rectify the problems I had in my new position, nor did it result in my being able to contribute meaningfully to the library's work with students. My coworkers publicly belittled my ideas and suggestions, and the administration told me that my thoughts were not worthy of the organization's time and effort in one way or another: my project was not a "priority," or it was not in line with "what we've always done." Despite multiple attempts and approaches, I could not contribute or grow in my new position. I began contacting my dean and HR as the problems persisted and worsened. They insisted that the library coordinator had no authority and was not a manager; therefore, the administration didn't have to correct or apologize for any negative interactions with them. Further, my only manager was the dean, who had no negative interactions with me and had never witnessed any negative interactions between library faculty. HR and the dean advised me to continue documenting my experiences and let them know when something happened. I did so, and the response was

---

12 Ahmed Alwan, Joy Doan, and Eric Garcia. "Microaggressions as a Barrier to Effective Collaboration Between Teaching Faculty and Academic Librarians: An Analysis of the Results of a US and Canadian Survey," *The International Journal of Information, Diversity, & Inclusion* 2, no. 3 (2018): 43, https://doi.org/10.33137/ijidi.v2i3.32191.

13 Jody Condit Fagan, et. al., "Librarian, Faculty, and Student Perceptions of Academic Librarians: Study Introduction and Literature Review," *New Review of Academic Librarianship* 27, no. 1 (January 2, 2021): 38–75, https://doi.org/10.1080/13614533.2019.1691026.

the same each time: "Thank you for letting us know." This response and the coordinator position itself shielded the administration from any responsibility for incidents of racism or other mistreatments and consequently perpetuated the racelighting in my workplace. Without validation, recognition, or support from upper management, I continued questioning my reality and blaming myself. I questioned my thoughts, reactions, perception of what was happening, and my worth and value as a librarian. I found that the very structure of the institution was a means of oppressing and silencing BIPOC library workers.

## *Combating Racelighting with Community*

Indeed, the work environment I found myself in was fraught with distrust and suspicion. It took me a while to make personal connections with my coworkers. Eventually, I befriended other BIPOC library workers, and once we overcame the distrust that permeated the environment, we shared our experiences. I came to learn that I wasn't the only one experiencing these issues; just about every other BIPOC library worker had similar negative interpersonal experiences while doing their work in this library. Additionally, we all shared some facet of racelighting because of these encounters.

Finding other colleagues and allies who could confirm, support, and validate my experiences was of enormous value. The racelighting and gaslighting process necessitates that the individual removes themselves from others who support or validate their experiences.[14] Once others confirm an individual's experience, thoughts, and reality, the spell of isolation is broken. Developing these connections and the validation that comes from sharing our stories allows us to "be seen as valued and respected contributors to the profession, increasing the potential for us to see ourselves as leaders who may inspire others."[15] In their work analyzing the experiences of BIPOC women science faculty, Rodrigues, Mendenhall, and Clancy found that "without sufficient social support, isolated faculty were more likely to internalize their colleagues' gaslighting and question their experiences," while "those faculty who did

---

14  Wood and Harris III, "Racelighting in the Normal Realities."

15  Torie Quiñonez, Lalitha Nataraj, and Antonia Olivas, "The Praxis of Relation, Validation, and Motivation: Articulating LIS Collegiality through a CRT Lens," in *Knowledge Justice: Disrupting Library and Information Studies through Critical Race Theory*, ed. Sofia Y. Leung and Jorge R. López-McKnight (The MIT Press, 2021), 258, https://doi.org/10.7551/mitpress/11969.003.0018.

have adequate social support better contextualized and externalized their experience by recognizing that the fault lay with systemic and interpersonal oppression, not their own abilities."[16] Once, I found supportive coworkers who validated my struggle and experienced it themselves. I no longer felt like I was the problem or that my work and efforts were worthless. Wood and Harris also encourage BIPOC to identify like-minded communities, explaining that community-building "dispel[s] the seeming legitimacy of microaggressive messages" by allowing BIPOC to confirm and validate each other's experiences.[17]

### Combating Racelighting with Self-Care

Wood and Harris recommend three other strategies to combat the effects of racelighting in addition to community-building; they are active proponents of self-care, encouraging readers to "care for themselves by exercising, meditating, praying, being part of a religious community, and practicing healthy eating patterns."[18] Certainly, self-care and mindfulness are powerful tools in dealing with stress, and there has recently been a surge of resources for library professionals on the topic, especially in the wake of the COVID-19 pandemic, including resources from ACRL, the *MindfulinLIS* blog, and *Renewals*.[19] I benefitted from my friends and family network, religious community, and creative outlets such as writing.

### Combating Racelighting with the Power of Naming

Further, they recommend that individuals affected by racelighting educate themselves on the mechanisms of racism, such as bias, racial microaggressions, racial battle fatigue, stereotype threat, and

---

16. Michelle A. Rodrigues, Ruby Mendenhall, and Kathryn B. H. Clancy, "'There's Realizing and Then There's Realizing': How Social Support Can Counter Gaslighting of Women of Color Scientists," *Journal of Women and Minorities in Science and Engineering* 27, no. 2 (2021), 18. https://doi.org/10.1615/JWomenMinorScienEng.2020034630.

17. Wood and Harris III, "Racelighting in the Normal Realities," 40.

18. Wood and Harris III, 39.

19. Chase Ollis, "LibGuides: Pandemic Resources for Academic Libraries: Self-Care and New Ways of Working," accessed July 30, 2021, https://acrl.libguides.com/pandemic/self-care-home; Kaetrena Davis Kendrick, Amanda M. Leftwich, and Twanna Hodge, "Providing Care and Community in Times of Crisis: The BIPOC in LIS Mental Health Summits," *College & Research Libraries News*, 82, no. 8 (September 3, 2021), https://doi.org/10.5860/crln.82.8.358; "Mindfulinlis," Mindfulinlis (blog), accessed February 4, 2022, https://mindfulinlis.wordpress.com; "Renewals," Renewals (blog), accessed February 4, 2022, https://renewerslis.wordpress.com/.

imposter syndrome. They argue that a deeper understanding of these issues "provide a sense of control and a language to discuss the issues BIPOC face in their lives."[20] This power of naming and enlightenment is real and quite substantial. Davis and Ernst assert that "recognizing the process and developing narratives to resist the confines of gaslighting—or at the very least name it as what it is—automatically diminishes some of its power."[21] When I first learned of racelighting and its role in BIPOC's daily lives, I felt a weight had been lifted. After attending a workshop on this topic, everything suddenly made sense after months of disoriented, disjointed interactions that left me wondering why all the pieces of my experience suddenly fell into place. I gained a fuller understanding of what was happening in my interpersonal interactions at work. That understanding allowed me to name and expel the racialized messages that were constant in my work life.

## *Combating Racelighting by Leaving*

Lastly, Wood and Harris encourage those who find themselves in especially harmful work environments to seek other employment if that is an option.[22] They argue that "long-term exposure to microaggressive messages must be avoided when there are the conditions and agency to do so."[23] Of course, this is a significant and deeply personal decision. The right decision for each person will vary widely and be dependent on various factors, such as library industry trends, personal financial and family obligations, or the ability to relocate, to name just a few.[24]

However, I found encouragement to remain in LIS from some advice from a prominent library leader in the American Library Association (ALA). I attended a webinar this leader gave to California community

---

20  Wood and Harris III, "Racelighting in the Normal Realities," 40.

21  Angelique M. Davis and Rose Ernst, "Racial Gaslighting," *Politics, Groups, and Identities* 7, no. 4 (October 2, 2019): 771, https://doi.org/10.1080/21565503.2017.1403934.

22  Wood and Harris III, "Racelighting in the Normal Realities," 41.

23  Wood and Harris III, "Racelighting in the Normal Realities"; Michelle A. Rodrigues, et. al, "There's Realizing, and Then There's Realizing," 18–19.

24  Kaetrena Davis Kendrick, "Leaving the Low-Morale Experience: A Qualitative Study." *Alki* 37, no. 2 (2021): 9–24.

college librarians in 2020. During the Q&A portion, I typed my response to a discussion about why there are not many librarians of color:

> Librarians of Color do not feel comfortable in the profession. I got my Master of Library and Information Science (MLIS) in 2012 and have had full-time positions in university/college libraries since then. But I am now reaching a point in my career where I can't stand the work environment any longer. There have been too many racist remarks, microaggressions, and questions about my race/background/legitimacy for me. I am seriously considering leaving the profession, even though I've already completed and paid for my very expensive master's degree.[25]

This person very patiently listened and compassionately responded to me. They empathized with my experiences and understood why I wanted to leave. Then, they offered an alternate perspective: I have worked hard to get where I am. I put in the time and work to complete my degree and progress to the position I found myself in. After all that hard work, I should not leave the career I had earned. I don't have to believe the idea that I don't belong because it simply isn't true. This person's help that day gave me strength. After all the destructive experiences I had as a BIPOC community college librarian who continually impressed upon me how insignificant, ineffective, and undeserving I was to be there, he heard me, validated me, and upheld my worth.

## The Community College Experience in Perspective

Multiple factors were at play in my experience. Not only was their interpersonal struggle compounded by the utter lack of leadership or administrative guidance, both in the department's personnel issues and in the department as a whole. Additionally, the institution took minimal action, ignoring repeated reports of incidences and pleas for help. However, after being able to identify what was happening in my work environment and being validated by my peers, in hindsight, this is an obvious reaction on the part of the administration. As Davis and Ernst repeatedly emphasize, "the process of racial gaslighting targets

---

25 Terezita Reyes Overduin in an anonymous question posed in an unrecorded webinar, December 2020.

those who resist" pathologizing those who dare challenge the dominant narrative."[26]

The lack of library leadership or administrative guidance seems to affect many library working environments, but especially in the community college environment.[27] Many community college libraries suffer under similar circumstances: the dean assigned to our department often needs a library degree and experience working in libraries and several other departments they oversee. Suppose academic libraries are lucky enough to have a dean who knows the library profession and can take the time to advocate for their library correctly. In that case, they have more significant potential to cultivate a much more student-focused, equitable, and enjoyable environment.

## Recommendations

Administratively, supporting BIPOC library workers is easy to do. So much of the racelighting experience depends on the response that managers, supervisors, deans, administrators, HR, and anyone with power lends to the situation. A manager or anyone in these roles should affirm the experiences of the affected person and do what they can to rectify the situation, even if it feels like they can't do much. Gaslighting is the effect of a non-response; the obvious solution is to have a response. This applies to colleagues as well. All people have the power to support a colleague just by speaking up instead of ignoring a situation. After an altercation, a simple "That was so inappropriate!" can help a colleague feel seen instead of ignored. Community college administration can support BIPOC library workers without platitudes. Supporting BIPOC library workers looks like:

- Publicly valuing library work.

- Acknowledging the adminstration's role in race lighting and its detrimental effects on their employees.

- Advocating for BIPOC by creating opportunities for employees to voice their concerns.

---

26  Angelique M. Davis and Rose Ernst. "Racial Gaslighting," *Politics, Groups, and Identities* 7, no. 4 (October 2, 2019): 761–74., https://doi.org/10.1080/21565503.2017.1403934.

27  Alma C. Ortega, *Academic Libraries and Toxic Leadership* (Cambridge, MA: Chandos Publishing, 2017), xii.

- Acknowledging voices once they have been heard by enacting change or validating experiences. Racelighting will occur if you invite employees to voice concerns and do nothing to recognize them.
- Respecting the communities that BIPOC creates for themselves.
- Speaking out against microaggressive or racist rhetoric, acts, and structures.

## Conclusion

In the process of writing this chapter, some updates have occurred I should include as a postscript. After receiving multiple complaints from different employees, my institution finally decided to open an investigation. Years after my initial experiences, my library hired a dean to oversee the library and tutoring services. Whether this will rectify the situation remains to be seen. However, the racelighting perpetuated by this work environment and the institution remains, and the damage to BIPOC workers still exists. A years-long delay in response does nothing to validate or affirm BIPOC experiences, and in fact, it leaves the feelings of neglect and impotence intact.

BIPOC community college library workers deal with racism and microaggressions in their daily lives and work. This can come from interpersonal interactions, but it is also compounded by the need for more knowledgeable administrative leadership and the institutional embrace of white-dominant structures. While the cumulative weight of these interactions and messages brings discouragement, desolation, and despair in the form of racelighting, there is also hope. By telling our stories, we send another message: You are not alone. You are not less worthy. Your work is valuable. Even though you may question yourself, your reality, and your work, know that others out there will support you, your work, and your growth in this profession.

We all can resist white dominance and systemic oppression collectively by learning, growing, and collaborating. BIPOC library workers can create community and safe spaces where we can hear each other's stories. White library workers can support their colleagues by supporting the creation of these spaces and making room for BIPOC voices and experiences in library work. We can learn about phenomena like racelighting, racial battle fatigue, and others to embrace and promote the power of naming. We can resist institutional oppression by challenging norms and advocating for ourselves and each other. Most importantly, we can lift these burdens from each other's shoulders by uplifting one another.[28] Once you find your people, create strong bonds and encourage them during hardships. As we advocate for each other and affirm each other's experiences and contributions, we will overcome the racial barriers in our profession and fully serve our students.

## Bibliography

Alabi, Jaena. "Racial Microaggressions in Academic Libraries: Results of a Survey of Minority and Non-Minority Librarians." *The Journal of Academic Librarianship* 41, no. 1 (January 1, 2015): 47–53. https://doi.org/10.1016/j.acalib.2014.10.008.

Alwan, Ahmed, Joy Doan, and Eric Garcia. "Microaggressions as a Barrier to Effective Collaboration Between Teaching Faculty and Academic Librarians: An Analysis of the Results of a US and Canadian Survey." *The International Journal of Information, Diversity, & Inclusion* 2, no. 3 (2018): 26–58. https://doi.org/10.33137/ijidi.v2i3.32191.

Arroyo-Ramirez, Elvia, Rose L. Chou, Jenna Freedman, Simone Fujita, and Cynthia Mari Orozco. "The Reach of a Long-Arm Stapler: Calling in Microaggressions in the LIS Field through Zine Work." *Library Trends* 67, no. 1 (2018): 107–30. https://doi.org/10.1353/lib.2018.0028.

Barton, R., and J. A. Whitehead. "The Gas-Light Phenomenon." *Lancet (London, England)* 1, no. 7608 (June 21, 1969): 1258–60. https://doi.org/10.1016/s0140-6736(69)92133-3.

Clance, Pauline Rose, and Suzanne Ament Imes. "The Imposter Phenomenon in High Achieving Women: Dynamics and Therapeutic Intervention." *Psychotherapy: Theory, Research & Practice* 15, no. 3 (1978): 241–47. https://doi.org/10.1037/h0086006.

Cooke, Nicole A. "Impolite Hostilities and Vague Sympathies: Academia as a Site of Cyclical Abuse." *Journal of Education for Library and Information Science* 60, no. 3 (July 1, 2019): 223–30. https://doi.org/10.3138/jelis.2019-0005.

---

28 Nicole A. Cooke, "Impolite Hostilities and Vague Sympathies: Academia as a Site of Cyclical Abuse," *Journal of Education for Library and Information Science* 60, no. 3 (July 1, 2019): 227–28, https://doi.org/10.3138/jelis.2019-0005.

Davis, Angelique M., and Rose Ernst. "Racial Gaslighting." *Politics, Groups, and Identities* 7, no. 4 (October 2, 2019): 761–74. https://doi.org/10.1080/21565503.2017.1403934.

Fagan, Jody Condit, Hillary Ostermiller, Elizabeth Price, and Lara Sapp. "Librarian, Faculty, and Student Perceptions of Academic Librarians: Study Introduction and Literature Review." *New Review of Academic Librarianship* 27, no. 1 (January 2, 2021): 38–75. https://doi.org/10.1080/13614533.2019.1691026.

Kendrick, Kaetrena Davis. "Leaving the low-morale experience: A qualitative study." *Alki* 37, no. 2 (2021): 9–24.

Kendrick, Kaetrena Davis, Amanda M. Leftwich, and Twanna Hodge. "Providing Care and Community in Times of Crisis: The BIPOC in LIS Mental Health Summits."*College & Research Libraries News*, 82, no. 8 (September 3, 2021): 358–61, https://doi.org/10.5860/crln.82.8.358.

Mindfulinlis. *Mindfulinlis* (blog). Accessed February 4, 2022. https://mindfulinlis.wordpress.com/.

Ollis, Chase. "LibGuides: Pandemic Resources for Academic Libraries: Self-Care and New Ways of Working." Accessed July 30, 2021. https://acrl.libguides.com/pandemic/self-care-home.

Ortega, Alma C. *Academic Libraries and Toxic Leadership*. Cambridge, MA: Chandos Publishing, 2017.

Overduin, Terezita Reyes, in an anonymous question posed in an unrecorded webinar, December 2020.

Quiñunez, Turie, Lalitha Nataraj, and Antonia Olivas. "The Praxis of Relation, Validation, and Motivation: Articulating LIS Collegiality through a CRT Lens." In *Knowledge Justice: Disrupting Library and Information Studies through Critical Race Theory*, edited by Sofia Y. Leung and Jorge R. López-McKnight. The MIT Press, 2021: 241–61. https://doi.org/10.7551/mitpress/11969.003.0018.

Renewals. *Renewals*(blog).Accessed February 4, 2022. https://renewerslis.wordpress.com/.

Rodrigues, Michelle A., Ruby Mendenhall, and Kathryn B. H. Clancy. 'There's Realizing and Then There's Realizing': How Social Support Can Counter Gaslighting of Women of Color Scientists." *Journal of Women and Minorities in Science and Engineering* 27, no. 2 (2021): 1–23. https://doi.org/10.1615/JWomenMinorScienEng.2020034630.

Smith, William. "Black Faculty Coping with Racial Battle Fatigue." In *A Long Way to Go: Conversations about Race by African American Faculty and Graduate Students*, ed. Peter Lang, 171–90. New York: Peter Lang Inc., 2004.

Steele, Claude M. "A Threat in the Air: How Stereotypes Shape Intellectual Identity and Performance." *American Psychologist* 52, no. 6 (1997): 613–29. https://doi.org/10.1037/0003-066X.52.6.613.

Sweeney, Miriam E., and Nicole A. Cooke. "You're So Sensitive! How LIS Professionals Define and Discuss Microaggressions Online." *The Library Quarterly* 88, no. 4 (October 1, 2018): 375–90. https://doi.org/10.1086/699270.

Wood, J. Luke, and Frank Harris III. "Racelighting: A Prevalent Version of Gaslighting Facing People of Color–Higher Education." *Diverse Issues in Higher Education* (February 12, 2021). https://diverseeducation.com/article/205210/.

Wood, J. Luke, and Frank Harris III. "Racelighting in the Normal Realities of Black, Indigenous, and People of Color: A Scholarly Brief." Racelighting. 2021. Accessed June 30, 2021. http://racelighting.net/wp-content/uploads/2022/06/CCEAL-Mar2021-update.pdf.

# About the Contributors

**Adriene Hobdy** is the Director of Talent Management & Leadership Development at Montgomery County Community College. Dr. Hobdy received her Doctorate of Education in Leadership and Innovation from Wilmington University, a Master of Business in Human Resources Management, and a Master's in Budget and Finance from the Lincoln University of Pennsylvania. She holds a Certificate of Leadership, Next Generation Leadership Academy, from Civitas Learning. Before that role, she was the AVP of Talent Management at Lambert Worldwide, Inc. In addition, Dr. Hobdy previously served as the Director and Associate Faculty of the Business Programs in the Schools of Graduate and Professional Studies at Rosemont College. Dr. Hobdy is very active in the community. She mentors high school and college students in Philadelphia, providing guidance and encouragement during their educational journey. She is the Vice-President of the National Association of University Women- Suburban Philadelphia Branch (NAUW) and a board member of the Abington School District Human Relations Council.

**Alyssa Jocson Porter** is a Filipina-American faculty librarian at Seattle Central College, where she is the liaison to STEM and creative arts programs. Her research interests include BIPOC hiring & retention in librarianship. She was once told years ago by a white male library administrator that this wasn't a worthy research topic. He's still wrong.

**Jess Koshi-Lum** is a branch manager at the San Mateo County Library system in the San Francisco Bay Area. Previously, she served as an associate dean of the library at Renton Technical College in greater Seattle and has worked in community colleges in Hawaiʻi and Washington for almost ten years. She received her MLISc from the University of Hawaiʻi at Mānoa in 2013 and is pursuing her Ed.D. in Leadership with a Higher Education focus at the City University of Seattle.

Her research interests include intersectional feminism, Asian American leadership, and library racial equity.

**Andrew Kuo** is an immigrant from Taiwan who spent half his childhood in Delaware County, Pennsylvania. He has served as the Library Coordinator of Contra Costa College (CCC), an HSI community college, in California since 2018. He is a writer and poet. He is a member of the CCC Asian Pacific Islander Faculty & Staff Association and CCC Friends of the Library.

**Dele Chinwe Ladejobi** is the Technical Services Librarian and professor at the Long Beach City College (LBCC), California. She currently serves as the Library Department Head. Dele has mentored several minority students and faculty from all over the world. She values the importance of literacy and access to information. Having experienced the frustrations of an environment where there are many barriers between students and the availability of critical resources, she has generously contributed thousands of essential educational materials to institutions in Nigeria, establishing her as an international educator who cares for the welfare and sound education for all societies. Several publications and instructional resources have cited her writings about the Nigerian-Biafran Civil War, African culture and traditions, especially the Igbo language, Igbo names, social life, and customs. Dele has served as a member on several campus-wide committees and task forces, including the Curriculum Committee; President's Task Force on Race, Equity & Inclusion; Faculty and Staff Diversity, Faculty Co-Chair, Student Equity Committee; LBCC Faculty Association (LBCCFA); Chair of the LBCCFA Faculty Equity; Co-Chair, Faculty and Staff Diversity; and more. She is also a member of the American Library Association (ALA) and the Black Caucus of the American Library Association (BCALA). She has served as the Vice President and President of the Southern California Technical Processes Group (SCTPG). She enjoys gardening, writing, traveling, and spending time with her family.

**Fran L. Lassiter** is an Associate Professor of English at Montgomery County Community College (MCCC). She received her Ph.D. in English from Temple University, specializing in African-American literature and early slave narratives. Her research and teaching focus broadly on questions of gendered and racialized identities in literature and Africanisms as a theoretical approach for the reclamation of understudied slave narratives. In 2008, she became the first Faculty

Diversity Fellow at MC3. She has presented papers at various national conferences on Black women writers and the rhetoric of nineteenth-century African American activists, and her paper entitled "Journey to Equality: From Maria W. Stewart to Barack Obama" received the Northeast Modern Language Association's CAITY Caucus Prize in 2010. In addition, her paper "From Toasts to Raps: New Approaches for Teaching the Harlem Renaissance," published in Pedagogy: Critical Approaches to Teaching Literature, Language, Composition, and Culture, offers a cross-disciplinary approach to teaching literature of the period. She is completing a book on a free-Black family in Colonial-era Virginia. She is married and lives with her husband in Montgomery County, Pennsylvania.

**Stephanie Nnadi** is an Assistant Professor of Biology at Montgomery County Community College. Stephanie holds a BA in Molecular Biology and Biochemistry from Rutgers University and a PhD in Genetics from Thomas Jefferson University, where she also completed her postdoctoral fellowship. Her research focused on using mouse models combining classical and molecular genetics to identify genes influencing intestinal cancer susceptibility. Stephanie found her calling in higher education. She is passionate about helping nontraditional college students find success through goal setting, mentoring, and networking. Additionally, Stephanie serves on the board of trustees of a small independent school. She resides outside of Philadelphia with her husband and two children.

**Evangela Q. Oates** is a scholar-practitioner and the Associate University Librarian for Student Success at the University of Minnesota Libraries. For the past 15 years, she has worked in various positions in academic libraries spanning all institutional types. Following a critical constructivist paradigm, her research primarily used necessary frameworks and methodological approaches centered on lived experience. Her main research areas are Black faculty and administrators, academic librarianship, and community colleges.

**Edeama Onwuchekwa Jonah** is the Equity and Engagement Librarian and Professor at the San Diego Mesa College. She has worked as an Academic Librarian and gained several years of experience actively working in the library, working and engaging with faculty and students towards promoting student success outcomes. She has a unique passion for serving the needs of students, significantly underrepresented, underserved students of color, and students from different socio-economic groups. Onwuchekwa Jonah has published in academic journals, presented in conferences, and has created and developed content for diverse professional groups. She currently serves on the Executive Board of the California Academic and Research Libraries Association. She is also on the Advisory Board of the Lifelong Information Literacy (LILi) Group. Before these roles, she served as Chair-Elect and Chair for the Diversity in Academic Libraries interest group in the California Association of Research Libraries. She is a member of the American Library Association (ALA) and the Black Caucus of the American Library Association. Besides her leadership role in the library, Dr. Onwuchekwa Jonah is the current President of the San Diego Chapter (Region X) of the American Association for Women in Community Colleges. Dr. Onwuchekwa Jonah is a voracious reader and an adept believer of the Maxim "Information Provision for All". She enjoys reading, writing, traveling, and spending time with her family.

**Terezita Reyes Overduin** is a first-generation college student and academic. She has been an academic librarian for seven years at both public and private institutions of various sizes. She works to better the research experiences of students, staff, and faculty through her teaching, reference, and research activities.

**Sally Najera Romero** is a Research and Instruction Librarian at California State Polytechnic University, Pomona (Cal Poly Pomona). She holds her BA in Communications from California State University, Fullerton, and her MLIS from San Jose State University. She is a first-generation Latina who aims to focus her teaching and scholarship on equity, diversity, and inclusion and uplifting the voices of the Latinx community.

**Shamika Jamalia Morris Simpson** is the Collection Development and Outreach Librarian and professor at Long Beach City College in Long Beach, California. Shamika is the current California Academic & Research Libraries (CARL), Vice President/President-elect, and a Booklist board member. Before this role, she served as an executive board member of the Black Caucus of the American Library Association (BCALA), Secretary/Treasurer of the Southern California Technical Processes Group (SCTPG), and has volunteered with a host of other professional library associations and groups. Simpson is passionate about engaging technologies in instruction, student wellness, social justice in librarianship, and continuous learning.

She holds Social Media and Marketing certificates from CSU Dominguez Hills, Diversity and Inclusion Skills from Library Juice Academy, and Diversity, Equity, and Inclusion in the Workplace from the University of South Florida Muma College of Business. She completed the 2021 CLA Developing Library Leaders Challenge and Dare to Lead certificate.

**Gerie Ventura** is a second-generation Pinay born and raised in Tacoma, Washington. She has been the Director of the Highline College Library in Washington State since 2018. Gerie is a writer and avid community volunteer with the Filipino-American National Historical Society and the Friends of the Tukwila Library.

# Index

#AcademicTwitter, 48
#EndCCStigma, 6-7
#LibraryTwitter, 48
#WeHere, 48
#WOCinLIB, 48

AACC. *See* American Association of Community Colleges
academic librarians. *See* librarians, academic
academic librarianship. *See* librarianship, academic
academic libraries. *See* libraries, academic
acculturation, 78-79
ACRL. *See* Association of College and Research Libraries
ACRL Framework for Information Literacy for Higher Education. *See* Association of College and Research Libraries Framework for Information Literacy for Higher Education
activist backgrounds, xvii-xviii
affinity groups, ix, xi
ALA. *See* American Library Association
ALA Emerging Leaders Program. *See* American Library Association Emerging Leaders Program
ALA's National Association of Librarians of Color. *See* American Library Association's National Association of Librarians of Color
American Association of Community Colleges, 3
American Indian Library Association, 35
American Library Association, 25, 114, 120-121
American Library Association Emerging Leaders Program, 38-39
American Library Association's National Association of Librarians of Color, 34
ancestral wisdom, xvii-xviii
anti-Blackness, 131-132
APALA. *See* Asian Pacific American Libraries Association
Asian American men. *See* men, Asian American
Asian American women. *See* women, Asian American

Asian Pacific American Libraries Association, 25, 34
Association of College and Research Libraries, 8, 39, 121
Association of College and Research Libraries Framework for Information Literacy for Higher Education, 56, 102
bamboo ceiling, xi, 19
BCALA. *See* Black Caucus of the American Library Association
belonging, xi, xii, 93, 101-102, 105-106
BIPOC. *See* Black, Indigenous, and People of Color
BIPOC librarians. *See* librarians, Black, Indigenous, and People of Color
Black Caucus of the American Library Association, 34
Black, Indigenous, and People of Color, ix, 12, 23
Black Lives Matter, 110, 140-141
Black women. *See* women, Black
blogs, 48
burnout, xvi

CALA. *See* Chinese American Librarians Association
California Community Colleges, 115, 116-118, 120, 149-150, 162, 185
California Upward Extension Act, 2
CCC. *See* California Community Colleges
Chicana identity, xv, 154-157
Chinese American Libraries Association, 34
class consciousness, 150-151
colleges, community
    absence of Black, Indigenous, and People of Color narratives in literature about, xviii, 2-5, 10, 47-48
    characteristics of, 40
    ethnic make-up of students at, 53, 68, 79, 149-150
    history of establishment of, 2 4, 116
    mission of, xvi, 127
    number in the United States, 4
    number of students in the United States attending, 115

questions for looking at with an equity lens, 116
reasons students decide to attend, xv
recommendations for Asian American librarians entering administration of, 33-34
recommendations for library administrators in, 34-35
retention of faculty at, 69
stereotypes and stigma about, xv, 4, 6-7
student success at, xii, xv
tenure process at, xvii, 45, 46, 135–138, 142-143
unique challenges of, xi, xv, 79, 194-195
colleges, technical, x, xi-xii, 19, 33-34
colonial mentality, 28-29
committees, x-xi
communities of practice, x, xi, xiii, 11, 40, 44-47, 54-61, 62-65, 67-69
community college librarians. *See* librarians, community college
community college librarianship. *See* librarianship, community college
community college libraries. *See* libraries, community college
community colleges. *See* colleges, community
commuter students. *See* students, commuter
Contra Costa College, 97
COP. *See* communities of practice
counter biases, 105
COVID-19 pandemic, xviii, 9, 33, 110, 138, 147
critical librarianship. *See* librarianship, critical
critical pedagogy. *See* pedagogy, critical
cultural competence, 118-119
cultural humility, 103-104
culture tax, 4, 53-54

deans, 21, 30
DEI. *See* Diversity, Equity and Inclusion
discrimination, ix
Diversity, Equity and Inclusion, 119

emotional labor, 5, 11

feminism, xii, 150-151, 152
feminist librarianship. *See* librarianship, feminist
Filipino American National Historical Society, 25

gaslighting, 184

George Floyd incident, 110, 138
glass ceiling, xi, 19-20
grind culture, 8

harmful systems, 11
HBCUs. *See* Historically Black Colleges and Universities
Highline College, 20-21
Hispanic Serving Institutions, 97-98
Historically Black Colleges and Universities, 2
Hobdy, Adriene, xi, 57, 201
HSIs. *See* Hispanic Serving Institutions
Hughes Jones, Kel, ix-xi

Implicit Association Test, 105
implicit bias, 105
imposter syndrome, xii, 28-29, 31, 75-77, 84-90
inclusivity, xii
information literacy, 39, 119
instructional design, 119
institutional oppression, 196-197
internalized oppression, 28-29
internalized racism, 88-90
intersectionality, xii, 88, 100
interviews, 19-37
invisible labor, 11
IS. *See* imposter syndrome

Jocson Porter, Alyssa, xi-xii, xvi, 20, 35, 201
Joliet Junior College, 2

Koshi-Lum, Jess, xi-xii, xvi, 20, 201-202
Kuo, Andrew, xii, xvii, 97-98

Ladejobi, Dele Chinwe, xii, xviii, 169, 202
Lassiter, Fran L., xi, 57, 202-203
Latina identity, xii, 76-77
Lee, Wai-Fong, 21
Leftwich, Amanda M., xi, xvi, 6, 9-11, 57
librarians, academic, xi, xvi-xvii, 41, 55-56, 119-120
librarians, Black, Indigenous, and People of Color
  as administrators, xvi
  as change makers in educational settings, xiii, xv-xvi
  community building for, x, xi, xii, 92, 185
  effect of administrators on, xvi, xvii, 195-196
  giving voice to, xi
  importance of affinity groups for, ix

*Index*

importance of positive work environment for, xii-xiii, 181
importance of support groups for, ix-x, 91-92
lack of attendance at library conferences, 1, 8-9
mentorship of, xvi, 35
need for space to express themselves, 2
onboarding for, xii, xviii, 170-172, 175, 177-180
retention of, xviii, 45, 169
work experiences, xvii, xviii, 7-8, 12
librarians, community college
  as administrators, 40, 41
  lack of attendance at library conferences, 1, 8-9, 40, 41
  mentorship of, 25
  need for space to express themselves, 2
  retention of, 45, 69
  types of labor, 1, 5
  work experiences, 7-8, 12
librarianship, academic, x, 45, 55-56
librarianship, community college, xi
librarianship, critical, 119-120
librarianship, feminist, 154
libraries, academic, xi, 118-120
libraries, community college, xi-xii, xiii, xv-xvi, xvii, 118, 122-123
libraries, technical college, xi-xii
library administration, xi, xvi
Library Bill of Rights, 114-115
library collection assessment, 123-125
library collection development, xii, 114, 118-119, 120-122, 125-127
library environment, 106-107
library funding, xii, 126
library outreach, xii, 126-127, 158-161
library space, 107-108
low morale, 5, 131

marginality, x, xii
men, Asian American, xii, 97-98
microaggressions, xii, xvi, xvii, xviii, 82, 98-99, 108-111, 189-190, 196
microassault, 108
microinsult, 108
microinvalidation, 108
Model Minority Myth, 28
Montgomery County Community College, 57
Morrill Act of 1862, 2-3
Morrill Act of 1890, 3
motherhood, xviii, 76, 81-84

Nnadi, Stephanie, xi, 57, 203

Oates, Evangela Q., xi, xvi, 5, 38-41, 203
OER. *See* open educational resources
onboarding, xii, xviii, 170-172, 175, 177-180
Onwuchekwa Jonah, Edeama, xii, 203-204
open educational resources, 45-46
oppression, xvi
Overduin, Terezita Reyes, xii, xvi, 204

pandemic pedagogy. *See* pedagogy, pandemic
passive-aggressive behavior, 29
patriarchy, 30-31
pedagogy, critical, 119
pedagogy, pandemic, 147-148
People of Color in Library and Information Science Summit, 1, 8, 9
Pierce College, 33
POCinLIS Summit. *See* People of Color in Library & Information Science Summit
productivity, 41-42
professional isolation, 42-44, 49

racelighting, xii, 184, 185, 187-190, 191-194
racism, ix, 5, 11, 29, 108, 111
REFORMA, 34
Renton Technical College, 20, 31
Rios-Alvarado, Eva M. L., xii, xvi, xvii-xviii, 9-11
Romero, Sally Najera, xii, xviii, 204
RTC. *See* Renton Technical College

SCC. *See* Seattle Central College
SEAP Program. *See* Student Equity and Achievement Program
Seattle Central College, 20, 21, 23
self-acceptance, xii
self-care, xii, 11, 131, 138-140, 192
self-worth, xii, 76, 90-91, 93
settler colonialism, 152, 154, 162-163
servant leadership, 27-28
service desks, 23-24
Servicemen's Readjustment Act, 3
sexism, 11
shame, 4
Simpson, Shamika Jamalia Morris, xii, xvii-xviii, 204-205
social capital, 39
social isolation, ix, xi, 4, 11, 43
Social Justice Leadership Institute, 31
social media, 6-7, 31, 48, 189
stereotypes, xi-xii, 28, 99-100, 109-110
stigma, 4, 100, 105

student diversity, xii
Student Equity and Achievement
    Program, 115
student success, xii, 122-123
students, commuter, x, xvii
support groups, ix-x, xi, 91-92
systemic oppression, 196
systemic racism, xii

technical college libraries. *See* libraries,
    technical college
technical colleges. *See* colleges, technical
tenure process, xvii
toxic work environment, xvi, xviii, 45, 46,
    135-138, 142-143
Truman Commission Report of 1947, 3
Trump era,110-111
Twitter, 6-7, 48

Ventura, Geri, xi-xii, xvi, 20-21, 35, 205

We Here, 1-2, 34
wellness, xii
white fragility, 29
white supremacy, xvi, xvii, 30-31
women, Asian American, xi-xii, 19-33, 35-36
women, Black, ix, xi
work attire, 30
work environment, xii
work-life balance, xvii-xviii

xenophobia, 110
Xicana identity, xii, 150-151, 155, 156-157

Zepeda, Lizeth, xv-xvii

www.ingramcontent.com/pod-product-compliance
Lightning Source LLC
Chambersburg PA
CBHW051356290426
44108CB00015B/2038